Library of
Davidson College

International Trade and Money

About the Editors

MICHAEL B. CONNOLLY is associate professor of economics at the University of Florida, Gainesville. From 1968 to 1972 he was assistant professor of economics at Harvard University, and, during the 1970–1 academic year, was visiting professor at the Graduate Institute of International Studies. He is the author of several articles dealing, in particular, with the theory of public goods, foreign lending, and international trade.

ALEXANDER K. SWOBODA is professor of international economics at the Graduate Institute of International Studies. He is also a visiting professor at the University of Geneva and the London School of Economics and Political Science. He has edited a number of books on international monetary economics and is the author of several articles on international finance and international monetary economics.

International Trade and Money
The Geneva Essays

EDITED BY

MICHAEL B. CONNOLLY
Harvard University

AND

ALEXANDER K. SWOBODA
Graduate Institute of International Studies

Published in collaboration with
the Graduate Institute of International Studies
Geneva

UNIVERSITY OF TORONTO PRESS

© George Allen & Unwin Ltd 1973

First published 1973
in Canada and the United States
by University of Toronto Press
Toronto and Buffalo

ISBN 0-8020-1969-2

ISBN (microfiche) 0-8020-0312-5

LC 72-97392

Printed in Great Britain

Contents

Editors' Preface *page* 9

PART I: INTRODUCTION

1. JOAN ROBINSON
   The Need for a Reconsideration of the Theory of
   International Trade — 15

PART II: INTERNATIONAL TRADE

2. ROBERT E. BALDWIN
   Customs Unions, Preferential Systems and
   World Welfare — 29

3. JAGDISH N. BHAGWATI
   The Theory of Immiserizing Growth:
   Further Applications — 45

4. MICHAEL B. CONNOLLY
   Induced Technical Change and the Transfer
   Mechanism — 55

5. THOMAS HORST
   The Simple Analytics of Multi-National
   Firm Behaviour — 72

6. JAN TINBERGEN
   Trends in Income Distribution in some
   Western Countries — 85

PART III: INTERNATIONAL MONETARY ANALYSIS

7. GIORGIO BASEVI
   A Model for the Analysis of Official Intervention in
   the Foreign Exchange Markets — 107

8. KARL BRUNNER
   Money Supply Process and Monetary Policy in an
   Open Economy — 127

Contents

9. RICHARD N. COOPER
   An Analysis of Currency Devaluation in Developing Countries — 167

10. JACQUES L'HUILLIER
    Some Misconceptions on the Sharing of the Burden of Adjustment between Deficit and Surplus Countries — 197

11. HARRY G. JOHNSON
    The Monetary Approach to Balance-of-Payments Theory — 206

12. ALEXANDER K. SWOBODA AND RUDIGER DORNBUSCH
    Adjustment, Policy, and Monetary Equilibrium in a Two-Country Model — 225

Index — 262

Editors' Preface

For a number of years, distinguished scholars have presented their research in various seminars in international economics at the Graduate Institute of International Studies. It seemed worthwhile to organise the research seminar for 1970-1 with publication of the papers in mind, and this volume is the result.

The organising principle in the selection of topics was a simple one. Each contributor was asked to present his views on a subject he was keenly interested in, the only two constraints being that the resulting papers deal with international economics and that they be of an analytical nature. The perhaps surprising result is a rather coherent collection of essays on international economics. Their coherence lies in three features shared in common: they reflect the belief that economic theory can help solve important and relevant problems in international economic relations, they represent original work on the frontiers of research in international economics, and they nevertheless use simple and understandable techniques to reach their conclusions.

The volume is divided into three parts. It opens with an introductory essay by Joan Robinson on the need for a reconsideration of the theory of international trade. She critically examines the treatment of foreign investment in the neo-classical trade model, and in particular argues that the gains from trade and investment to developing countries are exaggerated. Part II deals with five topics in trade theory. Robert Baldwin investigates the world welfare effects of customs unions and preferential trading arrangements, utilising both a very broad welfare criterion and a general equilibrium framework in contrast to the usual partial-equilibrium cardinalist approach. Baldwin shows that certain familiar conclusions concerning the welfare effects of customs unions hold even within this broad framework. Jagdish Bhagwati presents further applications of the theory of immiserizing growth. In the first part of his paper the theory is used to resolve two paradoxes in the analysis of growth and trade; in the second, the theory is generalised to include tariff-induced capital inflows. Michael Connolly applies the theory of public goods to the international dissemination of technical change. This enables Connolly to derive conditions for the optimum production of technical change and to analyse the spillover effects of induced technical change. Thomas Horst shows that multi-national company production decisions can be analysed with the help of a suitable modification of the standard tools of trade theory. He also investigates, and derives optimality conditions for, the multi-national firm's research and development strategy. Jan Tinbergen surveys the evidence on trends in income distribution on a cross-country comparative basis. He concludes that income inequality has unambiguously declined within a number of rich countries, in contrast to the trend in some developing countries, and examines the role played in this process by taxes and public finance.

The third part of the book is devoted to international monetary relations. It begins with Giorgio Basevi's analysis of the spot and forward markets for foreign exchange. Basevi presents a computable, though simple, model that relaxes the usual and damaging assumption that interest rates are exogenously determined. Karl Brunner's essay extends his well-known money-supply hypothesis to the case of an open economy. This makes possible a much more detailed and precise analysis of the financial sector than is usually incorporated in open-economy models. Richard Cooper applies economic theory and empirical analysis to a much neglected issue: the impact of devaluation on the economies of developing countries. Cooper's use of cross-section analysis enables him to squeeze interesting conclusions out of scant and rough data and constitutes an invitation to more detailed analysis. Jacques L'Huillier reviews critically some of the criteria that have been proposed for sharing the burden of adjustment between deficit and surplus countries and argues that the assessment of responsibility for disequilibrium should play a role in the definition of the proper sharing of the burden of adjustment. Harry Johnson presents a succinct but quite complete survey of the intellectual development of balance-of-payments theory and a simple but powerful mathematical model that summarises the emerging 'monetary' view of the payments adjustment process. This model yields highly significant conclusions on the role of devaluation, growth of income, domestic credit creation, and world money supply, and on the balance of payments under alternative international monetary systems. Rudiger Dornbusch and Alexander Swoboda use a Keynesian two-country model that incorporates a monetary mechanism of adjustment to reach similar conclusions in a comparative statics framework. They conclude that most of the one-country small

Editors' Preface

economy results hold qualitatively in a two-country framework, irrespective of the size of countries. In particular, the effect of monetary policy is independent of its national origin and the 'natural distribution of specie' will tend to reassert itself even in a Keynesian framework.

No preface is complete without acknowledgements. Thanks are due to Dee Ann Vavich for her assistance with readying the manuscript for publication and to Takahiko Mutoh who helped compile the index. In addition, we have incurred two main debts of gratitude in preparing this volume. The first is to the authors of the papers in this volume. The second is to the Graduate Institute of International Studies, which made this volume possible through its support of the research seminar and the editing process.

M.B.C.
A.K.S.

PART I

INTRODUCTION

1

The Need for a Reconsideration of the Theory of International Trade

JOAN ROBINSON
University of Cambridge

There is no branch of economics in which there is a wider gap between orthodox doctrine and actual problems than in the theory of international trade.

I

The argument is usually conducted in terms of static comparisons of equilibrium positions of a model which has the following characteristics: there are two countries which represent the whole trading world; each country is in stationary equilibrium with given 'resources' fully employed; there is perfect mobility of labour between occupations within each country and no mobility between countries; the value of imports is equal to the value of exports.

These characteristics of the model exclude discussion of any question which is interesting in reality.

Even within the terms of static comparisons, it is necessary to consider at least three countries before any general conclusions can be drawn. Propositions intended to show that some change is inevitably beneficial to all concerned cannot be demonstrated for more than two partners. For instance, an increase in efficiency in producing an export commodity in country A, within the conditions of the model, benefits B and C taken together, but if C was exporting the same commodity it is likely to be injured. Furthermore, the model applies only to trade between countries at the same level of industrial development; it was ill-suited to dealing with the importation into an industrial metropolis of primary products from colonial and quasi-colonial dependencies, though this in fact formed the great bulk of trade at the very time when teaching derived for the model was in its greatest ascendancy. (Nowadays the traditional arguments are being used to indoctrinate the intellectuals of the ex-colonial nations.)

The analysis conducted in terms of stationary states leaves out development, accumulation and technical change. It leaves out the shock effect of change and the process of readjustment. However drastic the change in the pattern of trade, equilibrium has always been restored before the discussion begins.

The assumption of full employment rules out the problems of effective demand. The capitalist world (except in rare moments of strong boom) is a buyer's market. Normally every industry has productive capacity for more output than it can sell. From the point of view of a national economy, exports promote employment and profits; imports reduce them. The comforting doctrines that a country 'cannot be undersold all round' was derived from the postulate of universal full employment. The argument consists merely in assuming what it hopes to prove.

Finally, the assumption that, for each country, the value of imports is necessarily equal to the value of exports rules out the problem of maintaining the national balance of payments which has been the great preoccupation of economic policy from the earliest times.

The aim of the traditional theory was to establish the beneficial effects of free trade. This was eagerly accepted by orthodox opinion in the country which had the most to gain from open markets for its exports. But in fact the case was made out by assuming away all the difficulties and all the aims which in reality give rise to protectionist policies.[1]

The model is usually operated in terms of a comparison between a situation in which each country is isolated, consuming only its own products, with a situation in which trade is taking place, in equilibrium, without any difference in the 'resources' or the 'tastes' of the two communities. Since the model was constructed for the purpose of a polemic against protection, the argument focuses on the case where the same commodities are produced in both countries. Protection would not arise unless a country could produce at home goods which others export. The import of exotic commodities did not need to be defended, and in any case, economic geography does not lend itself to the high abstractions of pure theory. Professor Samuelson's remark, that the production of tropical fruit in the

---

[1] Even within the terms of the orthodox model it could not succeed in proving that free trade is necessarily best for *each* country because of Bickerdike's objection. See Joan Robinson, 'The Pure Theory of International Trade', *Collected Economic Papers*, Vol. 1 (Basil Blackwell, Oxford, 1951), p. 197.

tropics is due to the prevalence of tropical conditions there, was not intended to draw the reader's attention to a major aspect of world trade, but rather to dismiss it as uninteresting.[2]

II

Ricardo set out the case against protection in terms of two countries, England and Portugal, each capable of producing both wine and cloth. The argument implies that there is a constant amount of labour in each country which can be shifted from one line of production to the other without difficulty or loss. (Even when he takes the example of wine, there is no problem of specialised land. Constant returns prevail for each commodity up to full employment of the whole labour force.) There are different production functions (in modern jargon) in the two countries. Output per head of wine in Portugal, relatively to output per head of cloth, is greater than in England. Thus total output is increased when trade permits labour to be moved into production of wine in Portugal and cloth in England.

The relative prices of the commodities in each country are proportional to labour cost. (The rate of profit and the value of capital per man, in each country, are the same for both commodities.) Since the relative prices are different, it is impossible for both to rule in a free market. To work out the equilibrium position that the assumptions entail, we have to introduce the conditions of demand. If England consumes more wine than Portugal can export, she must produce some wine herself. The world price of wine in terms of cloth, in the final position, is then set by conditions of production in England. Portugal becomes specialised, exporting wine and importing cloth. She gains on the terms of trade in respect of all her imports. (Portuguese wine sells at the same price as English, which is dearer in terms of cloth.) England gains in respect of the part of her requirements of wine which she can get by exporting cloth, since this uses less labour per unit than wine produced at home. The results are reversed when Portugal is the country producing both commodities. In the borderline case where each country produces only one commodity, the division of the benefit between them depends solely on the conditions of demand, and relative prices are no longer governed by costs of production.

[2] P. A. Samuelson, 'International Trade and Equalisation of Factor Prices', *Economic Journal*, Vol. 58, No. 230 (June, 1948), p. 182.

For Ricardo, the rate of profit on capital depends upon the labour-cost of producing the necessary real wage. Where the imported commodity is a wage good, trade tends to raise the rate of profit. (This was a point of great importance in his campaign against the corn laws.)

He provides a mechanism to ensure balanced trade. In his scheme the rate of profit, in general, will be different in the two countries; if this occurred between districts within one nation, there would be a movement to invest where the rate of profit was higher.

Experience, however, shews that the fancied or real insecurity of capital, when not under the immediate control of its owner, together with the natural disinclination which every man has to quit the country of his birth and connexions, and intrust himself with all his habits fixed, to a strange government and new laws, check the emigration of capital. These feelings, which I should be sorry to see weakened, induce most men of property to be satisfied with a low rate of profits in their own country, rather than seek a more advantageous employment for their wealth in foreign nations.[3]

It follows that an excess of imports has to be paid for in gold. The surplus country, receiving gold, experiences a rise of prices and the deficit country, losing gold, experiences a fall, until the value of goods traded between them is brought into balance.

Whether convincing or not, Ricardo's analysis is perfectly clear. The model in Marshall's *Pure Theory of Foreign Trade*, expressed in terms of 'offer curves', is not so easy to grasp. He refers to the *Pure Theory of Domestic Values* for the analysis of costs and prices in each country, but this theory is an inextricable mixture of static and dynamic elements. 'Increasing returns' is the result of investment and technical progress going on through time as the output of a particular commodity is growing. How can this be fitted in to the comparisons of static equilibrium? He was aware of the contradiction but did not feel able to deal with it.[4]

To make sense of his system, it seems to be necessary to confine the argument to the case in which each particular commodity is produced 'under conditions of diminishing returns', that is, where

[3] David Ricardo, 'On the Principles of Political Economy and Taxation', in Piero Sraffa and M. H. Dobb, eds. *Works and Correspondence*, Vol. 1 (Cambridge University Press, London, 1951), pp. 136–7.

[4] Alfred Marshall, *The Pure Theory (Foreign Trade-Domestic Values)* (London School of Economics and Political Science, London, 1930), p. 27.

labour cost per unit is an increasing function of the level of output, presumably because each requires some specialised ingredient which is in limited supply. (A footnote[5] promises an appendix which will explain the meaning of 'cost of production' but it is nowhere to be found.) On this basis, the analysis can be explained as follows. Two countries (which comprise the world) have different production functions for the various commodities. Each country has at least one commodity for which its productive capacity is limited relative to demand at home and at least one for which productive capacity exceeds demand. In a position of equilibrium with balanced trade, world prices (and the national incomes of the countries) are such that the cost at the margin of a unit of each commodity in each country is equal to its price in the world market (allowing for transport costs). Each country supplies part of its consumption of its high-cost commodity, importing the rest, and consumes part of its low-cost commodity, exporting the rest. The position of equilibrium is such that if either country were to export a little less, the cost at home of its commodity would be lower and the demand price abroad would be higher. Similarly, if it were to export a little more, its costs would be higher and its demand price lower; the equilibrium volume of trade is determined by the rule that supply price is equal to demand price for each commodity on the world market.

But this argument is completely hollow. There is no mechanism to make trade balance; it is merely assumed that the value of exports is equal to value of imports. Marshall refers to the fact that the rate of profit obtainable in one country must be the same for each commodity, but he says nothing about the rate of profit in the other. He does not discuss what would happen if the rates of profit were different. (Writing in the great age of British overseas investment, he could not very well use Ricardo's argument as an excuse for not discussing the subject.) In his monetary writings Marshall relied on the argument about flows of gold, but in his *Pure Theory* he merely postulates that trade is always balanced. The apparatus of offer curves was intended to elaborate and refine upon the simple system of labour-value prices but Marshall only succeeded in producing a degenerate version of Ricardo's model.

Samuelson's version of the Hecksher–Ohlin theory is still more degenerate.[6] In this model the production functions are everywhere

[5] *ibid.*, p. 2.
[6] Samuelson, *op. cit.*

the same; countries differ only in respect to their 'factor endowments'. It was on this basis that Samuelson produced the theorem that, in equilibrium with two factors, two countries and two commodities, either at least one country must be specialised, or, if both commodities are produced in both countries, the 'factor prices' must be the same in both countries. (Harrod pointed out that this depends upon one more assumption that Samuelson had slipped in – that the production functions are such that the commodity which is more labour intensive at one level of 'factor prices' is so at all levels.[7])

Samuelson called the factors of production labour and land but the argument is usually developed in terms of labour and 'capital'. Each country is endowed with a lump of 'malleable capital' which can be used in various proportions with labour and the 'factor prices' which are equalised, or not equalised, are the wage rate and the rate of interest. This was the neo-neoclassical system in its heyday. Recently, this conception of capital has retreated from criticism into a 'one-commodity world',[8] which presumably would not allow any scope for trade, though it has been argued that there might be a one-way movement of savings of the commodity from the country where its 'marginal productivity' was lower to be invested in the other where it was higher.[9]

III

Ricardo relied upon adjustments of the price levels to keep trade in balance. We can make some sense of this without resorting to the Quantity Theory of Money if we substitute money-wage rates for gold flows as the equilibrating mechanism. On this view, if there is near-full employment when trade is balanced, a surplus of exports generates an excess demand for labour which drives up money costs and (with fixed exchange rates) reduces the competitive advantage of the country. In a very broad, long-run historical sweep, this tendency evidently works – high output per head, comparing one region with another, goes with high money-wage rates and therefore high real wages in terms of tradable goods. But the tendency is weak, sluggish and irregular. At any moment there is certainly not balanced trade

[7] R. F. Harrod, 'Factor-Price Relations Under Free Trade', *Economic Journal*, Vol. 68, No. 270 (June, 1958), pp. 245–55.
[8] Cf. R. M. Solow, *Growth Theory: An Exposition* (Oxford University Press, London, 1970).
[9] See below p. 23.

Reconsideration of Theory of International Trade

between the various areas of the habitable globe that happen to be under separate national governments – there is an ever-changing pattern of deficits and surpluses.

Moreover, Ricardo's doctrine that gold flows in when there is a surplus of exports and out when there are surplus imports, which may have been not far wrong in his day, was quite false when it was repeated by Marshall and Pigou. An inflow of gold (or gain of reserves) occurs when the outflow of finance is less than the surplus in the balance on income account (including interest and dividends as well as visible and invisible trade), or when the inflow of finance is greater than the deficit on income account. The operation of the gold standard mechanism was to keep flows of lending in line with income balances. A centre that was lending too much or borrowing too little raised its interest rate. Since there was perfect confidence in exchange rates, small differences in interest rates were sufficient to redirect the flow of finance. But this mechanism would not have been strong enough to do its work if there had not been harmony in the main between flows of trade and flows of finance.

In the latter part of the nineteenth century, the appearance of equilibrium was maintained just because trade was not balanced. The British economy had a continuous surplus on income account which was matched by an outflow of finance. The borrowing countries enjoyed a surplus of imports while investment was being carried out within their frontiers and since the main aim of investment was to open up sources of primary products for which there was a profitable market at home, the subsequent development of an export surplus permitted the service of loans to be financed.

Since 1914 the kaleidoscope of economic history has been continually shaken; the pattern today is greatly changed.

There is no longer any underlying harmony between the flows of finance and the pattern of surpluses and deficits on income account. For instance, sterling is weakened by institutions and habits geared to overseas investment while the British economy suffers from a chronic tendency to run into a deficit, and Germany fails to develop a sufficient outflow of finance to prevent her surplus from making the mark exchange rate uncomfortably strong. The British economy goes through agonies to get rid of an unwanted deficit while fear of inflation prevents the German authorities from playing the old rules of the game, that is to lower interest rates when reserves are accumulating. The new rules of the game – changing exchange rates – are slow, clumsy, and uncertain. The international monetary mechanism is being set problems too hard for it to solve.

There is a further source of discrepancy in balances of payments. Just as the issue of currency notes represents an interest-free loan from the citizens of a country to their government, so the reserves and working balances of foreign and colonial institutions and businesses, held in a metropolitan financial centre, represent loans to that economy. The country whose currency is used as a world medium of exchange is able to support an outflow of finance in excess of its surplus on income account as long as the world's requirement for balances is growing.

The prestige of sterling survived the strength of the British economy; for long periods her deficits were partly covered by loans from her dependencies, and, after 1947, from the so-called developing nations which succeeded.[10] The role of sterling as a reserve currency came to a final end with the devaluation of 1967. Now sterling balances have to be guaranteed in terms of dollars. The American dollar is effectively the only world currency.

The appetite of the great American corporations for overseas investment is strong; the American economy can support an outflow of finance greatly in excess of its surplus on income account, the difference being offset by an accumulation of foreign-owned dollar balances. This system is known as 'borrowing short and lending long'. It undermines confidence and threatens the stability of the currency so long as there is something to fly into; for the time being the demand for dollars has been propped up by effectively demonetising gold, but this system somehow lacks the appearance of the solid respectability of the old gold standard managed from London before 1914, and doubts are expressed from time to time as to how long it will continue.

The greatest obfuscation of the orthodox theory was in its treatment of foreign investment. The concept of 'capital' as a factor of production implied that when one country lends to another it is transferring real resources to it.

In the neo-neoclassical revival of pre-Keynesian theory, investment is determined by the desire of society to save, under the influence of time preference. Capital consists of lumps of putty and the

---

[10] However, the great bulk of wartime borrowing in the form of accumulated balances was paid off in 'unrequited exports' which made a contribution to the development of the countries concerned.

rate of interest is determined by the ratio of putty-capital to labour, being equal to the marginal productivity of putty.

In this scheme of ideas, international capital flows consist of exports of putty from one country to another.[11] A rich, high-wage country has a high putty-labour ratio and a low rate of interest. Therefore it exports its putty-savings to a country with a higher rate of interest. Savings of putty, it seems, are put onto a boat and sent to be used as putty-capital in the low-wage country.

Now, it is true that 'capital' in the sense of capital goods, say steel ingots or machine tools, may be put onto a ship and sent from one country to another, but this is not necessarily associated with a movement of 'capital' in the sense of finance, for the goods may be paid for by visible or invisible exports going in the opposite direction. On the other hand, finance may pass from one country to another to be expended exclusively in employing labour and buying property on the spot, so that there is no movement of capital goods.

A country which receives an inflow of finance is not receiving a supply of a factor of production called 'capital', it is enjoying the possibility of running a surplus of imports or amassing monetary reserves.

The latter case has been much discussed in recent times. Under the old gold standard, net lending for any country was restricted to equality with its surplus on income account. Nowadays the operation of the international monetary system permits an outflow of long-term lending from the United States in excess of its surplus; it follows that other countries are receiving loans in excess of their deficits. Thus the French complain that the American corporations take over businesses in France or instal branches to compete in their market, while all that the French economy gets in exchange is dollar balances of which they have too much already. Their proper reply, of course, within the rules of the game, would be to set about buying up American industry in return; or like Japan, they might excuse themselves from the rules and keep foreign capital out; since the French do not feel able to do either the one or the other, they complain that the game is unfair.

In the case where borrowing is covering a deficit on income account, there is a certain sense in which savings are being exported from one country to another. The deficit country is absorbing more, taking

[11] Cf. N. C. Miller, 'A General Equilibrium Theory of International Capital Flows', *Economic Journal*, Vol. 78, No. 310 (June, 1968), pp. 312–19.

consumption and investment together, than its own production. In this sense its economy is drawing upon savings made for it abroad. In return it has a permanent obligation to pay interest or profits to the lender. Whether this is a good bargain or not depends upon the nature of the use to which the funds are put. If they merely permit an excess of consumption over production, the economy is on the road to ruin. If they permit an excess of investment over home savings, the result depends upon the nature of the investment. The colonial type of investment, developing animal, mineral, and vegetable products to supply the metropolitan market, and transport to move them, was, of course, made in search of profits and was generally handsomely rewarded, but it could, in a certain sense, be said to 'create wealth' which would not otherwise have come into existence. When the colonial regions became independent 'developing countries' the consequent export earnings, minus the profits being remitted, provided ammunition for their development plans; some make bold to keep the profits as well.

The colonial type of investment is still going on (notably from Japan in Australia) – but nowadays (apart from oil) the greater part of overseas investment is looking for markets rather than supplies of materials.

When an American corporation sets up a subsidiary to sell consumer goods say, in Mexico, what does the local economy gain? There is an inflow of finance, which will have to be paid for later by remission of profits. This is a very expensive form of borrowing. The inflow of finance is generally only a small part of the capital acquired, for it is supplemented by borrowing locally. Part of profits may be reinvested on the spot. This may be a benefit to the local economy as far as it goes, but the new capital so created belongs to the parent corporation; it will give rise to additional profits which will increase the amounts to be remitted in the future. Perhaps the corporation supplies know-how and efficient management, so that, while paying the same wages, it can make a higher rate of profit than local industry. This is the point claimed in its favour. But the local economy is charged with the whole profit on the investment, not only with the extra bit due to its embodying foreign methods of production. Legally the local government is free to tax profits accruing within its borders but, for obvious reasons, this power is sparingly used. Moreover, the remission of profits is likely to involve a 'transfer burden' since investments of this type are not directly building up future export earnings to implement the remission of profits. There is a strong presumption that the so-called developing countries would be better off if they financed their investments themselves, even though at a slower rate and with less advanced technology than the foreign firms provide. The doctrine of the advantages of free trade favoured the country which was first in the field with manufacturing industry; the doctrine of the advantage of free capital movements favours the country whose firms command the greatest fund of finance.

Once we have seen through the neo-neoclassical fallacy that 'capital' is a factor of production there is a great deal of rethinking to be done.

PART II

INTERNATIONAL TRADE

2
Customs Unions, Preferential Systems and World Welfare

ROBERT E. BALDWIN
University of Wisconsin

I

A drawback of much of the literature analysing the welfare implications of customs unions and other second-best policy measures is its reliance upon the assumptions that an individual's utility is cardinally measurable and that different individuals' utilities can be added together to obtain a social welfare function.[1] The reason these implausible assumptions have been long used in customs union theory seems to be a widely-held belief that they are necessary if any very meaningful welfare statements are to be made in this field.[2] It is generally accepted that meaningful welfare statements based on ordinal measurement of utility can be made when comparing such situations as no-trade with some-trade or free trade with an optimum tariff, but in comparing second-best situations most writers abandon the ordinalist method.

Two notable exceptions to this general practice of using the cardinalist method of analysing the economic effects of customs unions are the comparatively recent monographs of Jaroslav Vanek[3] and Murray Kemp.[4] Both writers show that it is possible to abandon the dubious assumptions of the cardinalists and still make meaningful policy statements about customs unions. A limitation of much of Vanek's analysis, however, is that it is conducted under the assump-

[1] The work of J. E. Meade, e.g. *The Theory of Customs Unions* (North-Holland Publishing Company, Amsterdam, 1955), is, of course, the best-known example of this approach.
[2] Jagdish N. Bhagwati, 'The Pure Theory of International Trade: A Survey', in American Economic Association, *Surveys of Economic Theory*, Vol. 2, pp. 211–13.
[3] Jaroslav Vanek, *General Equilibrium of International Discrimination – The Case of Customs Unions* (Harvard University Press, Cambridge, 1965).
[4] Murray C. Kemp, *A Contribution to the General Equilibrium Theory of Preferential Trading* (North-Holland Publishing Company, Amsterdam, 1969).

tion of fixed output levels in the countries under consideration. Moreover, when he does lift this assumption, he assumes for the most part that output proportions remain unchanged before and after the customs union is formed.[5] The welfare test that he uses in deciding if a customs union increases or decreases world welfare is whether the world utility-possibility function based upon the world output bundle associated with the customs union is above or below the utility-possibility function based upon the output bundle attained prior to the formation of the customs union. If the utility function derived from the collection of goods achieved with the customs union is entirely outside that based upon the pre-union collection, it is possible to make each country (and the individuals within each country) better off with the customs union bundle of goods than the pre-union bundle no matter how this pre-union bundle was distributed among the countries initially.

The procedure of comparing only the bundles of commodities obtained before and after the customs union is open to the objection made by Samuelson of the Hicks and Scitovsky welfare criteria.[6] The particular world output bundle selected by the various countries in the pre-union situation is only one of many that could have been selected in this situation. There is a whole range of production possibilities open to the world, given a particular tariff policy. If income within the countries is distributed in a different manner this will change the world production point selected under the particular tariff levels set in each country. The same will be true under the customs union situation. Thus, to be as free as possible from the constraints of a particular pre- and post-customs union distribution of income one should compare every attainable production point in the pre-customs union situation (and every possible distribution among all individuals for each of these output points) with every possible production point under the customs union situation (each output bundle again being redistributed among all individuals in every possible way). Such a procedure will give two 'situation' utility-possibility curves. Unless one is outside the other over its entire range, one cannot say that one policy situation is better than the other.

Kemp permits production to vary as relative prices change but

[5] Vanek, *op. cit.*, p. 138.
[6] P. A. Samuelson, 'Evaluation of Real National Income', *Oxford Economic Papers*, Vol. 2, No. 1 (January, 1950), pp. 1–29.

uses a more restrictive welfare criterion than Vanek. In particular, he assumes lump-sum transfers are made within a country such that for any bundle of goods consumed by the country other than the initial one all individuals are either better off, worse off, or as well off as they were originally.[7] Thus, he is able to draw a set of community indifference curves that do not intersect. However, if the initial distribution pattern within the country is changed, a new set of community indifference curves is obtained. Moreover, a particular post-union collection of goods can represent an increase in welfare on the basis of one initial distribution pattern but a decrease in welfare on the basis of another. Thus, unless one is prepared to introduce a social welfare function explicitly and thereby make interpersonal utility comparisons – a step that Kemp does not wish to take – his procedure is open to the objection that it implicitly assumes the initial income distribution to be better than others that might have prevailed.

II

This paper follows the ordinalist approach of Vanek and Kemp in further investigating the welfare effects of customs unions and preferential trading arrangements. In particular it follows Kemp's study in permitting production always to vary but uses the concept of 'situation' utility possibilities curves in making welfare comparisons. Since this is the framework within which the welfare effects of free trade and tariff policies are analysed, it is also the appropriate one for investigating the welfare implications of customs unions and preferential trading arrangements. As will be shown, when this framework is utilised, a few simple and familiar principles are the main determinants of whether customs unions and preferential trading arrangements raise world welfare.

A simple example illustrates the major relationships that can be established about world welfare changes under this broad welfare criterion. Suppose that the production possibilities curves of three countries, A, B, and C, are identical and that the rate at which the curves change direction, i.e. their curvature, is a constant. This latter assumption concerning production possibility curves seems a reasonable one to make in the absence of special information about their shape. Since by appropriate choice of measurement units the distance

[7] Kemp, *op. cit.*, p. 25.

INTERNATIONAL TRADE AND MONEY

representing the maximum output of x can be made equal to that for y, the production curves can be represented as in Figure 2.1 by the portion of a circle PP'.[8] To make the analysis as general as possible suppose that the slope of the production possibility curve varies from zero at its intersection point on the y axis to infinity at its intersection point on the x axis.[9]

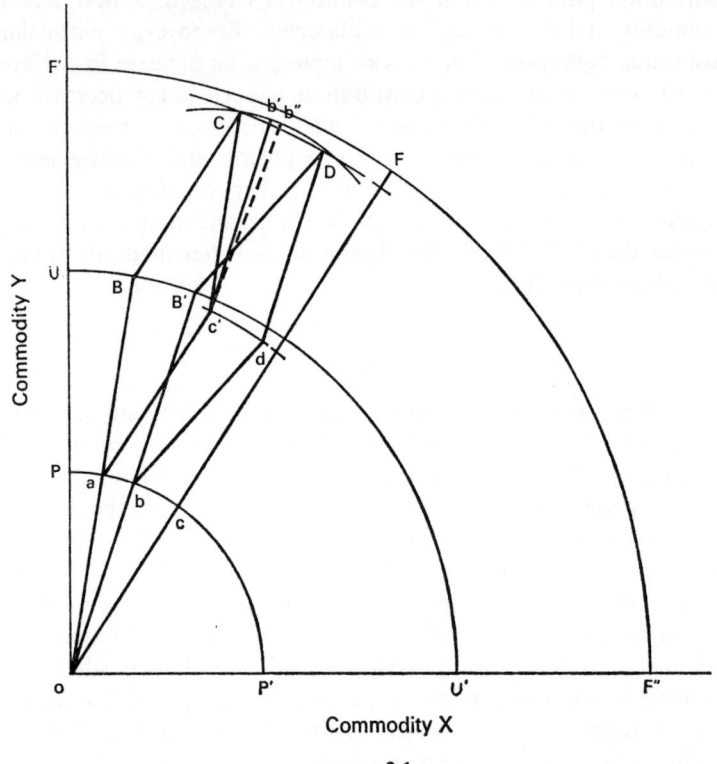

FIGURE 2.1

[8] One characteristic of a circle is that its curvature is constant.
[9] Ordinarily, the slope of the curve at its intersection points with the x and y axes will be negative and between zero and infinity. With non-identical but circular production-possibility curves, the convention would be to choose x and y scales such that for one of the production-possibility curves the distances from the origin of the figure to the intersection points of the curve with the x and y axes were the same. This would then mean that these distances would generally differ for the other two production-possibility curves. The welfare conclusions to be drawn about identical, constant-curvature production-possibility curves also hold for non-identical, constant-curvature curves.

Customs Unions

Next assume that tastes differ among the three countries so that international trade takes place under free trade conditions. Since in the absence of trade impediments the marginal production costs of (say) x in terms of y for both countries will equal the common domestic price of x in terms of y, each country produces at the same point on the common production curve, e.g. c. The combined production and consumption for the three countries is three times this output, i.e. F. The points c and F are, however, only one possible set of outputs for each country individually and combined, respectively. If lump-sum taxes are used to redistribute income among the residents of each country, new reciprocal demand curves (not shown) would be generated for each country along with new international prices and different common production points. To make the analysis as general as possible suppose that appropriate lump-sum taxation and distribution can cause production to take place at any point on the common production possibility curve. This means that the range of possible output for the three countries combined can be depicted by the curve $F'FF''$.

If international trade were not permitted and yet tastes differ among the three countries, each country's no-trade production point would differ. The production levels represented by the points oa, ob, and oc, for example, might represent the no-trade production points for countries A, B, and C, respectively. By constructing the line ac' so that it is parallel and equal in length to oc and the line $c'b'$ parallel and equal in length to ob, the combined output of the three countries under these circumstances can be represented by the point b'. Other possible total output points (brought about by redistributing income within each country) under a no-trade policy could be determined in a similar manner. As is apparent from Figure 2.1, they would all lie below the curve $F'FF''$, since in general marginal costs and domestic prices would differ among the three countries.

One can readily see from the figure why we can say that a policy of free trade is better in a world welfare sense than no trade. By appropriate lump-sum redistribution it is possible to reach points on $F'FF''$ northeast of the point b'. Since more of both goods are available at these points, it is possible by appropriate redistribution of these totals among the three countries to make everyone in all the countries better off than they are with the no-trade collection of goods regardless of the manner in which the no-trade bundle is initially distributed among the three countries and the individuals within these countries.

The same is true for any other no-trade point located below the potential free trade output levels.

Instead of regarding the points a, b, and c, as the no-trade production points for the three countries, suppose they represent equilibrium production points for the three countries when trade takes place but each imposes a different *ad valorem* duty on its imports. The differences in the slopes of the production possibility curve at the three points reflect the differences in domestic prices among the countries that are caused by the separate tariff policies. Country A exports commodity x for y, country C exports y for x, and country B could export either y or x. In both circumstances the point b' again represents the combined output level of the three countries. With a given directional pattern of trade among the three countries and given *ad valorem* duties, other possible total output points under this particular tariff situation could be represented by a curve (not shown) passing through b' and approaching F'' and F' on the x and y axes respectively. The ratio of the slopes at the production possibility points on which any particular point on this world output curve is based will always bear the same proportionate relationship to each other. The curve will, however, lie entirely below the free trade world output curve, $F'FF''$.

Suppose next that countries A and B form a customs union and adopt A's import duties as their common external tariff. With a customs union countries A and B will both produce at the same point on the common production possibilities curve. The distance oB, which is twice the distance oa, represents a possible combined output level for the two union members. Other potential output levels for the customs union are depicted by the curve $UBB'U'$. By letting the line BC be parallel and equal in length to oc, the point C then represents a possible combined output point for the union plus country C. By taking all possible combinations of production points at which the ratio of the slope of the union curve, $UBB'U'$, and the slope of country C's production possibility curve, PP', is the same, a combined world output curve under the customs union situation can be generated. The curve CD represents a portion of such a curve.

As the curve CD is drawn in the figure it passes below b' and therefore indicates that the customs union formed from the initial tariff situation is inferior in a world welfare sense to this tariff arrangement at the output proportions represented by the point b'. Actually, it can be shown that there is always some pre-customs union tariff situation which is superior to the customs union formed and based upon the higher of the two members' tariffs. To demonstrate this, consider again the point C, which indicates the combined output of the customs union and country C. Instead of indicating the output of country C at the customs union point C as the distance BC, represent this output by a line ac' from a equal in length and parallel to BC (and also oc). Then represent the output of country B by a line $c'C$ from c' that is equal in length and parallel to aB. Since the line $c'C$ also terminates at C, one can think of reaching the combined customs union plus country C output by either going along the lines oa, aB, BC, or oa, ac', $c'C$.

Next place the origin of country B's production possibility curve at c' and let $Cb'b''$ indicate this production possibility curve as it would pass through C. If the tariff situation were such that domestic prices in countries A and C were the same as initially depicted but the domestic price of x in country B was only slightly higher than in country A, a possible combined output point of the three countries could be indicated by a point on the curve $Cb'b''$ slightly to the right of C.

This point must be to the northeast of a portion of the world output curve CD that is based on the customs union between countries A and B for the following reasons. The slope of CD at C will be a weighted average that lies between the slope of the customs union output-curve $UBB'U'$ at B and the slope of country C's production possibilities curve at c. On the other hand, the slope of country B's production-possibilities curve $Cb'b''$ drawn from c' will at C equal the slope of $UBB'U'$ at B. This means that the absolute value of the slope of the curve $Cb'b''$ at C must be less than that of CD at C and therefore that there must be points along $Cb'b''$ after it cuts through CD from below (moving from left to right) which are northeast of points along CD. In turn this implies that for given tariff rates for the customs union and the rest of the world there is always some different duty level for one of the customs union members that will increase potential world output.[10]

There is, moreover, some (but changing) duty level for this former member of the customs union that maximises world output at any ratio of commodity y to commodity x given the tariff rates of the

---

[10] This point has also been made by C. A. Cooper and B. F. Massell, 'A New Look at Customs Union Theory', *The Economic Journal*, Vol. 75, No. 300 (December, 1965), pp. 745–6.

other two countries. Consider, for example, the point c' which represents the combined output of countries A and C under the initial tariff rates for these countries. If these tariff rates are held constant and other international prices and production possibilities points for each country are considered, a curve $c'd$ through c' is generated which represents all possible output points for countries A and C with the given *ad valorem* duties. The origin of country B's production possibility curve can be placed at any point on this curve and a combined output possibilities curve, e.g. $Cb'b''$, then depicted. The envelope of such curves, as the origin of country B's production curve is placed at different points along the curve $c'd$, indicates the maximum output levels attainable with a fixed ratio between the domestic prices of countries A and C and all possible domestic price ratios in country B. If a straight line between o and c' were extended a distance equal to the radius of country B's production possibilities curve, the resulting point b'' would be on this envelope. As the production curves are drawn the extended line would divide the angle aoc in half, and the slope of $c'd$ at c' will equal the slope of B's production possibility curve at b''.[11]

A constant ratio of relative domestic prices between any two countries does not mean that the angle between the corresponding output-ratio rays, e.g. between oa and oc, remains constant for all possible output combinations. If it did all the curves such as CD and $c'd$ would also be circles of a given radius. Instead, the length of a ray from the origin to the world output curves based on the customs union, CD (and the same holds with respect to $c'd$) decreases as the ray moves from the vertical axis to somewhat before a 45° position and increases thereafter.[12] Because of this relationship, a particular

---

[11] See R. E. Baldwin, 'Equilibrium in International Trade: A Diagrammatic Analysis', *Quarterly Journal of Economics*, Vol. 62, No. 5 (November, 1948), p. 754 for a proof of this relationship.

[12] If θ is the (acute) angle of inclination between a tangent line to the production-possibility curve and the x axis, $m = \tan \theta$ is the slope of the production-possibility curve at the point of tangency and $dm/d\theta = \sec^2 \theta / \tan \theta$ is the proportionate rate of change of the slope. This ratio is negative as the angle θ (in radians) goes from 0° to $-90°$, and its derivative, i.e. $d/d\theta = (\sec^2 \theta / \tan \theta) = \tan^4 \theta - 1/\tan^2 \theta$ is negative between 0° and $-45°$ and positive between $-45°$ and $-90°$. Consequently, with a common circular production curve and a fixed domestic price-ratio relationship between any two countries, the production points on PP' for any two countries become farther apart as the average slope rises from zero to minus unity and then closer together as the slope approaches minus infinity. This means that if the total output of the two countries, e.g. countries A and C, is represented in Figure 2.1 in the manner described in explain-

set of *ad valorem* tariffs for the three countries can result in total output levels that at some output ratios are northeast of points on the world output curve based on a customs union but at other output ratios are southwest of the output points on the customs union curve.[13] The closer country *B*'s tariff brings its domestic price ratio to the domestic price ratio prevailing in country *A*, the greater the likelihood that the world output curve based on this tariff (given the tariffs in countries *A* and *C*) is to the northeast of the world output curve based on the customs union at all possible output ratios.[14] Expressing the same point in a more familiar form, the greater the proportion by which the domestic price of *x* in country *B* exceeds that in country *A* under the pre-union situation, the greater the range of output ratios at which world output under the customs union exceeds that obtained under the tariff arrangement.

Another well-known principle that can be established easily from

ing the curve $c'd$, the length of a ray from the origin to $c'd$ decreases between the vertical axis and a 45° line and increases thereafter. When the output of another country, e.g. country *B* is added to the output of the other two countries in such a way that its domestic price ratio of *x* always equals that of the two countries with the lower domestic price of *x*, e.g. a union between *A* and *B* is formed, the length of a ray from the origin to the resulting world output curve will begin to lengthen before a 45° line is passed.

[13] For example, if the curve *CD* in Figure 2.1 were a circle of radius *OC*, the representation of country *B*'s production curve using c' as the origin, i.e. $Cb'b''$, would intersect *CD* again at a point on the extension of the line ac', whose slope is country *C*'s output ratio. Since the *CD* portion of the actual world output curve based on the customs union is in the range where the length of a ray from the origin is decreasing as the output of *x* increases and *y* declines, it will cut $Cb'b''$ below and to the right of where the extension of ac' intersects $Cb'b''$. However, if the point *C* on the customs union curve was below the 45° line so that points below it on this curve would be outside of a circle of radius *OC*, the curve $Cb'b''$ would cut the customs union world-output curve above where the extension of the appropriate ac' line cuts the customs union curve. Thus, domestic price ratios in country *B* that are near the domestic price ratios in country *C* but still between the ratio in countries *A* and *C* will be above the customs union curve at relatively high y/x output ratios and below the curve at low y/x output ratios.

[14] As the average domestic price ratio of *x* for *y* in countries *A* and *C* rises beyond a certain point (the proportionate relation between them being held constant), not only does the distance on the production possibilities curve between successive sets of production points for the countries decrease but a given domestic price-ratio relationship in country *B* that is between those in countries *A* and *C* will be represented by points on the production possibility curve that become relatively closer and closer to country *C*'s production point. This means that the closer country *B*'s domestic price ratio is to country *A*'s domestic price ratio, the smaller the output range in which world output under a tariff situation may be less than under a customs union between countries *A* and *B*.

Figure 2.1 is that the smaller the rest of the world in relation to the customs union the more likely the union will increase world welfare. A decrease in the size of country C (the rest of the world) can be shown by moving $c'C$ in a parallel fashion to the left and thus decreasing the size of the parallelogram $aBCc'$. As the line BC becomes shorter the slope of country C's production possibility curve will have less weight in determining the slope of the world output curve under the union. Therefore, the slope of the curve CD at the point C will become less and reduce the range in which the curve $Cb'b''$ lies above CD.

Since curves such as $Cb'b''$ will always cut the curve CD at C from above (moving from right to left) throughout the range of possible output ratios, any customs union that reduces the degree of disparity between the domestic prices of one member and the rest of the world (country C) always increases world welfare. For example, if the line ob were to the left of oa a customs union between countries A and B in which country A's duties become the common external tariff will be unambiguously better in a world welfare sense than the tariff situation.[15] Another implication of the same point is that not only is there some tariff situation yielding greater world output than any particular customs union situation but there is always some customs union situation that results in a greater world output than any particular tariff situation. If the world economy moves back and forth between these two policies in such a way as always to increase world welfare, it would move toward the free trade world output curve.

III

The same framework outlined in analysing customs unions can also be used in studying the world welfare implications of preferential

---

[15] However, because the curvature of a world output curve based on a customs union is not constant, it cannot be said that a customs union between country A (with A's duties as the common external tariff) and another country B whose domestic price of x is greater than in either countries A or C results in an unambiguous increase in world welfare. Actually, in Figure 2.1 the CD portion of the world output curve under the customs union is drawn in the y/x output range where it is possible for a domestic price of x in country B higher than in country C (and, of course in country A) to yield a world output point above the customs union world-output curve. More specifically, a line from c' representing country B's output that is somewhat less steep than ac' – and thus representative of a higher domestic price of x in country B than in C or A – can cut $Cb'b''$ to the northeast of part of the curve CD.

trading relations. Suppose, for example, that country A, which trades with both countries B and C, eliminates its import duties on commodities exported from B but retains these duties on goods exported from C. Country B also retains its imports duties on goods coming from country A.

The initial world output level can be illustrated by the point b' in Figure 2.1. After the preferences are granted to country B by A, the domestic price ratio in the former country will move toward that in country A, but not to a position of equality because of B's duties on A's exports. In the figure world output will shift from positions like b' to points on the curve $Cb'b''$ between C and b'.

In general, the statements that can be made about world welfare changes are the same as in the case of customs union. In particular, unless country B's domestic price ratio under preferences is such that world output is maximised for the given tariff rates and production levels in countries A and B, there will be some non-preferential arrangement among the three countries that will increase world output. Moreover, since the domestic price ratio in country B which maximises world output with given tariffs in countries A and C shifts as the world output ratio changes, some non-preferential arrangement can always increase world output at all other output ratios even if the preference point is on the maximum output curve at some particular output ratio. The same statement can be made in reverse, namely, that some preferential arrangement among the three countries can always increase world output over that reached by a particular tariff arrangement, except perhaps at one output ratio.

No simple statement about whether the particular preference arrangement adopted is better than the particular initial tariff situation can be made because, as in the tariff vs. customs union case, the world output curves based on these two situations may cross. However, the larger country A in relation to country B and – as in the customs union case – the smaller the rest of the world in relation to country B, the greater will be the range of output ratios at which world output under the preferential arrangement exceeds world output under any particular tariff arrangement which fixes country B's domestic price ratio between that of countries A and C. If countries A and B did not trade with each other but traded the same goods with country C, a preference arrangement in which both countries A and B reduced their duties to zero on C's exports would reduce the degree of price distortion in world trade and unambiguously increase world welfare by shifting the world output curve outward. Still another principle similar to the customs union case is that in the situation where country A grants preferences to country B but not to country C, the higher the tariff initially imposed by A the more likely the preference arrangement will raise world welfare.

IV

Once the assumption of production-possibility curves with constant curvatures is dropped, the wide range of possibilities for intersections between the world output curves based on a particular set of tariffs and a customs union derived from this tariff arrangement make attempts to generalise about world welfare changes over the whole output range very difficult. However, one can still say that there is always some tariff situation that will increase the level of world output achieved with a particular customs union situation. The reason is that, as at point C in Figure 2.1, with increasing-cost production possibility curves the world output curve based on a customs union will at any point be cut from above (moving from right to left) by a curve depicting the world output possibilities attainable by raising the domestic price ratio in country B (the country whose domestic price ratio was between the domestic price ratios in the other two countries in the pre-union situation) relative to this ratio in the other member country. For similar reasons one can also say that there is always some customs union that will increase the level of world output achieved with a particular tariff situation. In addition, the remarks previously made concerning the size of the rest of the world relative to the union as well as the initial degree of pre-union price disparity for the union members also apply in judging particular tariff and customs-union situations.

V

The manner in which any particular bundle of goods on the pre- and post-union world production possibility curve is allocated among the three countries depends upon the distribution policies followed in the countries, since these influence the shapes of their offer curves. However, by assuming that the internal distribution policies of other countries remain unchanged, it is possible to assess the effect of a customs union on a particular country. Consider, for example, the

CUSTOMS UNIONS

effect of a customs union on the rest of the world. Prior to the union country C (the rest of the world) faces a given net offer curve from A and B.[16] Depending upon the redistribution policies followed in country C, the offer curve of C could intersect A's excess offer curve at any point along it and thus give a range of possible international price ratios. However, given the level of *ad valorem* duties imposed by country C on imports from country A, the domestic price ratio in C will always differ from the international ratio by a fixed percentage. Figures 2.2a and 2.2b illustrate the pre-union transformation

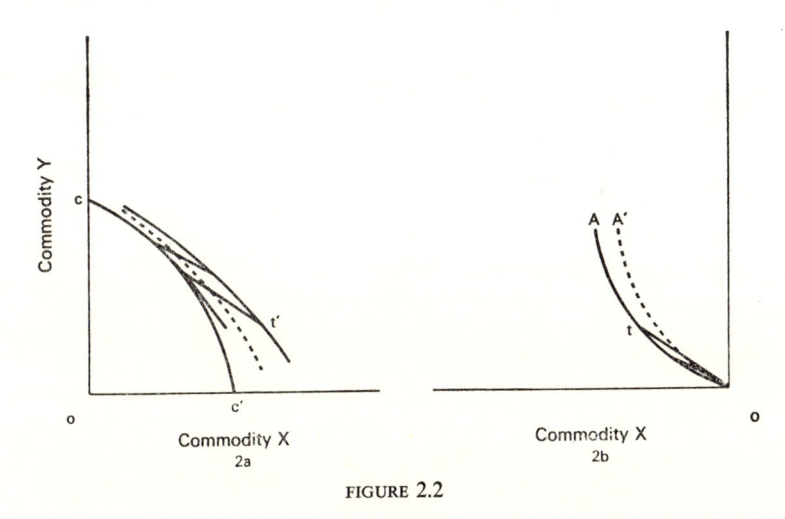

FIGURE 2.2

possibilities open to country C, given its duty levels and country A's post-tariff excess offer curve. A point on this curve, e.g. t', is determined by taking a particular offer of A, e.g. Ot, and placing it on C's production possibilities curve, cc', at the point where the domestic price ratio in C that would be associated with this international price is tangent to C's production curve. (The domestic price exceeds the international price by the given duty imposed by C.) The post-union transformation possibilities for C are determined in the same way except that A's post-union excess offer curve is used. Since, as Vanek points out, this excess offer curve OA', 'almost necessarily'[17] lies

[16] Under the assumption that countries B and C trade in the same direction, the net offer curve facing C is determined by subtracting B's post-tariff offer curve from A's post-tariff curve. This gives A's excess offer curve in the pre-customs union tariff-situation.
[17] Vanek, *op. cit.*, p. 106.

below *A*'s post-tariff excess offer curve, it follows that the post-union transformation possibilities curve open to *C* almost always lies below the pre-union curve facing *C*.

Ascertaining the combined welfare potential for countries *A* and *B* before and after the formation of the customs union is more complicated. The pre-union transformation curve for the two countries is determined by combining country *C*'s post-tariff offer curve and

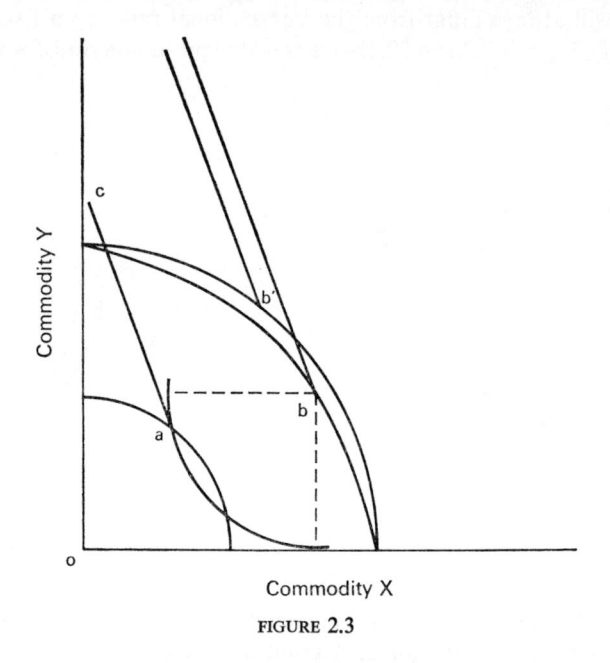

FIGURE 2.3

the appropriate joint production possibilities of *A* and *B* under their given tariffs. In combining these curves country *C*'s offer curve is added to the joint production curve in the same way described above with reference to combining *A*'s excess offer curve with *C*'s production curve. The resulting transformation curve indicates the various quantities of *x* and *y* that *A* and *B* together could obtain given their own tariff levels as well as their trading possibilities with *C*. The post-union transformation curve will be determined in the same manner except that *C*'s offers will be combined with a larger joint production possibility curve for *A* and *B*.

An example where the post-union situation gives *A* and *B* less potential welfare along part of their transformation possibilities curve is given in Figure 2.3. Country C's offer curve is assumed to be infinitely elastic. Thus, given a particular *ad valorem* duty in A against imports from C, there will be only one production point in A from which trade with C will take place. (Country B is assumed not to trade with country C.) This is shown by point a in the figure with ac indicating A's trading possibilities with C. Country B's production curve is assumed to intersect A's at the angle indicated at point a, thus given the combined production curve on which b is a point. Transferring ac to b indicates the trading possibilities of the two countries with the outside world. When they form a customs union (using A's duties as the common external tariff) and A and B production costs become equal, the line ac would shift to b' to show their combined trading possibilities. Since the extension of ac from b' is below that from b, their welfare possibilities in this direction are lower. Of course, by reducing the slope of ac it would be possible to reverse these results. As Vanek points out, when less than infinitely elastic offer curves are introduced, decreasing the elasticity of C's offer curve rapidly reduces the possibility that post-union welfare potential for A and B is less than pre-union welfare opportunities.[18] The other main factor affecting the outcome is the extent to which A's and B's combined production possibilities expand after the union. The greater this expansion (which means the higher the initial duties between A and B) the more likely is the post-union welfare situation to be an improvement over the pre-union situation.

VI

To summarise, the main purpose of this paper has been to investigate the world welfare effects of customs union and preferential trading arrangements utilising both a very broad welfare criterion and a general equilibrium framework in contrast to the usual partial-equilibrium, cardinalist approach. More specifically, the world output-possibilities associated with a particular customs union or tariff situation are taken to be all the possible output combinations that are consistent with a fixed set of domestic price-ratio relationships among all countries. Only if the utility-possibilities curve based on all of these output possibilities lies entirely outside that based upon a different customs union or tariff situation is the former trading situation regarded as superior in a world welfare sense to the latter.

[18] Vanek, *op. cit.*, p. 107.

Even within this broad framework it is still possible to derive certain familiar principles concerning the likelihood that a customs union or preferential arrangement will raise world welfare when each country produces all goods. In particular, two important principles which still apply are that the larger the pre-union (or pre-preferential arrangement) discrepancy in relative prices between the union members and the smaller the rest of the world's production possibilities compared to the production potential of the countries in the union (preferential arrangement) the more likely it is that a customs union (preferential arrangement) will raise world welfare. A specific case where world welfare is unambiguously raised is when the customs union members adopt a common external tariff that reduces the discrepancy between domestic prices of the union members and those in the rest of the world. In comparing all possible customs union and tariff situations another conclusion which emerges (and the same applies to preferential arrangements) is that it is always possible to find some particular tariff arrangement that will yield a larger bundle of all goods for the world than those achieved at any particular production point under a specific customs union arrangement. Similarly, any specific tariff arrangement can be improved upon in the same sense by some appropriate customs union. Only when a free-trade policy is reached is it impossible to raise world welfare further.

3

The Theory of Immiserizing Growth: Further Applications[1]

JAGDISH N. BHAGWATI
Professor of Economics (MIT)

In this paper, I consider two applications of the theory of immiserizing growth (Bhagwati, 1968).

In Section I, I examine mainly the paradox of a reduction in the welfare of a 'small' country, with a domestic distortion in production, when its terms of trade improve exogenously. This, and related, paradoxes are seen to be nothing but special cases of the general theory of immiserizing growth.

In Section II, I examine the paradox of a reduction in the welfare of a country following a tariff-induced inflow of capital. This paradox again follows from the theory of immiserizing growth; besides, it is clearly of immediate and direct relevance to policymaking.

I. WAGE DIFFERENTIALS, TERMS OF TRADE IMPROVEMENT, AND IMMISERIZING GROWTH

Batra and Pattanaik (1970) have produced recently the paradoxical proposition that an exogenous improvement in the terms of trade can worsen, rather than improve, welfare if a country has a distortionary wage differential. Batra and Scully (1971) have now added yet another paradox to the theory of trade and welfare in showing that immiserizing growth can occur, *despite endogenous-growth-induced improvement in the terms of trade*, if wage differentials are present. It is easy to provide the underlying rationale for these two paradoxes by drawing on recent insights into the theory of immiserizing growth.[2]

---

[1] Thanks are due to the National Science Foundation for research support. Thanks are due to Michael Connolly for helpful comments.

[2] The substance of the following argument is now summarised in Batra–Scully (1971).

Batra–Pattanaik paradox

Let me first examine the Batra–Pattanaik (1970) paradox. It can easily be shown that this paradox is, paradoxically enough, yet another instance of the generalised theory of immiserizing growth.

This theory (Bhagwati, 1968) states that if growth takes place in a country characterised by (a distortion and hence by) a sub-optimal policy, then immiserizing growth can ensue; conversely, growth cannot be immiserizing if optimal policies are pursued (before and after growth). Growth can only improve welfare if optimal policies are pursued; however, if sub-optimal policies are followed before and after growth, immiserizing growth will ensue if the primary gain from growth, measured as the gain which would accrue if optimal policies were followed, is outweighed by the *incremental* loss that could arise from the pursuit instead of sub-optimal policies.

As Batra and Scully have noted, I have used this theory elsewhere (Bhagwati, 1968) to show that in the presence of a wage differential, immiserizing growth can occur for a country with *given* terms of trade and *laissez-faire* as its economic policy. The reason is that *laissez-faire* is a sub-optimal policy when a distortionary wage-differential is present, as argued by Hagen (1958) in a classic paper.

But I have also noted elsewhere (Bhagwati, 1971) that the theory of immiserizing growth can be used to illuminate, and prove, other propositions of trade theory where no growth, in an obvious sense, is involved. Thus, the classic propositions of Gottfried Haberler (1950), which compare free trade (i.e. *laissez-faire*) with no trade (i.e. autarky) and demonstrate that the two policies cannot be ranked uniquely if production externalities or factor–price rigidities are present, can be readily seen to be examples of the theory of immiserizing growth. This is because, as Baldwin (1948) has shown, the free-trade-situation availability locus lies uniformly outside (except for overlaps) the production possibility curve which is, of course, the no-trade-situation availability locus. Thus, the no-trade and free-trade policies are conceptually the same as pre-growth and post-growth situations. Hence, if a distortion is present in the two situations, so that the two situations are sub-optimal, immiserizing growth can follow: that is to say, free trade can be inferior to no trade.

The Batra-Pattanaik paradox also falls into place in a similar fashion. The exogenous improvement in the terms of trade implies an outward shift of the Baldwin availabilities locus, implying 'growth'; the presence of the distortionary wage differential implies that this

The Theory of Immiserizing Growth

'growth' is occurring in the presence of sub-optimal policies. Hence 'immiserizing growth' can occur: that is to say, an exogenous improvement in the terms of trade can worsen welfare.

Batra–Scully paradox
The Batra–Scully proposition involves a paradox within a world of paradoxes. While it has been shown (Bhagwati, 1968) that the

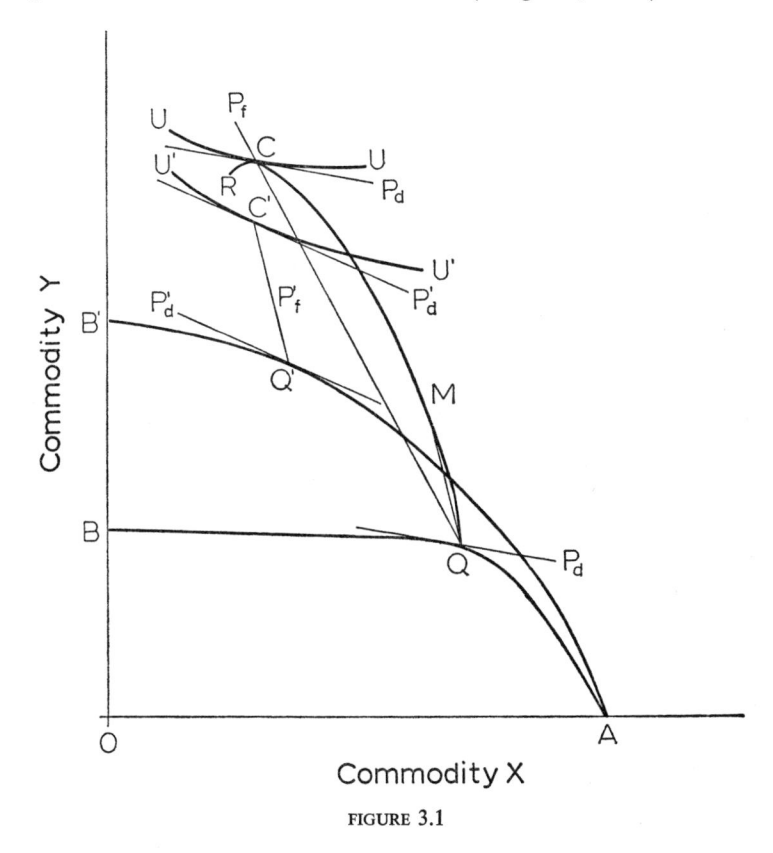

FIGURE 3.1

presence of wage differentials in a 'small' country can lead to immiserizing growth, they demonstrate that such immiseration can arise even when, for a 'large' country, the terms of trade have *improved* as a result of this growth.

The Batra–Scully paradox is, however, similar to my other demonstration (Bhagwati, 1968) of the possibility of immiserizing growth when, for a large country, the pre-growth optimal tariff is kept unchanged after growth and ceases to be optimal in the post-growth situation. In the geometrical illustration (Figure 2, Bhagwati, 1968) of this possibility, reproduced here as Figure 3.1 for convenience, the terms of trade actually improved in the post-growth situation and yet growth was immiserizing;[3] however, the paradoxical phenomenon of improvement in the terms of trade was neither noted nor explained.

And yet this paradox is readily resolved. When the growth occurs and the tariff (which is optimal in the initial, pre-growth situation) is kept unchanged, the tariff ceases in general to be optimal.[4] Hence the loss from this sub-optimal policy can outweigh the gain from growth (measured as when an optimal tariff were levied in the post-growth situation as well). That this can happen when the terms of trade improve is, in turn, seen as follows. If the growth is heavily biased in favour of the importable good,[5] then the marginal rate of domestic transformation improves in favour of the importable good thus implying that the optimal tariff should be increased. Since it is not, there is a loss of welfare which outweighs, when large enough, the gain from growth. At the same time, given the foreign offer curve facing the country and the country's unchanged tariff, the growth (which is, in the illustration, ultra-biased in favour of the importable good and hence shrinks the country's own offer curve) will improve the terms of trade. Hence the phenomenon of terms-of-trade improvement can arise simultaneously with the phenomenon of immiserizing growth.

The Batra–Scully paradox is to be explained in similar terms. Their analysis is for a large country with *laissez-faire and* with a distortionary wage differential: hence they are comparing the pre-growth and the post-growth situations which are both characterised, in general, by sub-optimality arising from *two* distortions: failure to offset the wage differential and failure to pursue a policy designed to exploit

[3] Thus, in Figure 3.1, AB is the pre-growth production possibility curve, AB' the post-growth production possibility curve, $QMCR$ the super-imposed foreign offer curve facing the country, the post-growth equilibrium shows lower welfare level implying immiserising growth $(U > U')$ and the terms of trade have improved after growth (from QC to $QM = Q'C'$).

[4] Note that the foreign offer curve facing the growing country is taken, as always, to be given in the analysis.

[5] In Figure 3.1, the growth is ultra-biased in favour of the importable good so that, at constant commodity prices, growth actually reduces the output of the exportable good.

The Theory of Immiserizing Growth

the country's largeness (i.e. its monopoly power in trade). Hence immiserizing growth is possible. At the same time, growth may shrink the country's offer curve, causing the terms of trade to

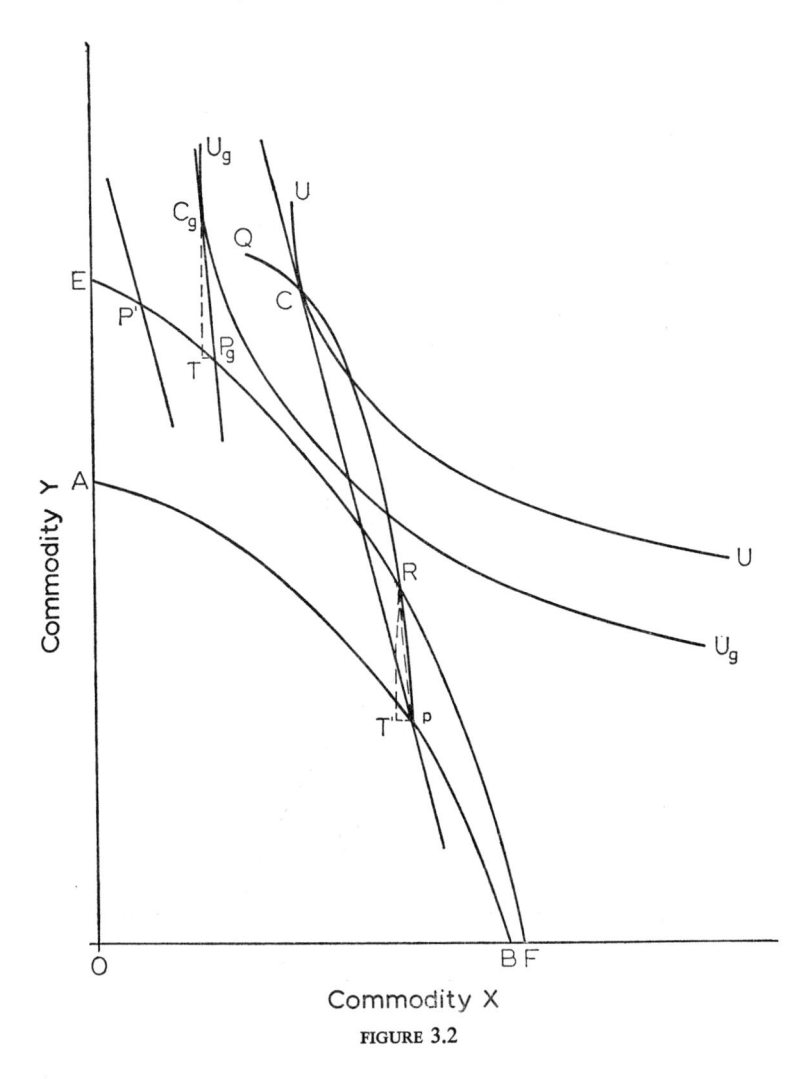

FIGURE 3.2

improve. Hence arises the possibility illustrated in Figure 3.2, where the production possibility curve shifts with growth from *AB* to *EF*, the initial terms of trade are *PC*, the initial welfare level at *U*, and the new equilibrium is at improved terms of trade $P_g C_g$ but at reduced welfare level U_g, implying immiserizing growth.[6]

II. TARIFF-INDUCED CAPITAL INFLOW AND IMMISERATION

The second application of the theory of immiserizing growth arises from Harry Johnson's (1967) demonstration that a 'small' country, growing subject to a constant tariff, can experience immizerising

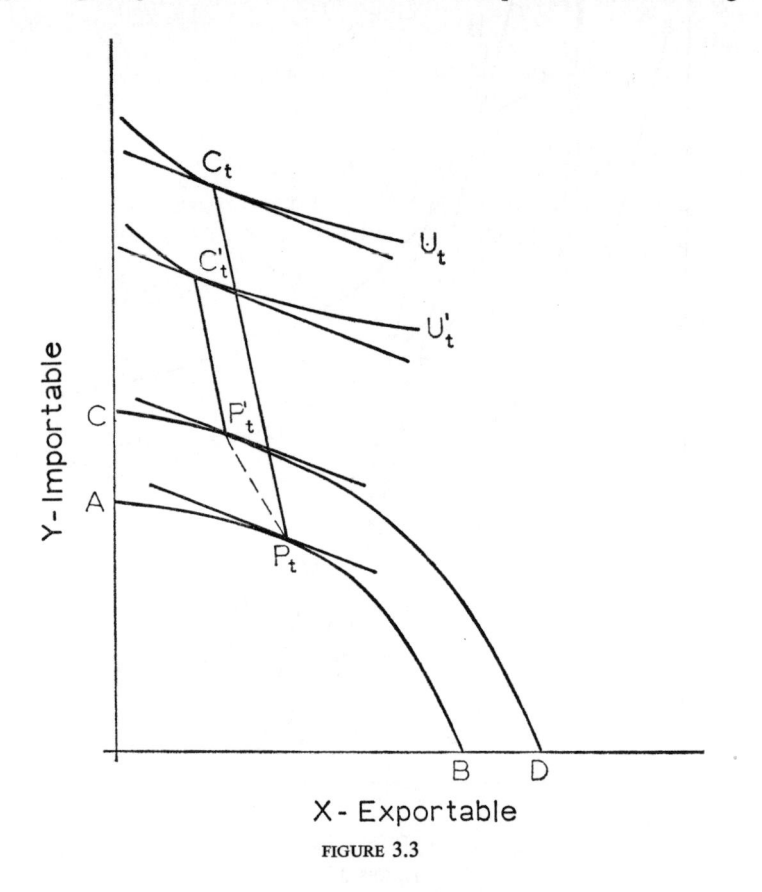

FIGURE 3.3

[6] P' shows the production point after growth if terms of trade were held constant, implying that growth is ultra-biased in favour of the importable commodity Y; and $PRCQ$ is the given foreign offer curve, with $P_g C_g$ parallel and equal in length to PR, implying that the illustrated post-growth equilibrium is consistent with the given foreign offer curve.

growth. His analysis clearly points to the possibility of immiseration following from a tariff-induced inflow of capital. However, the analysis cannot be carried over identically and fully as Tan (1969), in his subsequent examination of the conditions for Johnson's possibility to occur, has implied.[7]

Johnson's analysis relates to a comparison of the pre-growth and post-growth situations, both subject to a given tariff. On the other hand, the analysis of tariff-induced capital inflow and (resulting) immiseration requires a comparison of the free-trade situation with the tariff-inclusive, post-growth (*via*-capital-influx) situation. I now explore this particular comparison and discuss the conditions under which immiseration will follow.

Johnson's paradox

In Johnson's paradox, illustrated in Figure 3.3, the pre-growth tariff-inclusive production is at P_t, the given international price-line is $C_t P_t \| C'_t P'_t$, the pre-growth consumption is at C_t and welfare is at U_t. With capital accumulation, the production possibility curve shifts from AB to CD, production to P'_t, consumption to C'_t and welfare is reduced to U'_t ($<U_t$). It is clear that a necessary and sufficient condition for such immiseration is that the Rybczynski-line $P_t P'_t$ be less steep than the international price-ratio $P_t C_t$; a necessary condition for such immiseration is that the output of the exportable good must fall at constant, tariff-inclusive prices (i.e. growth should be ultra-biased in favour of the importable good).

Tariff-induced capital inflow

When, however, we wish to examine the conditions under which the possibility of immiseration will emerge if we have a tariff-induced capital inflow, we have the following four welfare elements in the transition from an initial free-trade situation to the tariff-and-capital-inflow-inclusive situation:

(i) The tariff imposes a production cost by distorting the prices faced by producers.
(ii) The capital influx implies 'growth', at constant tariff-inclusive

[7] Bertrand and Flatters (1971) also have, subsequent to Tan's work, explored the conditions for Johnson's paradox to occur when capital accumulation is responsible for the growth. Bhagwati (1968) has provided the general theory of immiserizing growth which reduces Johnson's and other earlier (Bhagwati, 1958) paradoxes to special cases.

domestic prices faced by producers, which may imply a welfare gain or a welfare loss.

(iii) The tariff imposes a consumption cost by distorting the prices faced by consumers; and

(iv) The tariff-induced capital influx earns a reward which must be reckoned as a cost and hence a welfare loss to the tariff-imposing country.

These elements are illustrated in Figure 3.4. The initial free-trade equilibrium with production possibility curve AB and the fixed

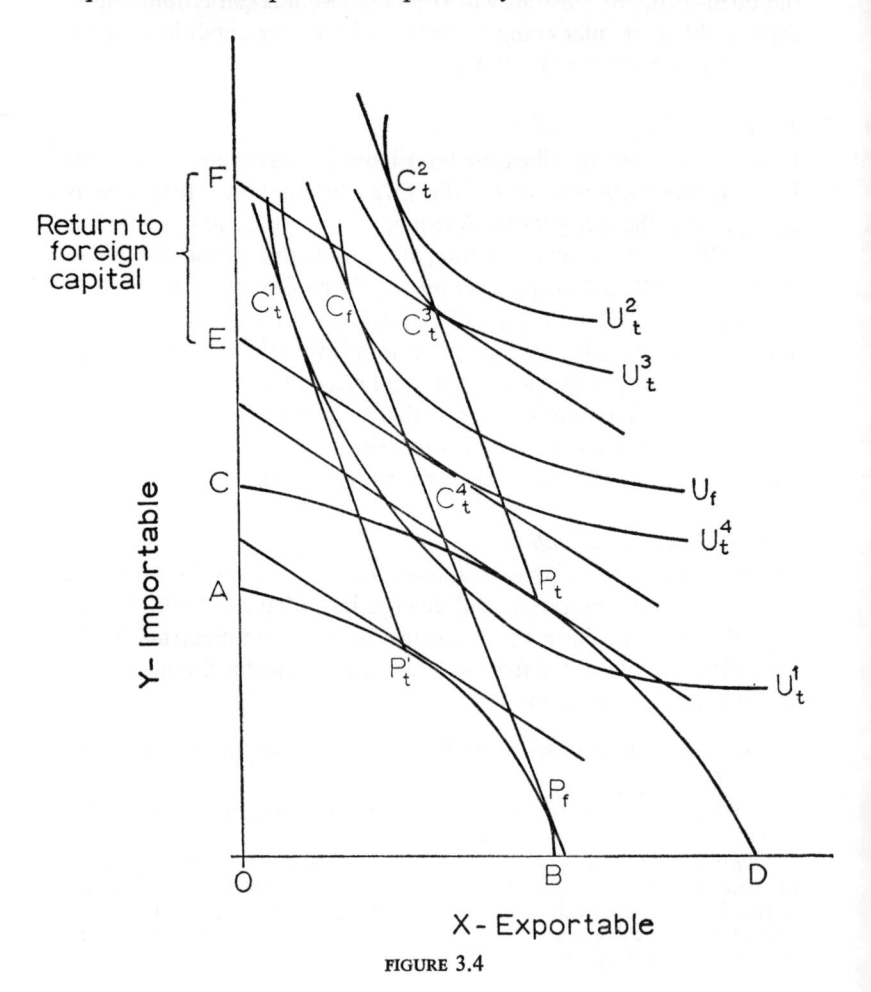

FIGURE 3.4

international price-line $P_f C_f$, is characterised by production at P_f, consumption at C_f and welfare at U_f. The tariff-plus-capital-influx equilibrium is, with the foreign-capital-augmented production possibility curve CD, at P_t, $C^4{}_t$ and $U^4{}_t$ ($< U_f$) and shows, in consequence, immiseration. The transition from U_f to $U^4{}_t$ can be built up through the four elements we have already distinguished:

(i) The tariff shifts production from P_f to P'_t along AB, leading to a decline in welfare from U_f to $U^1{}_t$; this is the result of the production distortion.
(ii) The influx of foreign capital shifts production, at tariff-inclusive prices, from P'_t to P_t and therefore welfare from $U^1{}_t$ to $U^2{}_t$; this welfare-shift, *identical* with the one underlying the Johnson paradox (which involves immiserizing growth under a given tariff), may be positive (as in Figure 3.4) or negative (as in the Johnson paradox).
(iii) Consumption must also be shifted because it will occur at tariff-inclusive prices; this reduces the economy from $U^2{}_t$ to $U^3{}_t$; and finally
(iv) The return to the foreign capital inflow, measured at EF amount of Y-goods in domestic prices,[8] will reduce the economy still further to $U^4{}_t$.[9]

It is clear, therefore, that the tariff-induced-capital-inflow immiseration requires far less stringent conditions than the Johnson case. The latter must rely entirely on effect (ii) being negative, this being a necessary and sufficient condition for the immiserizing phenomenon. On the other hand, in the present case, effects (i), (iii) and (iv) being necessarily negative, effect (ii) can be positive and yet be compatible with immiseration, as is in fact depicted in Figure 3.4. It should be possible to set down formally the necessary and sufficient conditions for immiseration in this case; but this has not been attempted here.

---

[8] While capital will earn the value of its marginal product, the return would have to be modified by phenomena such as corporation taxes. We must therefore take the *net* return into account.

[9] An alternative way to get from U_f to $U^4{}_t$ would be to (i) go from U_f to $U^*{}_f$ on assumption that capital has come in but that we are still in free trade; this would be done by putting the international price-line tangent to CD and then tangent, in turn, to $U^*{}_f$; this is necessarily a welfare gain; (ii) go from $U^*{}_f$ to $U^2{}_t$, which would be the production loss associated with the tariff, but now taken at CD; (iii) go from $U^2{}_t$ to $U^3{}_t$, which is the consumption loss; and (iv) go finally from $U^3{}_t$ to $U^4{}_t$, which would be the loss from netting out the reward to foreign capital.

REFERENCES

1. R. Baldwin, 'Equilibrium in International Trade: A Diagrammatic Analysis', *Quarterly Journal of Economics*, Vol. 62, No. 5 (November, 1948), pp. 748–62.
2. R. Batra and P. Pattanaik, 'Domestic Distortions and the Gains from Trade', *Economic Journal*, Vol. 80, No. 319 (September, 1970) pp. 638–49.
3. R. Batra and G. Scully, 'The Theory of Wage Differentials: Welfare and Immiserizing Growth', *Journal of International Economics*, Vol. 1, No. 2 (May, 1971), pp. 241–7.
4. T. Bertrand and F. Flatters, 'Tariffs, Capital Accumulation and Immiserizing Growth', *Journal of International Economics*, Vol. 1, No. 4 (November, 1971), pp. 453–60.
5. J. Bhagwati, 'Immiserizing Growth: A Geometric Note', *Review of Economic Studies*, Vol. 25, No. 68 (June, 1958), pp. 201–5.
6. J. Bhagwati, 'Distortions and Immiserizing Growth: A Generalization', *Review of Economic Studies*, Vol. 35, No. 104 (October, 1968), pp. 481–5.
7. E. Hagen, 'An Economic Justification of Protectionism', *Quarterly Journal of Economics*, Vol. 72, No. 4 (November, 1958), pp. 496–514.
8. H. G. Johnson, 'The Possibility of Income Losses from Increased Efficiency or Factor Accumulation in the Presence of Tariffs', *Economic Journal*, Vol. 77, No. 305 (March, 1967), pp. 151–4.
9. A. H. Tan, 'Immiserizing Tariff-induced Capital Accumulation and Technical Change', *Malayan Economic Review*, 1969.

4

Induced Technical Change and the Transfer Mechanism[1]

MICHAEL B. CONNOLLY
University of Florida

The purpose of this paper is to examine three aspects of technical change in an international setting. First, technical advances are frequently produced through research and development. Second, technical advances are often, if by no means always, sold or traded through a patent system designed to make appropriable the external gains inherent in their development. (Patents are designed to prevent the *free* adoption of innovations, not to exclude their adoption altogether.) Third, and perhaps most important, new techniques can, in many instances, be applied to productive processes throughout the world, independently of their place of origin or discovery. From this standpoint, one can consider new advances as having public or collective characteristics. This aspect of technology has been recognised for some time, and is clearly stated, for example, by Marshall in *Industry and Trade*:

> Broad ideas and knowledge, which when once acquired pass speedily into common ownership; and become part of the collective wealth, in the first instance of the countries to which the industries specially affected belong, and ultimately to the whole world (p. 175).

In fact, this is one way of looking at the often cited characteristic of information and knowledge: namely, the same bit of knowledge can be applied many times over.[2] In what follows, we examine the

[1] I am pleased to acknowledge the helpful suggestions of Thomas Horst, Harry G. Johnson, Irving Kravis, Robert A. Mundell and Stephen Ross. I would also like to express my gratitude to members of seminars at the University of Chicago and the University of Pennsylvania before whom earlier versions of the paper were presented, and to the Graduate Institute of International Studies, Geneva, where the final draft was completed. Thanks are also due to a Ford Foundation International Studies Grant.

[2] Putting the accent on the *collective* nature of certain technical changes does not diminish the possibility and importance of *localised* technical progress, as

implications of these three aspects of technical change. The analysis focuses upon two major issues: (1) the appropriability of the gains from new techniques, and (2) the impact on welfare of changes in the *commodity* terms of trade due to technical change. The paper abstracts from problems frequently associated with technical change, such as uncertainty [2] and learning by doing [1], as well as from problems associated with the lag between the devotion of resources to the development of new techniques, and their appearance and eventual adoption [10, 16, 19]. It is assumed rather that innovations can be produced continuously, and are capable of being immediately adopted wherever they are found to be of use. We ignore completely, therefore, any costs associated with adapting an innovation to its different uses, for instance, domestic and foreign. This further restricts the analysis by partially eliminating the problem of time, one which may be particularly present in transmitting advances from one country to another.[3] In order to completely eliminate the problem of time, it is assumed that there is only one period relevant to the analysis, and that the technical progress takes place then and only then, and can be measured by its impact on production patterns in that time period.[4] In return for the loss in generality implied by these restrictions, we gain in focusing attention on the explicit and intended production of technology, on its public characteristics, and its export by sale, licence, or use by subsidiaries in foreign countries.

Part I sets out the conditions for the optimum production of technical change in a framework in which new techniques can be exported abroad in exchange for payments. Rather than treating technical change as an observable magnitude that enters production functions much like produced capital, we adopt as a measure of technical progress its *effects upon production* at home and abroad. Consequently, payments for the import of new techniques take the form of a *transfer* of goods, and can thus be incorporated into the

recently stressed in [3]. Indeed, a localized technical change in their sense may be collective for firms elsewhere that operate under broadly similar technical and factor use conditions.

[3] For our purposes, the problem of time in an international setting is a separate one. It can, however, be approached in a Fisherian framework [4, 7, 14 and 20].

[4] This assumption precludes the possibility that technical advances typically yield a stream of increased output over time. From the point of view of a firm which takes interest rates or the terms of trade over time as parameters the problem is easily solvable. In the general equilibrium approach taken here, the relative price of time is a variable and makes for difficulties that we do not wish to take up here. Once again, refer to [4, 7, 14 and 20].

classical two-good trade model without having to add a third commodity.[5] At the optimum position, the value of the change in *world* production due to the appearance of new techniques must just be offset by the cost of producing more of them. Further, a departure from the optimum position in the direction of increased production, sale and transfer of technology from country to country is shown to involve the *sum* of three effects for which the standard trade apparatus has a ready answer: (1) a *decline* in production in the country in which innovations are produced, (2) a *rise* in production in the country which adopts them, and (3) a *transfer* of income from the adopting to the innovating country. The outcome is shown to involve changes in the commodity terms of trade, thereby highlighting an important consideration in the choice of new techniques in an open economy. Throughout, payments for the use of new techniques are linked directly to the classical transfer mechanism.

In Part II, we take up the implications of a *free* spillover of induced technical change, and reach the conclusion that, at the margin, an increase in the production and spillover of new techniques can be treated simply as an increase in productivity abroad, at no change in productivity at home. We also compare the results with the standard approach of an exogenous increase in productivity that is assumed to occur at no cost in terms of the investment of resources in technical change. Part III extends the analysis to the case of incomplete specialization, thereby allowing for the possibility that advances in technology may be of use only in the production of a specific commodity.

I. TRADE IN TECHNICAL CHANGE

A. *The optimum conditions* (*ignoring monopoly power*)

The approach taken here is to specify the conditions for the efficient production of technology; then to examine the consequences of departures from such efficient patterns by making use of the efficiency characteristics. We take up the simplest case first, namely that of

---

[5] An alternative approach would be to treat technical change as a measurable input, so that trade in technical progress would be treated like trade in an intermediate good that has public characteristics.

A defect of that approach is that one cannot easily quantify new ideas because of their intangible nature, but rather can measure them by their impact on production. Thus, making available an idea abroad is basically dissimilar to exporting a tangible commodity.

complete specialisation in production. Country A produces only its national product, Y. To maximise output, resources can be employed directly in the Y industry, or they can be diverted to the production of new techniques which in turn increase the productivity of factors employed in producing Y. We can call this subsidiary industry the R/D (research and development) sector. In the absence of foreign trade, it is very easy to specify the efficiency condition: resources must be diverted to the R/D sector to the point where the extra gain in increased production due to the new techniques is just cancelled by the fall in production induced by the diversion of resources from direct employment in the Y industry. Letting dY_t represent the rise in production due to the new techniques, and dY_r the absolute value of the fall in production due to the diversion of resources to the R/D sector, the maximum condition for a closed economy is: $dY_t = dY_r$. It is simply a question of shuffling resources about so as to maximise income; there is only one product, and time does not enter the analysis.

Now consider the possibility of trade in technology. To do this, assume that the newly appearing techniques of production resulting from the R/D industry in A can be profitably put to use in the production of the national product, X, in country B. In addition, suppose that the transfer of technology takes the form of an export: that is, techniques flow from A to B, and in return, payments flow from B to A. To be specific, assume that the R/D sector in A enjoys patent or property rights to the techniques, and further, appropriates for itself the full value to production in B, indicated by dX_t, of the adoption of the new techniques. Under these circumstances, it will pay to produce more new techniques than justified solely by the domestic increase in productivity. In particular, resources must now be devoted to the production of new techniques up to the point where the *sum* of the extra gains due to new techniques (increased productivity at home, plus royalties from abroad) are just offset by the further decline in production due to the diversion of additional resources to the R/D sector. If A does in fact appropriate the full gains to the export of new techniques, its revenue from the export of new technology will equal the increase in production in B, dX_t, brought about by the import of the new techniques, so that the maximum conditions become:

$$dY_r = dY_t + p\,dX_t,$$

INDUCED TECHNICAL CHANGE AND TRANSFER MECHANISM

where p is the relative price of X in terms of Y. This would represent a case of full internalisation of the worldwide gains to the production of new techniques, and, neglecting the terms of trade effects taken up shortly, the optimum conditions from the standpoint of the two countries taken together would be the same as those dictated by the competitive profit-maximising production and export of new techniques: namely, that the extra sacrifice in terms of Y due to the production of new techniques, dY_r, equals the *sum* of the value of the increase in production of Y in A and X in B, $dY_t + pdX_t$.[6]

Notice that while we have not mentioned trade in final products, the existence of such trade in no way changes the maximum conditions. Indeed, trade in commodities is necessary to give us the price, p, at which imports of X from B due to the export of techniques are to be valued. To simplify matters, we can choose commodity units such that at the initial pattern of trade in commodities and technology, one unit of Y is worth one unit of X, e.g. $p = 1$. Thus, at the efficiency position, the extra sacrifice in Y entailed by a marginal diversion of resources in A to the R/D industry is just offset by the sum of the domestic and foreign increases in production due to the adoption of new techniques.

To summarise, we have a situation in which A, the innovating country, exports both Y and new techniques to B, the adopting country. In exchange, B exports X, some of which is in payment for imports of Y, and the remainder is in the form of a transfer for use of new techniques of production. Further, trade balances when A's exports of Y are just cancelled by the sum of imports and transfers of X from B.

B. *Effects on terms of trade of departure from efficiency position* (*with monopoly power*)

The next step in the analysis is to examine the implications of a departure from a position of equilibrium in which the efficiency condition holds. To do this, notice that the efficiency condition can be expressed in a slightly different manner. By deducting the *increase* in production of Y in A brought about by the new techniques from the *fall* in production of Y due to the diversion of resources to the R/D industry, one arrives at a measure of the *net* marginal cost of

[6] This criterion corresponds to the well-known Samuelson one for the optimal provision of a public good. Here, the criterion refers to the manufacture of techniques of production which have public characteristics.

developing new techniques: $dY_n = dY_r - dY_t$. As before, if foreign trade did not exist, efficiency would entail that the two just cancel, i.e. that the net cost be zero at the margin. However, with trade and the export of techniques, it is worthwhile for A to produce at a position in which there is a positive net marginal cost in terms of Y of producing new techniques. The reason for this is that the marginal decline in output of Y is compensated for by imports of X from B due to the sale of the new techniques. In fact, at the optimum position, the net marginal cost of new techniques (decline in production due to fewer resources being employed in Y, less the rise in production due to increased productivity of remaining resources) is just equal to the value of the increase in production of X in B. That is

$$dY_n = pdX_t = dX_t \text{ since } p = 1.$$

In short, the net marginal decline in the production of Y is compensated for by the increased production of X in B which, in turn, is sent to A in payment for the import of techniques. This implies that, departing from the efficiency position, the increased production and the export of new techniques causes (1) a (net) decline in the production of Y in A, the innovating country, (2) an *equal* rise in the production of X in B, the adopting country, and (3) an *equal* transfer of X from B to A in payment for the imported techniques. Further, note that the increased production of new techniques over the efficiency position causes no change in real income, either in A or B, *at constant terms of trade*. This is so since the marginal loss to A in terms of Y is just compensated for by increased imports of X. From B's standpoint, the entire increase in production of X due to the import of the new techniques is transferred to A in the form of royalty payments, so real income is unchanged there also. Consequently, *if demand patterns in A and B depend solely on the value of domestic income and relative prices*, the increased production of new techniques will leave demand patterns unchanged in both A and B at the initial terms of trade. However, the marginal increase in the production of technology causes a (net) decline in the production of Y, and a rise in the production of X. Since the world demand for X and Y is unchanged, and the supply of Y has fallen while that of X has risen, *the relative price of Y must increase*. In short, A's commodity terms of trade improve, and consequently, it realises gains from the extra export of techniques, while B suffers a loss in welfare.

We can express the outcome in terms of the impact on A's balance of trade. Note that we can measure A's trade balance solely in terms of one good as the excess *world* demand for its export, Y (or as the excess world supply of X).[7] Since world demand patterns are unchanged, the surplus generated in A's trade balance departing from the efficiency position is equal to the decline in production of Y in A, or equivalently, to the value of the rise in production of X in B. Or, since the increase in production in B is transferred to A in the guise of a royalty payment, A's trade balance improves by the full amount of the transfer payment for the import of new techniques. To eliminate the surplus, the terms of trade must consequently move in A's favour. More precisely, to eliminate the disequilibrium, the terms of trade of A must rise by an amount equal to the transfer, divided by the elasticity factor $I_a(\eta_a + \eta_b - 1)$, where I_a represents A's import of X, and η_a and η_b are the price elasticities of demand for imports in A and B respectively.

The argument can be made graphically. For simplicity, assume that there is initially no (net) trade in technology, but that the efficiency conditions apply.[8] At the outset, the trading point is at P in Quadrant II of the Figure 4.1 (p. 62) determined by the intersection of the initial offer curves (not drawn in). The corresponding production pattern in B is represented in Quadrant I by the point M, the consumption pattern by the point N, exports equal OT units of X, and imports equal PT units of Y. Similarly, in Quadrant III the initial production and consumption patterns in A are indicated by the points V and W respectively, A's exports of Y being equal to TP and her imports of X are OT. The equilibrium terms of trade indicated by the slopes of the parallel lines MN, OP and VW are initially assumed to equal unity.

Since we assume that the efficiency condition applies, a rise in the

---

[7] See [15]. Briefly, A's trade balance is
$$B_a = (y_b - Y_b) - p(x_a - X_a - T).$$
The income equation is
$$y_a + px_a = Y_a + p(X_a + T) \text{ or } p(x_a - X_a - T) = (Y_a - y_a)$$
Together, they imply
$$B_a = (y_a + y_b) - (Y_a + Y_b)$$
where small letters indicate consumption, capital ones production, the subscripts refer to the countries, p is the relative price of X, and T indicates the net transfer of X from B to A in payment for imported techniques. (X_a and Y_b are zero in the case of complete specialisation discussed here.)

[8] It will become apparent in the analysis that this assumption does not affect the generality of the argument.

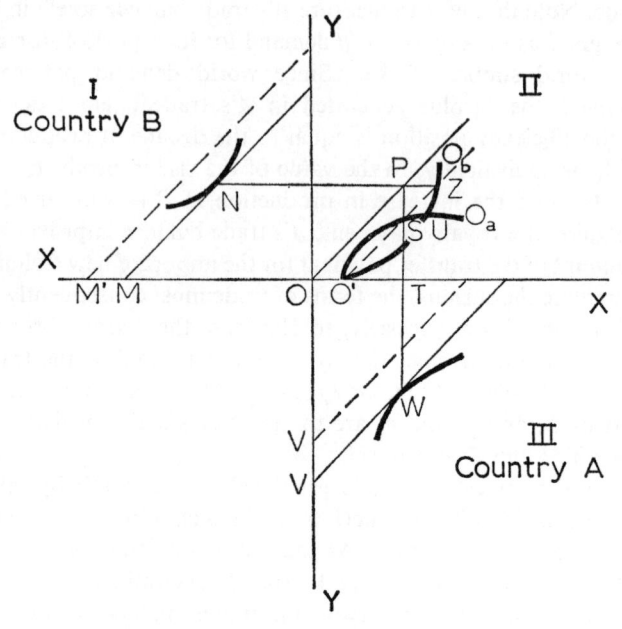

FIGURE 4.1. TRADE IN TECHNICAL CHANGE

The initial production and consumption patterns in country A are points V and W in Quadrant III. In country B, the corresponding production and consumption patterns are indicated by points M and N respectively in Quadrant I. Accordingly, the initial trading equilibrium is at point P in Quadrant II, and the terms of trade are indicated by the slope of the parallel lines OP, MN, and VW, assumed to equal unity.

The existence of trade in innovations makes it profitable for the innovating country, A, to produce new techniques up to the point where the extra (net) decline in home production of Y is just compensated for by the rise in production of X in B since the latter is transferred to A in payment for the new techniques. Therefore, a marginal increase in the production of new techniques in A will cause a fall in production of Y equal to VV', an *equal* rise in the production of X in B indicated by MM', and an *equal* transfer of OO' of X from B to A in payment for the increased import of new techniques. At constant terms of trade, the marginal departure from the efficiency position causes no change in incomes, and consequently demand patterns remain at N in B and W in A. Thus, the incoming transfer of OO' of X in A must be supplemented by $O'T$ of imports at the initial terms of trade, OP or $O'Z$, so that point S is on A's new offer curve. Similarly, at unchanged terms of trade, B demands the same amount of imports of Y, as indicated by the point A on B's new offer curve. A enjoys a surplus equal to PS units of Y, or PZ units of X, and the terms of trade move in her favour till equilibrium is reached at point U. A's welfare rises while B's falls. In short, the extent and direction of trade in technology can be measured by the value and direction of the net transfer payment for techniques along the axes in Quadrant II.

62

production of technology in A will cause a *net* decline of production of Y in A equal to VV', a corresponding *equal* rise MM' in the production of X in B, and an *equal* transfer of X from B to A of OO'. That is, at constant terms of trade, the income line in A would decline to V', but this is compensated for by an equal incoming transfer of X equal to OO' ($= VV'$). For this reason, there is initially no net change in income in A, and the demand pattern W is maintained. Similarly, the rise in production of X in B equal to MM' or OO' is transferred to A, so that income is unchanged and the demand pattern in B remains at N. The transfer of X in payment for the imported technology, however, causes the origin of the offer curves to shift to the right by OO'.

At the initial terms of trade, indicated by the slope of $O'Z$, the same amount of X (OT units) is demanded in A, so that imports of $O'T$ would have to supplement the transfer. A's new offer curve must therefore pass through S (the intersection of the lines PW and $O'Z$). By the same token, we can extend the line NP to the right till it intersects the old terms of trade OZ at Z, thereby arriving at the new point on B's offer curve. That is, at the initial terms of trade $O'Z$, and with the transfer, income is unchanged in B, so the demand for imports of Y remains the same at Z as at P.

Further, at those terms of trade, Country B now has a deficit of PZ units of X, or PS units of Y, an amount exactly equal to the transfer payment for the import of new technology. Consequently, *the terms of trade must move in favour of Country A, the innovator, to restore equilibrium in the balance of trade*. The exact improvement necessary is one which brings the supply and demand for imports into equality at point U. Welfare in A must therefore rise, while it falls in B.

Having found the value of the initial disequilibrium (a surplus of PS units of Y in A's trade balance, or $dB_a = dT$) brought about by the increased production of technology, we may calculate the improvement in A's terms of trade necessary to restore balance by setting the surplus $dB_a = dT$ equal to the deficit caused by the improvement in A's terms of trade, $dB_a = I_a(\eta_a + \eta_b - 1)dp$ and solving:

$$\frac{dp}{dT} = -\frac{1}{I_a(\eta_a + \eta_b - 1)}, \quad (1)$$

where dT represents the additional transfer of X from B to A in payment for the increased import of technology. Furthermore, the rise in A's real income, and the fall in B's can be measured by the initial volume of trade multiplied by the change in its terms, $I_a dp$, or:

$$\frac{dU_b}{dT} = -\frac{1}{(\eta_a+\eta_b-1)} = -\frac{dU_a}{dT} \qquad (2)$$

It is instructive to compare these results with those of the traditional transfer analysis where transfer proceeds are collected by taxes in B and are re-distributed by subsidies in A, and expenditures fall and rise respectively in the two countries by the full amount of the transfer. Under these conditions, a strict transfer of income from B to A of dT units of X causes a disequilibrium in A's balance of trade equal to $(1-m_a-m_b)dT$, where m_a and m_b are the marginal propensities to import in the two countries. Consequently, to eliminate the disequilibrium caused by the transfer, the price of B's export good must change by

$$\frac{dp}{dT} = -\frac{1-m_a-m_b}{I_a(\eta_a+\eta_b-1)}.$$

We can now make clear a point stressed earlier, namely that the departure from the efficiency position can be decomposed into the sum of three effects: a decline in production in A, a rise in B, and a transfer from B to A, all of the same amount. A decline in production in A of dY_a units would tend to improve its trade balance by an amount equal to $m_a dY_a$, and a rise in production in B of dX_b units would tend to improve A's balance by $m_b dX_b$. A transfer of dX_b from B to A would, however, have the effect of improving A's balance of trade by $(1-m_a-m_b)dX_b$. Since the terms of trade are initially assumed to be unity, optimal production of exported technology requires $dY = dX_b$, the *net* disturbance in A's trade balance is the sum of the three effects, or in tabular form:

EFFECT ON A'S TRADE BALANCE OF:

(1) Decline in production in A of dY_a	$+m_a dY_a$
(2) Rise in production in B of dX_b	$+m_b dX_b$
(3) Transfer from B to A of dX_b	$(1-m_a-m_b)dX_b$
Net effect (noting that $dY_a = dX_b$ at the efficiency position)	dX_b

Essentially, the income effects of the transfer have been netted out and consequently, demand patterns are unchanged. The terms of trade change, therefore, by

$$\frac{dp}{dT} = -\frac{1}{I_a(\eta_a+\eta_b-1)}$$

where dX_b has been replaced by the equivalent term dT. It is as though there were a pure transfer of income where the transferring country does not reduce its expenditure, nor does the receiving country increase its expenditure. Thus, the marginal propensities to consume do not play a role, only the value of the transfer does.

Notice that we have assumed full internalization of the gains to the production of new technology, none of which assumes the form of a free spillover of knowledge. That is, the full rise in production of X in B is shipped to A in payment for the use of the new techniques. It is also important to stress that the additional export of technical change in this simple framework causes secondary gains in real income to A since the commodity terms of trade improve as a result. From the point of view of B, however, the transfer of the increase in production has by itself the effect of leaving income there unchanged, so that the consequent worsening of the terms of trade actually acts so as to reduce real income in B.

In conclusion, we might remark that B could produce and export technology to A as well, so that the distance and the position of the offer curves along the axes can be used to represent the *net* balance of trade in technology. If the 'technology gap' were in B's favour, the initial origin of the offer curves would lie on the Y axis, and a marginal increase in production of techniques in A would shift the offer curves downward towards the origin, and also improve A's terms of trade in the same manner as above. Or, with the transfer of OO' and the efficiency conditions holding, a *reduction* in the production and export of new techniques would reduce the transfer, move the origin of the offer curves towards the origin, and worsen A's terms of trade.

II. THE IMPLICATIONS OF A FREE SPILLOVER OF INDUCED TECHNOLOGY

In many instances the transmission of technology from one country to another takes the form of a free spillover of knowledge rather than the export of techniques. This is so for many reasons; one can imitate or adapt a product in one country without actually infringing legally upon patent rights, or the costs of pursuing legal action in a country with another legal framework and perhaps another language may be forbidding, or a technique of production may not be inherently patentable. For whatever the reason, the consequences of the inappropriability of the external gains inherent in the spillover of technology are immediately obvious: an innovating country would fail to take into account (marginal) gains in production abroad due to its research and development efforts.[9] That is, the conditions of resource allocation that are optimal *from the standpoint of an innovating country taken in isolation* require that resources be diverted to R/D till the point where *domestic* gains and losses just balance each other. It follows that a marginal departure from what is *viewed by A* as the efficiency position in the direction of increased production of technology would leave income and production in the innovating country unchanged. Consequently, neither supply nor demand conditions there would vary. However, the change would entail an increased spillover of techniques abroad. Therefore, both foreign production and income rise at the initial terms of trade. This implies that we can analyse the increased free spillover of new techniques at the margin in a very familiar manner; namely, as an increase in foreign productivity combined with no change in productivity at home. To stress the point, it is as though the foreign country grows while the home country does not.

Without treating the case in detail, we may note that A's initial offer curve passing through point P in Quadrant II is left unchanged since neither production nor income initially change. In B, however, the value of production rises, as does income, at the initial terms of trade since the adoption of the new techniques is in the form of a spillover. As a result, the demand from imports of Y rises by a proportion equal to m_b. In short, the induced deficit in B's trade balance is $m_b dX_b$, and her terms of trade must deteriorate by an amount equal to

$$\frac{dp}{dX_b} = -\frac{m_b}{I_b(\eta_a+\eta_b-1)}. \tag{3}$$

That is, the effect on the terms of trade of the increased production and spillover of technology is identical to the outcome of an exogenous increase of productivity in one country, productivity in the other being held constant. A's welfare rises due to the improvement,

[9] In [6], I treat a case of mutual spillovers of a consumption good, television, in a two-country setting under a similar assumption.

while in B, it is possible that the loss in welfare due to the worsening of the terms of trade offsets the gains due to the marginal spillover of knowledge.[10]

Allowing for spillovers of technology produced in both A and B would not change the results. Indeed, a situation of bilateral spillovers of technology would have the same characteristics as simultaneous, exogenous growth in both countries. The interpretation would, however, differ considerably. In the spillover instance, there is a sort of invisible trade in technology, while in the standard analysis, improvements occur exogenously.[11]

III. INCOMPLETE SPECIALIZATION AND COMMODITY SPECIFIC TECHNOLOGY

The case of complete specialisation discussed in the previous section serves the purpose of highlighting some broad issues that one might expect to play a role in the production and transmission of technology. In particular the simple case has served to illustrate the point that if all the gains inherent in the production of technology are internalized by the innovator, departures from an optimum position have no effect upon demand patterns but do change supply patterns. And, in instances where the domestic gains are internalised, but the foreign ones are not, a departure from what is viewed as the optimum position by the innovating country leaves supply and demand patterns unchanged there, but has the effect of an increase in productivity in the foreign country. In both cases, the innovating country's terms of trade improve. This results because we have worked within the simple framework of complete specialisation which forces us to consider new techniques that are of use in the Y industry in one country, and the X industry in the other. In a sense, the techniques under consideration are of a very general sort.

However, one might expect that technical advances produced by research and development in the X industry in one country could be put to use in the X industry in other countries, but may be of little use in other industries. In this section, we briefly discuss a strict case

---

[10] Indeed, this possibility would correspond precisely to that of immiserising growth. See [5].
[11] Evoking this sort of intangible trade, David Hume particularly stresses in [9] spillovers of technology as an important source of the gains from trade.

in which technical advances apply only to a particular commodity. By necessity, we must consider the case of incomplete specialisation. This does not prevent us, however, from taking along as much information as possible from the case of complete specialisation. For example, the full internalisation of gains to new techniques when both goods are produced in both countries does not really pose any new problems from the point of view of the efficient production of technology: the opportunity costs of producing additional technology must just be offset by the value of the sum of the change in world production. Thus, any departure from this position will leave income and *hence* demand patterns unchanged at the initial equilibrium terms of trade.[12] In other words, at the margin we need only focus upon the change in the *composition* of world supply, as in the previous instance of complete internalisation of gains. As before, a departure from the efficiency position can be broken down into two components: (1) the impact of *the diversion of resources* from direct production to the improvement of the state of the arts, and (2) the impact of *the adoption of new techniques* when they appear. Furthermore, with full internalisation, the value of the decline in production due to the diversion of resources will exactly equal the value of the increase in world production due to the improvement of the state of the arts.

However, while the value of production remains the same, its composition need not. For example, in the Heckscher–Ohlin model, if the R/D sector in a country uses a higher capital/labour ratio than the factor endowment ratio of the economy as a whole, the impact of the increased diversion of resources to R/D would, along the lines of the Rybczynski theorem [17], reduce the ratio of the output of the capital intensive good to the output of the labour intensive good at the initial set of commodity prices. With no change in techniques of production, at the initial terms of trade factor returns would remain the same. The appearance of the new techniques in a particular industry would have the effect of increasing the ratio of output of that industry to the other at constant commodity prices.[13] In

[12] This ignores feed-back effects on the demand pattern as a result of the redistribution of factor income due to changes in techniques of production. See below.

[13] In fact, provided that the new techniques are neutral, saving in the factor intensive to the innovating industry, or not disproportionately saving in the other factor, output of the other industry must actually contract. See [8]. However, even if the other industry does not contract, as is possible in the third case, the ratio of output of the innovating industry to the other may still rise. And in this context, it is the final effect on the *ratio* of outputs that counts.

addition, at given commodity prices, it would have the effect of shifting income in favour of the factor used intensively in the innovating industry.[14] Ignoring any impact on the demand pattern due to this redistribution of income among factors, the value of income in the two countries would be unchanged, so the same quantities of the goods would be demanded at the initial terms of trade. Once again, we need only examine the change in the composition of world supply. And, as indicated above, the bias due to the Rybczynski effect can be in either direction depending on the factor-proportions of the R/D sector versus that of the endowment of the innovating country.

If, however, the technical bias is in favour of a particular industry in one country, for example, the import-competing one, it would be in favour of the corresponding export industry in the other country. In other words, the technical bias would mitigate unambiguously in favour of one good. However, not being able to single out a particular good as being a more likely candidate for innovative activity, combining the resource bias with the technical bias leaves us, not surprisingly, with an ambiguous result. We can no longer specifically state the direction of the change in the balance of trade nor in its terms due to a marginal increase in innovative activity in either country. Clearly, then, the increased production and export of technical change by one country need not improve its balance of trade. To cite an example: if expansion of the R/D sector in A served to increase the relative abundance of the abundant factor, and the new techniques were largely applicable to the export industry in A (and if commodity-specific) also to the import-competing industry in B, the increased technical progress would worsen A's terms of trade.

Similarly, in the case of the free spillover of new techniques, the final impact on the terms of trade is ambiguous. However, once again, a marginal increase in the production of new techniques in A would leave the value of its income constant, but the spillover would raise income and production in B at constant terms of trade. Thus, a departure in the direction of increased production of techniques over that where *domestic* gains and losses just cancel out would have the effect of *increasing the value of world income*.

---

[14] This is true for all types of technical progress in the Heckscher–Ohlin trade model. See [8], Part I. Essentially, this means that a bias toward labour-saving innovations as discussed in [12] and [18], for example, would not have the effect of shifting income from labour to capital if the innovative activity takes place in the labour-intensive industry.

IV. CONCLUDING REMARKS

To the extent that the production, export and/or spillover of new techniques of production tends to have the side effect of improving an innovating country's terms of trade, the gain to the country of additional technology can be underestimated at the margin. A subsidy to the production of new techniques which facilitate import substitution at home, and whose adoption abroad induce increased export supplies from foreign sources might be in order. Conversely, a tax on the production of techniques having the effect of worsening the country's terms of trade might serve to limit the corresponding losses.

More important, a country which essentially pays the full value of imported techniques of production tends to gain little in the process, and in fact, may suffer losses. Put bluntly, arguments such as the technological externality one that favour direct foreign investment rest on weak ground when the foreign firm captures the bulk of the profits attributable to the new techniques.

Finally, a word of caution. This analysis stresses marginal changes from efficiency positions. Its sole purpose has been to focus attention upon the collective nature of technical change, the problem of appropriability, and the importance of associated changes in the commodity terms of trade.

NOTE

It has just come to my attention that Harry G. Johnson anticipated many of the results reached in my paper in his 1955 'Economic Expansion and International Trade'. See, in particular, Part III, 'Economic Expansion and International Trade' in *International Trade and Economic Growth*, Harvard University Press, Cambridge, Mass. 1967.

REFERENCES

1. K. J. Arrow, 'The Economic Implications of Learning by Doing', *Review of Economic Studies*, Vol. 29 (3), No. 80 (June, 1962), pp. 155–73.
2. ——, 'Classificatory Notes on the Production and Transmission of Technological Knowledge', *American Economic Review Proceedings*, Vol. 59, No. 2 (May, 1969), pp. 29–35.
3. A. B. Atkinson, and J. E. Stiglitz, 'New View of Technological Change', *Economic Journal*, Vol. 79, No. 315 (September, 1969), pp. 573–8.

4. R. E. Baldwin, 'The Role of Capital-Goods Trade in the Theory of International Trade', *American Economic Review*, Vol. 56, No. 4, Part 1 (September, 1966), pp. 841–7.
5. J. Bhagwati, 'Immiserizing Growth: A Geometrical Note', *Review of Economic Studies*, Vol. 25, No. 68 (June, 1958), pp. 201–5.
6. M. B. Connolly, 'Public Goods, Externalities, and International Relations', *Journal of Political Economy*, Vol. 78, No. 2 (March/April, 1970), pp. 279–90.
7. M. B. Connolly and S. Ross, 'A Fisherian Approach to Trade, Capital Movements, and Tariffs', *American Economic Review*, Vol. 60, No. 3 (June, 1970), pp. 478–84.
8. R. Findlay and H. Grubert, 'Factor Intensities, Technological Progress, and the Terms of Trade', *Oxford Economic Papers*, Vol. 2, No. 1 (February, 1959), pp. 111–21.
9. David Hume, 'Of the Jealousy of Trade', *Essays and Treatises on Several Subjects* (Thomas Nelson & Sons, London, 1955). See pp. 78–9, in particular.
10. H. G. Johnson, 'Comparative Cost and Commercial Policy Theory for a Developing World Economy', *The Wicksell Lectures for 1968*.
11. R. W. Jones, 'The Role of Technology in the Theory of International Trade', in *The Technology Factor in International Trade*, edited by Raymond Vernon (National Bureau of Economic Research; Columbia University Press, New York, 1970), pp. 73–92.
12. C. Kennedy, 'Induced Bias in Innovation and the Theory of Distribution', *Economic Journal*, Vol. 74, No. 295 (September, 1964), pp. 541–7.
13. A. Marshall, *Industry and Trade* (Macmillan and Co., London, 1919), p. 175.
14. N. C. Miller, 'A General Equilibrium Theory of International Capital Flows', *Economic Journal*, Vol. 78, No. 310 (June, 1968), pp. 312–19. N. C. Miller, 'A General Equilibrium Theory of International Capital Flows: Reply', *Economic Journal*, Vol. 80, No. 319 (September, 1970), pp. 747–9. J. R. Melvin, 'A General Theory of International Capital Flows: A Comment', *Economic Journal*, Vol. 80, No. 319 (September, 1970), pp. 742–6.
15. R. A. Mundell, 'The Pure Theory of International Trade', *American Economic Review*, Vol. 50, No. 1 (March, 1960), pp. 67–110.
16. M. V. Posner, 'International Trade and Technical Change', *Oxford Economic Papers*, Vol. 13, No. 3 (October, 1961), pp. 323–41.
17. T. M. Rybczynski, 'Factor Endowment and Relative Commodity Prices', *Economica*, Vol. 23, No. 88 (November, 1955), pp. 336–41.
18. P. A. Samuelson, 'A Theory of Induced Innovation Along Kennedy–Weisacker Lines', *Review of Economics and Statistics*, Vol. 42 (XLVII), 1965, pp. 343–56.
19. R. Vernon, 'International Investment and International Trade in the Product Cycle', *Quarterly Journal of Economics*, Vol. 80, No. 2 (May, 1966), pp. 190–207.
20. L. R. Webb, 'The Role of International Capital Movements in Trade and Growth: The Fisherian Approach', in *Studies in International Economics: The Monash Conference Papers, 1969*, edited by I. A. McDougall and R. H. Snape (North-Holland Publishing Company, Amsterdam, 1970), pp. 225–66.

5

The Simple Analytics of Multi-National Firm Behaviour

THOMAS HORST
Harvard University

INTRODUCTION

The formal analysis of multi-national firm decision making tends to be rather complex.[1] On the one hand, much of this complexity would seem to be inherent in the topic itself: the typical multi-national firm is presiding over a very complicated set of decisions in seeking an optimal strategy for its global operations. But on the other hand, international trade theory has traditionally dealt with an analogous set of questions in analysing the general equilibrium position for two or more countries trading with one another. This paper pursues an analogy between the general equilibrium theory of international trade and the partial equilibrium theory of the multi-national firm in order to show how analytical tools familiar from the former can be properly used in understanding the latter.

The first section of the paper considers how a firm selling its product in two countries decides how much to produce, sell, and export (or import) in each country. My objective will be to derive a marginal-cost-of-exporting schedule for one country and a marginal-revenue-from-importing schedule for the other which will correspond closely to the reciprocal supply and demand curves of traditional trade analysis. This process will also reveal an appropriate transfer price for intra-firm exports, which can then be compared to the price a multi-national firm might choose in actual practice.

The second section of the paper extends the analysis to a situation in which the parent firm by investing in new research and development renders all its operations, foreign and domestic, more profitable

[1] See, e.g. Guy Stevens, 'Fixed Investment Expenditures of Foreign Manufacturing Affiliates of U.S. Firms: Theoretical Models and Empirical Evidence', Yale Ph.D. Dissertation, New Haven, 1967; or my paper, 'The Theory of the Multi-national Firm: Optimal Behavior under Different Tariff and Tax Rates', *Journal of Political Economy*, Vol. 78, No. 5 (September/October, 1971).

than they would otherwise have been. This analysis is interesting primarily for what it reveals about the proper charge for the international transfer of technology. I will argue, in particular, that a 'fair-share' rule, under which a subsidiary's share of the cost of an R & D programme would equal its share of the benefits from that programme, provides a feasible and equitable method for pricing the technology transferred in the direct investment process.

I. A SIMPLE MODEL OF MULTI-NATIONAL FIRM BEHAVIOUR UNDER FIXED TECHNOLOGY

This section explores a simple model of a firm with a given technology selling in two countries simultaneously.[2] In both the home country (country *1*) and the foreign country (country 2) the quantity sold, S_i, depends on the price charged, p_i:

$$p_i = p_i(S_i), \quad \frac{dp_i}{dS_i} < 0, i = 1, 2 \qquad (1)$$

Assuming the firm has some monopoly power in both countries (as multi-national firms invariably do), the demand curve in each country has some downward slope. The firm is also able to produce in either country with total production costs, C_i, depending solely on the volume of production, X_i, in that country:

$$C_i = C_i(X_i) \quad i = 1, 2 \qquad (2)$$

I will permit the marginal cost, c_i, of production to be either increasing or decreasing as the volume of production is expanded. For reasons which will soon be apparent, the analysis of multi-national firm behaviour depends crucially on the slopes of the two marginal cost curves.

With only two countries in the model, the foreign subsidiary's net imports must equal the difference between its own sales and production as well as the difference between its parent's production and sales:

$$M = S_2 - X_2 = X_1 - S_1 \qquad (3)$$

Finally, there are tariffs and taxes imposed by the governments of

[2] This model has been explored in greater detail and rigour in my paper cited above.

the two countries in which the firm is operating. For convenience, I will assume that the rates at which profits are taxed, t, is the same in each country, either because the actual tax rates are the same or because the home country in taxing foreign profits allows full credit for taxes paid to the foreign government. If τ is the tariff on imports and π is the transfer price the firm chooses for its intra-firm imports, then the total tariff duties paid by the firm will be $\tau\pi M$.

The assumed objective of the firm is to maximise the value of its after-tax earnings, E, which will be the after-tax share, $(1-t)$, of total revenues from sales, $p_1 S_1 + p_2 S_2$, less the total costs of production, $C_1 + C_2$, and less the tariff duties, $\tau\pi M$:

$$E = (1-t)(p_1 S_1 + p_2 S_2 - C_1 - C_2 - \tau\pi M) \qquad (4)$$

Since tariff duties, the last item in (4), are a dead-weight loss from the firm's point of view, the firm will obviously want to set the transfer price of intra-firm exports as low as it possibly can. How low it can actually go depends on what the tariff and tax authorities in the two countries will permit. Since most exports are highly tangible (unlike the technology to be considered in the next section), something like the marginal or average cost of production in the exporting country may set the lower limit for the transfer price, π.

The next step in determining the firm's maximising strategy is to determine how many degrees of freedom the firm has in choosing its strategy and then apply the calculus of maximisation. The important issue here is whether the firm can set prices in the two countries independently or whether the choice of a home price effectively limits the choice of a foreign price. The latter possibility opens up many theoretically interesting possibilities, but also serves to make the formal analysis exceedingly complex. I want to assume, therefore, that the firm is always free to act as a discriminating monopolist, to choose its price in each country independently of its choice in the other. Such is a reasonable assumption if existing tariffs, transport costs, or consumer ignorance is high enough to insulate the markets from one another, or if other terms of a sale besides the price (e.g. servicing) discourage buyers from doing their own importing, or if the elasticities of demand in the two countries are similar enough that the firm does not wish to maintain a very large international price differential.

If the firm is free to discriminate perfectly between the two markets, it has three degrees of freedom in choosing an optimal strategy for serving the two markets. Taking the volume of sales in each country and the subsidiary's production as the control variables yields three first-order conditions for an earnings maximum:

$$r_1 = c_1 \quad (5)$$
$$r_2 = c_2 \quad (6)$$
$$r_2 = c_1 + \tau\pi \quad (7)$$

These conditions require that marginal revenue, r, should equal marginal cost, c, in the home and foreign markets respectively, and that the marginal revenue from the subsidiary's sales should also equal the marginal cost of the parent's production plus the unit tariff duty on intra-firm imports.

Deriving these conditions is one thing, seeing what levels of prices, sales, production, and exports they imply is another. Figures 5.1A, 5.1B, and 5.1C depict the optimal strategy graphically. Figure 5.1A shows the demand curve, the corresponding marginal revenue curve and the marginal cost curve in the home country. According to Condition (5) above, no matter how much the parent firm exports, it will always want to keep its own marginal revenue equal to its own marginal cost. The horizontal distance from the marginal revenue curve out to the marginal cost curve, which is shown as the $c_M c_M$-curve in Figure 5.1B, gives us the parent firm's marginal-cost-of-exporting schedule. The area under this curve, naturally enough, is the total cost of exporting, where *the total cost of exporting includes both the additional costs of production and the foregone sales revenues incurred by the parent*. There is, as one can see, a close analogy between this marginal-cost-of-exporting curve and the reciprocal supply curve used in traditional international trade analysis, but the monopoly power of the multi-national firm precludes our treating any marginal cost curve as a supply curve in a behavioural sense.

The foreign subsidiary's marginal-revenue-from-importing curve may be derived in a similar fashion. Figure 5.1C depicts the demand curve, the corresponding marginal revenue curve and the marginal cost curve in the foreign country. According to Condition (6), the subsidiary should always keep its marginal revenue equal to its marginal cost. The horizontal distance from the marginal cost curve out to the marginal revenue curve, which is shown as the $r_M r_M$-curve in Figure 5.1B, gives us the subsidiary's marginal-revenue-from-importing schedule. The area under this curve is the total revenue to the subsidiary, where *the total revenue from importing includes both the additional revenues from subsidiary sales and the decreased costs of*

FIGURE 5.1

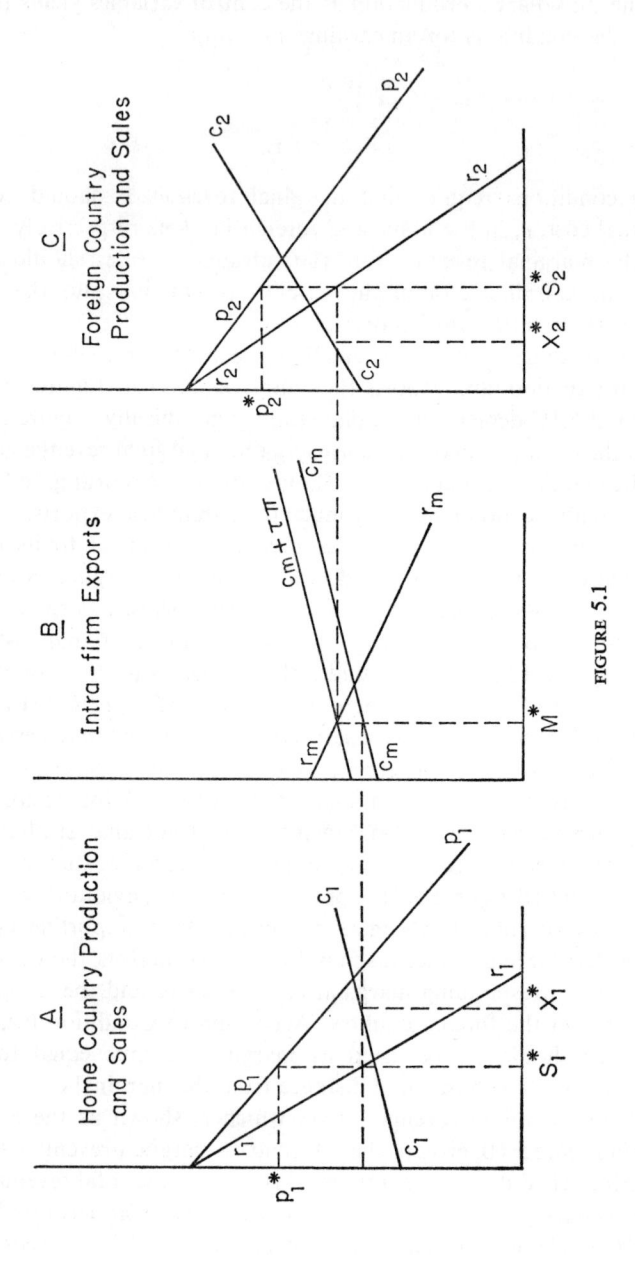

subsidiary production. Pursuing the analogy suggested above, this marginal-revenue-from-importing curve is closely akin to the traditional excess demand curve, but once again the presence of monopoly power precludes our interpreting it as such in a behavioural sense.

The third step in this process is to put the marginal-cost-of-exporting curve together with the marginal-revenue-from-importing curve to find the optimal strategy. According to Condition (7), the firm will want the marginal cost of exports *including the tariff* to equal the marginal revenue from imports. By shifting the $c_M c_M$ curve up by the amount of the unit tariff duty, $t\pi$, we find the optimal volume of imports at the intersection of the shifted marginal-cost-of-exporting curve and the original marginal-revenue-from-importing curve. The optimal levels for production, sales, and prices in the home and foreign countries are then found by tracing back to Figures 5.1A and 5.1C respectively. Were we able to interpret marginal revenue and marginal cost curves as market demand and supply curves respectively, then the process by which we found an optimal strategy for a multi-national firm would be identical to the process by which excess supply and demand curves are used to find a general equilibrium for two countries trading with one another.

The preceding analysis describes the optimal strategy for a firm whose marginal costs are increasing with the level of its production in each country. Should the firm enjoy decreasing marginal costs of production, the analysis proceeds along somewhat different lines. Rather than seeking an optimal mix of imports and subsidiary production for supplying its foreign market, the firm will want to choose among three fundamentally different supply strategies: (1) produce all its output in the home country and serve the foreign market entirely with exports; (2) produce in both countries, but refrain from exporting between the two; and (3) produce all its output in the foreign country and serve the home market entirely with imports. In short, imports will never be mixed with local production in either country.

The nature of this choice is depicted in 5.2A, showing the marginal revenue and cost curves in the home country, and 5.2B, showing the same for the foreign country. Once again the horizontal distance from the marginal revenue curve out to the marginal cost curve yields a marginal-cost-of-exporting-to-the-other-country schedule which, when shifted up by the amount of the unit tariff duty, can be

FIGURE 5.2

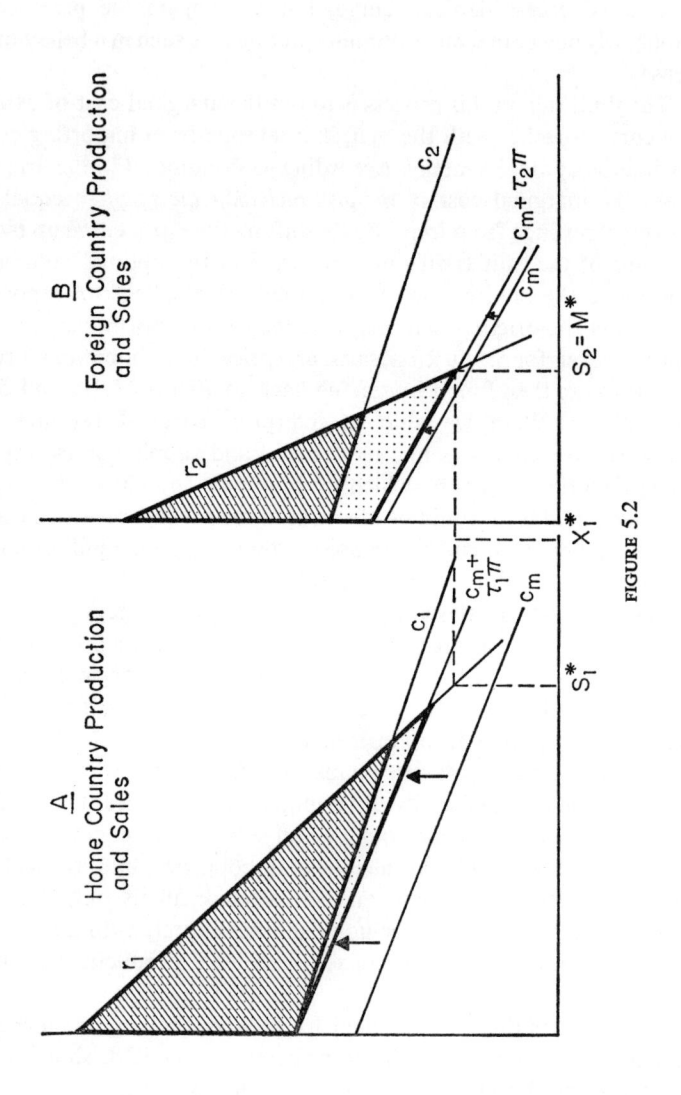

compared to the marginal-cost-of-local-production schedule. Since the triangular area between a marginal revenue and a marginal cost curve measures total profits, the firm will choose among the three different supply strategies by comparing the total areas of the two profit triangles yielded by each of the three alternatives. Strategy *1* yields the smaller triangle in Figure 5.2A and the larger triangle in 5.2B. Strategy *2* gives the smaller triangles in 5.2A and 5.2B, while strategy *3* allows the larger triangle in 5.2A and the smaller in 5.2B. Given the demand, cost and tariff conditions depicted in Figures 5.2A and 5.2B, strategy *1* is clearly the best of the three in this instance.

With decreasing costs the firm's optimal strategy depends not only on the underlying costs of production and the tariffs on imports, but also on the relative size of the two markets. There is a clear tendency, unit cost structures and tariff duties being relatively equal, to locate production facilities in the country with the larger domestic market and thereby avoid the tariff duties on a large volume of imports from the other country. Notice that in the situation depicted in Figures 5.2A and 5.2B, the foreign country is able to produce any given level of output at a lower total cost than the home country can, and yet because of the home country's tariff and relatively larger market, the firm has not only declined to import foreign produced goods, but has actually chosen to serve the foreign market with goods produced at home. All of this is to suggest that the assumption of increasing marginal costs of production may lead us to underestimate the sensitivity of international trade to market size and tariff structures.[3]

Before concluding this section, let me comment briefly on the indeterminacy of transfer prices in even this simple model. The legal requirement that the firm set the same price for an *intra*-firm transaction as it would have set for an *inter*firm transaction – the 'arm's length' rule – is undeniably ambiguous. Were the parent and subsidiary independently owned, we would be confronted with a bilateral monopoly situation in which the outcome could not be fully determined *a priori*. Notice, however, that the marginal cost of production in the exporting country does determine an 'efficiency' price for exports in the firm's own cost-minimising calculation. If the

---

[3] This sensitivity of trade flows to tariff rates and market size when marginal costs are decreasing would also occur in a general equilibrium setting. See Murray Kemp, *The Pure Theory of International Trade and Investment*, Chapter 8 (Prentice-Hall, Inc., Englewood Cliffs, 1969).

ambiguity surrounding the notion of an arm's length price permits the multi-national firm to set the transfer price of exports equal to the marginal cost of production, then economists should be satisfied. But it still remains true that the home country could gain tax revenues and foreign exchange at the direct expense of the foreign country if transfer prices could somehow be raised.

Once the nature of the optimal strategy choice is understood, many of the comparative statics questions of policy interests can be easily answered. The impact of growth in the demand in one market, or of a reduction in the costs of production, or an increase in unit tariff duties can be determined by shifting the appropriate demand or cost curve and tracing out the resulting adjustment in the optimal sales-production-export strategy. Needless to say, with decreasing marginal costs of production, marginal changes in tariff rates or underlying demand and cost conditions may result in quantum shifts in the firm's operations. Although the preceding analysis concentrated on the production and export of finished goods, by making a few obvious adjustments, one could apply this analysis to the export of capital goods, intermediate inputs to the production process, investable funds and many other transactions undertaken by multi-national firms.

II. OPTIMAL STRATEGY WHEN TECHNOLOGY CAN BE IMPROVED

The preceding section investigated the optimal strategy for a firm facing static demand and cost conditions in the two countries in which it is operating. The present section introduces the possibility that the firm by investing in new research and development can either make its product more attractive to its buyers in both countries or reduce the cost of producing a given product both at home and abroad. Given certain assumptions about how the new technology shifts existing demand or cost curves, I will (1) show what the optimal research and development expenditure is, and (2) determine what an appropriate transfer price for the international transmission of technology might be.

In order to demonstrate certain basic principles as clearly as possible, I will make a few restrictive assumptions. In order to get around problems of uncertainty and of discounting a stream of future returns to current technological investments, let me assume that the returns to current research and development expenditures are known with certainty at the outset and will accrue to the firm entirely within the time period referred to by the demand and cost functions. With these two rather messy problems assumed away, the optimal strategy for a bi-national firm can be determined in a rather straightforward manner.

Consider a research and development expenditure whose sole benefit is to make the firm's product more attractive to buyers in both countries. This shift in buyers' preferences may be incorporated directly into the demand functions for the firm's product:

$$p_i = p_i(S_i, D) \quad i = 1, 2 \tag{8}$$

where D is the firm's total expenditure on research and development. The fact that the same D enters both demand functions simultaneously reflects the 'public-good' nature of technology within the multi-national firm.[4]

Since research and development expenditures offer the firm an additional degree of freedom in maximising after-tax earnings, we must add a fourth first-order condition to conditions (5) to (7) derived above:

$$S_1 \frac{\partial p_1}{\partial D} + S_2 \frac{\partial p_2}{\partial D} = 1 \tag{9}$$

This new condition states that for a given volume of sales in each market, the firm should set the *sum* of the marginal revenues in each country from spending one more dollar on research and development equal to unity. This summing of marginal benefits is a familiar rule in the theory of public goods.

In order to show the optimal research and development expenditure implied by this first-order condition, let me use Figures 5.3A and 5.3B which are closely analogous to those employed above. Assume that the firm has already determined the optimal sales volume in each market. Figure 5.3A shows the marginal revenue in the home country of additional research and development as well as the marginal cost of those expenditures. By taking the *vertical* distance from the marginal cost curve down to the marginal revenue curve, we can derive the parent's marginal-cost-of-providing-technology schedule.

[4] Harry Johnson has explored the role of the multi-national firm in transmitting existing technology in 'The Efficiency and Welfare Implications of the International Corporation', in C. P. Kindleberger, ed., *The International Corporation; A Symposium* (MIT Press, Cambridge, 1970) pp. 35–56.

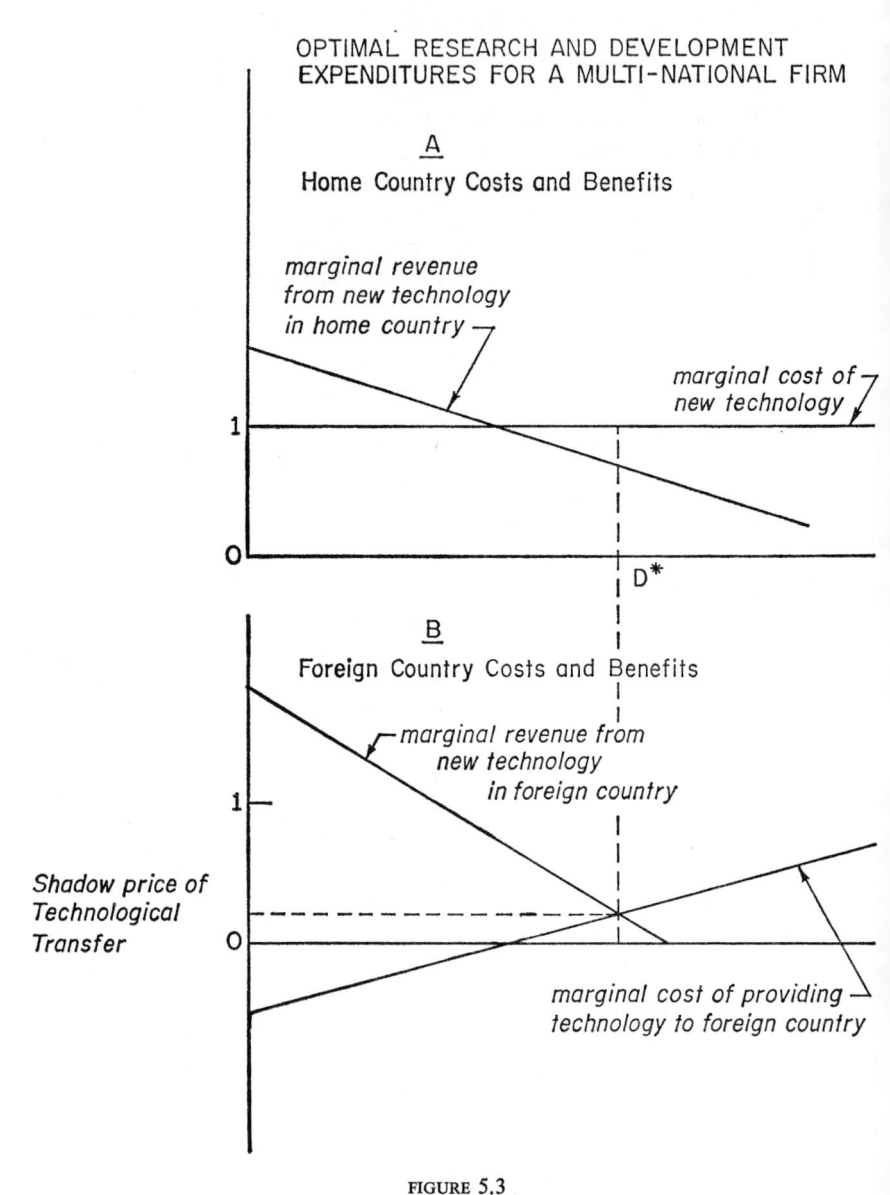

OPTIMAL RESEARCH AND DEVELOPMENT EXPENDITURES FOR A MULTI-NATIONAL FIRM

A
Home Country Costs and Benefits

marginal revenue from new technology in home country

marginal cost of new technology

1

0

D*

B
Foreign Country Costs and Benefits

marginal revenue from new technology in foreign country

1

Shadow price of Technological Transfer

0

marginal cost of providing technology to foreign country

FIGURE 5.3

The area under this curve (shown in Figure 5.3B) equals the total cost of providing technology, which is the difference between the total cost of the R & D programme and the total benefit of that programme to the parent. Assuming that there is no tariff on the actual transfer of technology, the optimal R & D programme is determined by the intersection of the marginal-cost-of-providing-technology schedule with the marginal-revenue-from-new-technology schedule for the foreign subsidiary.

Figures 5.3A and 5.3B are useful not only for determining the optimal research and development programme, but also for seeing what an appropriate charge for the technology developed in one country and transferred to the other might be. In the present problem the shadow price of the technological transfer is given by the intersection of the marginal-revenue-of-technology and the net-marginal-cost-of-technology schedules, and this shadow price would seem to offer an appropriate basis for charging the subsidiary for its share of the R & D programme.[5] Firstly, and least importantly, it is an efficiency price and would appeal to economic purists. Secondly, on the additional assumption that each country's demand curve is shifted up by a uniform amount, the appropriate charge is remarkably easy to calculate. Since $\partial p_1/\partial D$ would equal $\partial p_2/\partial D$, the firm allocates the costs of the R & D programme on the basis of the parent's and the subsidiary's share in total sales. Finally, this charge satisfies one's notion of international equity by treating the parent and subsidiary symmetrically. That is to say, were the same research and development programme undertaken at the same cost in the foreign country, the parent and the subsidiary would continue to pay the same shares of their common programme, and the taxes collected in each country would be unaffected.

Although the preceding analysis focused on research and development expenditures which make the firm's product more attractive to its customers, the analysis could easily be applied to cost-reducing technological expenditures, head-office expenditures, managerial training programmes, and all other joint costs of a multi-national firm.

[5] At first glance this rule would appear to contradict Harry Johnson's claim that the efficiency price for the transfer of technology is zero. The crucial difference between his analysis and mine is that he is concerned with the transfer of *existing* technology while I am focusing on the production of *new* technology. Since the former requires no use of scarce economic resources while the latter does, the efficiency price will be zero in the first instance and positive in the second.

Notice, however, that if a program is directed towards reducing costs and not increasing demand, the 'fair-share' transfer price would be based on production instead of sales.

The benefits of applying this 'fair-share' rule, under which joint costs are allocated in proportion to separate benefits, contrast rather sharply with the current chaos stemming from the arm's length rule. As the Canadian Finance Minister recently stated:

It is generally impossible for the revenue authorities in any country to determine the reasonable amount that should be charged for technical or managerial know-how by a parent company to its subsidiaries except, perhaps, in the very rare instance where there is a comparable arm's length transaction to use as a yardstick.

It is also difficult to determine whether or not any charge is appropriate. For there is a basic inconsistency in the attempt to force an arm's-length standard on transactions between related entities when the transactions result from an arrangement which is peculiar to the non-arm's-length situation.[6]

The fair-share rule appears to offer some resolution for the present difficulties stemming from the arm's length rule.

CONCLUSION

Over the last two decades the significance of the multi-national firm in all phases of international exchange has grown tremendously. The very size of these firms clearly indicates that the perfectly competitive behaviour assumed in traditional international trade and investment theory is no longer fully appropriate in the analysis of current international economic phenomena. But while many of the traditional linkages between domestic *prices* and the direction, composition, and extent of international trade are severed by the presence of monopoly power in multi-national firms, many of the linkages between domestic *costs* and international trade not only remain, but are even reinforced by the ability and willingness of multi-national firms to make rational cost calculations in determining a global supply strategy. This paper has sought to show how these linkages in costs between countries provide a basis for using the familiar analytical tools of traditional international trade analysis in the study of multi-national firm decision making.

[6] 'Notes for an Address by Finance Minister E. J. Benson to the Advisory Board of Tax Management, Waldorf Astoria, Thursday, 24 June 1971, New York City', Department of Finance, Ottawa, 1971, p. 9.

6

Trends in Income Distribution in some Western Countries

JAN TINBERGEN
Netherlands School of Economics

I. PURPOSE OF THIS SURVEY

This article tries to present in comparable form a considerable number of figures collected by other authors and by institutions on income distribution in Western countries over the past decades. In addition, these figures are contrasted with data for India and with one comparison over a longer period. Income distribution is treated here only as the frequency distribution over households or persons and not as the distribution over factors of production. The purpose of this survey is to put in perspective trends in this distribution over the past decades.

As is well known, income distribution is one of the important social aspects of our economies. Most critics of the nineteenth- and twentieth-century Western societies have selected income distribution as one of their main targets. Some of our recent problems, such as wage claims, strikes and inflation, are rooted in continuing dissatisfaction with income distribution, and understandably so. The main question behind this survey therefore is: Where do we stand with respect to this important feature of Western society? This question cannot be answered adequately by only considering primary income distribution. In most countries a considerable degree of redistribution occurs as a consequence of various reforms in the field of taxation, social security and other government intervention.

Even though considerable work has been done in recent decades the available material shows important lacunae. This implies that for many countries there is scope for undertaking more research in this field. This will be clear from the limited number of countries considered, especially in the tables dealing with redistribution. The phenomenon is of course related to the degree of tax discipline existing in various countries.

Throughout this essay countries will be indicated by their motor car symbols. For the readers not acquainted with them, they are listed below.

BR	Brazil*	RCH	Chile*
RA	Argentina*	N	Norway
MEX	Mexico*	IND	India*
H	Hungary*	J	Japan*
DK	Denmark	CDN	Canada
USA	United States	D	Germany (F.R.)
F	France*	S	Sweden
GB	United Kingdom	NL	Netherlands

* Countries mentioned occasionally only. Most of the evidence collected refers to countries without asterisk.

II. SOME DEFINITIONS

Since I have only used material collected by others I will not discuss here a number of subtleties considered by the original authors, especially with regard to the inclusion or exclusion of some items from the income concept used. This study focuses on three income concepts only: *primary income*, that is, income before taxes; *income after tax*; and *income after complete redistribution by public finance*. The latter concept includes the imputed values of services rendered to the person or persons considered below cost, minus the amounts actually paid by the recipients. Possible redistribution effects of social insurance institutions of an autonomous character have been neglected. It is often assumed that these redistribution effects are not considerable. For some continental European countries, however, this remains an open question.

Among the authors surveyed, Bentzel [3] explicitly states that the concept of income after complete redistribution equals consumption expenditure plus savings. Some other sources, namely some of the family budget inquiries, in particular Dandekar and Rath [9], only collect data on consumption expenditures; for low incomes the deviation from income will be small.

The other main concepts this study concentrates on are *income recipients* as different from *households, families*, and *consumers*. By far the greatest part of the studies quoted deal with one of the first three concepts as their units of observation; only a few consider the individual consumers as their units. There is a difference between households and families in that most sources do not include single person households as families. Only Nicholson [18] explicitly uses households and families as synonymous. Families may not be identical to income recipients as one family may count several income recipients. Fairly precise information on this point is available in many cases. The difference between households and income recipients on the one hand and *persons consuming* on the other hand is much larger, however, than the difference between the number of households and of income recipients. Households of five persons are no exception and the average size of households in lower and higher income brackets has developed differently (cf. below, Section VI).

The figures below will be presented as far as possible in the form of deciles (tenths) and quintiles (fifths) of the total number of units present in the country and year studied. These percentages are not always clearly defined in the sources we used, but as a rule they are parts of the total number of households or of income recipients. All figures of this kind have been expressed as per mils (‰) of total income. Moreover, in some cases, total income has been replaced by median income times total number of income recipients yielding a figure difficult to use in comparisons. The only figures not affected by this last operation are the ratios between deciles or quintiles, and it is on these that our conclusions concentrate.

III. SOURCES AND ERRORS – INDICATORS OF INEQUALITY

Sources used by the authors quoted may either be 'complete' inquiries, such as census and tax statistics, covering in principle all objects under investigation or 'samples', such as family budgets, sample censuses (cf. [26]) or *ad hoc* inquiries (for instance, Nicholson [18]). Sampling techniques have advanced sufficiently in order to keep sampling errors under better control than the main source of error: tax evasion. Increased efficiency of tax collection may give some hope that tax evasion is declining and some checks have been possible, from time to time, to estimate its extent. The increased role of corporations as compared with private firms may also have been a favourable development. The subject remains one where more research is highly desirable.

Even though the absolute figures contain considerable errors, the errors in some of the derived figures are considerably smaller. This applies to comparison over time, or estimates of the influence of redistribution, which are the main objects of this study.

Several indicators of inequality have been used. The main yardstick used in this survey, however, consists of quintile or decile ratios, between upper and lower. They are shown in Tables 6.I.A, 6.II.A, 6.III.A, 6.IV and 6.V. For comparison some other indicators have been collected in Tables 6.I.B, 6.II.B and 6.III.B though for well-known reasons, Pareto's has not been used. These other indicators are:

(i) d, the relative average deviation, that is the average absolute deviation each income shows from average income expressed as a portion of average income. Its lower limit is zero (equality of all incomes), its upper limit 2 (a large number of incomes zero and one non-zero).

(ii) P_5, the upper fifth percentile income as a percentage of median income. Of course one could have used other percentiles as well.

(iii) R, the inequality index derived from the Lorenz curve and representing the ratio of the area between the diagonal and the curve, divided by the area of the triangle under the diagonal. Its limits are 0 (equality) and 1 (a large number of incomes zero and one non-zero).

(iv) E, the maximum equalisation percentage, that is, the percentage of total income that must be taken from the higher and given to the lower incomes in order to make them all equal. Its limits are 0 and 100 per cent.

IV. INCOMES OF INCOME RECIPIENTS, HOUSEHOLDS OR FAMILIES BEFORE TAX

Tables 6.I.A and 6.I.B summarise the information collected from the sources quoted.[1] Table 6.I.A shows clearly that, on the whole, the trend of the lower incomes has been upward and for the highest incomes downward, if expressed in terms of average or median incomes. The most notable exception is for the Netherlands in 1935. This may be due partly to the Great Depression, during which profits

---

[1] Canadian data, unlike that from other countries, has been included, even though it consists only of one observation.

Income Distribution in some Western Countries

TABLE 6.1.A
INCOME BEFORE TAX FOR LOWER AND UPPER DECILES OR QUINTILES OF INCOME RECIPIENTS (R), HOUSEHOLDS (H) OR FAMILIES (F), ‰ OF TOTAL INCOME OF COUNTRY, SELECTED COUNTRIES AND YEARS

Country	CDN (Wages+salary)		D (R)			DK (R)			GB (R)		
Year	1930–1	1951	1936	1950	1939	1952	1963	1938	1949	1957
Decile 1			10	10	14	16				
Decile 2			20	30	30	32				
Quint 1	21	39	30	40	44	48	52		72	
Decile 9			140	140	158	154	166	120	145	
Decile 10			390	340	352	286	260	380	330	280
Quint 5	485	399	530	480	510	440	426	500	475	
Source	[10]		[24]			[24]	[21]	[16]	[24]	[16]

Country	N (sample)		NL (H)		S (R)			USA (F)			
Year	1840	1960	1935	1946	1962	1935	1948*	1954*	1935–6	1946–7	1959	1960–1
Decile 1				10	15			12	20			
Decile 2				22	30			33	36			
Quint 1			59	32	45		32	45	56	41	50	45	46
Decile 9			366	147	151	166	163	152	155			
Decile 10	570	240		383	318	395	303	300	273			
Quint 5			512	530	469	561	466	452	428	517	460	457	455
Source	[22]		[23]	[24]	[19]	[3]	[24]		[24]	[11]	[11]	[11]	[1]

* Unadjusted tax records.

TABLE 6.1.B
REDUCTION IN INEQUALITY

Indicator	Country	Length of period of observation (in years)	Fall in indicator, per cent over total period	Fall in indicator, per cent per year	Average for indicator per cent p.a.
d	GB	17	17	1·0	⎫
	NL	43	33	0·8	⎬ 1·0
	USA	18	24	1·3	⎭
R	D	14	8	0·6	⎫
	DK	13	12	0·9	
	GB	26	5	0·2	
	NL	22	6	0·3	⎬ 0·6
	S	28	26	0·9	
	N*	85	36	0·4	
	USA†	53	34	0·6	⎭
E	DK	26	18	0·7	⎫
	GB	17	10	0·6	⎬ 0·6
	S	13	7	0·5	⎭

* Sample of 2 towns only. † Wages only.

TABLE 6.1.C
OTHER INEQUALITY INDICATORS, INCOME BEFORE TAX

(1) Relative average deviation (d)

Country	GB		NL				USA		
Year	1949	1966	1921	1927	1933	1938	1950	1964	1948	1955	1966
Lower income limit	£250	£300			f1400		f3000	f5000	$2500	$2500	$3000
Rel. av. dev.	0·58	0·48	0·72	0·73	0·65	0·68	0·62	0·48	0·59	0·60	0·45

Source: CBS [8].

(2) Upper 5th percentile income, as a percentage of median (earnings only) P_5

Country	BR	CDN	F	GB	H	J	MEX	RA	RCH	S (all incl.)		USA	
Year*		1961								1930	1960	1939	1959
P_5	380	205	280	200	180	280	450	215	400	303	222	267	206

Source: Lydall [17] (only countries for which also indicators of education inequality are given by Lydall).
* Years not mentioned: near 1960.

TABLE 6.1.C (cont.)

(3) Inequality Index (Concentration ratio of Lorenz curve) R, per cent

Country	D		DK		GB		NL		S		N*		USA†	
Year	1936	1950	1939	1952	1938	1964‡	1938	1962‡	1935	1963†	1865	1950	1903	1956
R	49	45	50	44	43	40	48	44	54	40	50	32	50	33

Source: UN [24] ch. IX p. 6; for N: Soltow [22] p. 55; for USA: Keat [13].
* Average of 2 towns (Østfold, Vestagter).
† Wages only.
‡ Supplementary information from United Nations.

(4) Maximum equalization percentage (E)

Country	DK		GB		NL		S	
Year	1939	1965	1938	1955	1950		1935	1948
E	33	27	30	27	31		38	31

Source: UN [24]; for DK: [21].

were low or negative and a considerable number of households received unemployment 'benefits', and partly to the family size situation, to be discussed in Section VI. A further interesting common feature of the figures is that before World War II half of national income went to the 20 per cent highest income recipients, families and households. Finally, the Norwegian sample by Soltow is interesting for several reasons. It covers by far the longest period available and shows a clear equalitarian trend, typical of the Scandinavian countries and Britain. Tables 6.I.B and 6.I.C show similar trends extending also to the Netherlands and the United States and possibly to (Western) Germany.

From these tables, it is possible to conclude that if the percentage fall of inequality in primary incomes were to continue, a reduction to one-half of existing inequality would take 50 to 85 years to achieve.

V. INFLUENCE OF TAXES OF COMPLETE REDISTRIBUTION

Tables 6.II.A and 6.II.B partly repeat the figures of Tables 6.I.A and 6.I.B, but add income-after-tax figures where they are available. From these tables we note that taxes have reduced everywhere the share of the highest decile and, after World War II, raised the share of the lowest decile. Since the decile data do not cover many cases, the other indicators, shown in Table 6.II.B, deserve some more attention.

The after-tax inequality index R for Britain fell by 8 percentage points over 21 years, for Denmark by 7 points over 13 years and for Sweden by 11 points over 13 years; the average picture being 9 points in 16 years, hence half a point per annum. If this (linear) trend could go on, the inequality in after-tax incomes could be reduced to half its British value in 1959 during a period of 27 years or one generation. A similar exercise for the maximum equalisation percentage E tells us that in fourteen years a reduction in E by 6 points took place and hence a reduction to half its present value of, say, 20, would take, if the trend continues, 23 years, a comparable figure.

Tables 6.III.A and 6.III.B show the influence of 'complete redistribution' neglecting possible further redistribution by some autonomous social security institutions. The case of Denmark, based on a very careful inquiry [21] is particularly interesting. The quintile ratio (upper/lower) of 8·2 before tax is reduced to 2 or 3, depending on the

TABLE 6.II.A

INCOME BEFORE (B) AND AFTER (A) TAX, LOWER AND UPPER DECILES AND QUINTILES, ‰ OF TOTAL INCOME OF COUNTRY, SELECTED COUNTRIES AND YEARS; INCOME RECIPIENTS (R) OR FAMILIES (F)

Country	DK				GB				NL				S			
Year	1939(R)		1952(R)		1938(F)		1955(R)		1957(F)		1946(R)	1950(R)	1962(F)		1935(R)		1948(R)	
B or A	B	A	B	A	B	A	B	A	B	A	B	A	B	A	B	A	B	A
Decile 1	14	14	16	17							10		28	33				
Decile 2	30	27	32								22		47	52				
Quint 1	44	41	48								32	48	75	85			32	35
Decile 9	158	162	154		120	128	144	149	135	145	147	150	144	145	166	172	163	161
Decile 10	352	350	286	275	380	336	293	245	280	235	383	300	298	251	395	369	303	270
Quint 5	510	512	440		500		437	394	415	380	530	450	439	397	561	541	466	431
Source:	[2]	[24]	[4]	[24]	[16]		[24]	[25]	[16]		[24]	[25]	[19]		[24]	[25]	[24]	[25]

INCOME DISTRIBUTION IN SOME WESTERN COUNTRIES

assumption made with regard to the gains derived by the various income groups from some or all of the public expenditures. The corresponding figures for the Netherlands indicate a less impressive, but still considerable redistribution; one wonders whether the Swedish figures by Bentzel are as comparable to those for Denmark and the Netherlands as their description suggests [3].

TABLE 6.II.B
OTHER INEQUALITY INDICATORS, INCOME BEFORE AND AFTER TAX

(1) *Inequality Index (Concentration ratio of Lorenz curve) R, per cent*

Country Year	DK 1939 1952	GB 1938 1955 1959	NL 1950	S 1935 1948
R, pre-tax	50 44	43 41 32	45	54 44
R, after tax	47 40	38 34 30	41	52 41

Source: UN [25]; GB, 1959 Nicholson [18].

(2) *Maximum equalisation percentage (E)*

Country Year	DK 1939 1952	GB 1938 1955	NL 1950	S 1935 1948
E, pre-tax	36 31	30 27	31	38 31
E, after tax	34 28	27 24	28	37 28

Source: UN [25].

Turning to Table 6.III.B, the inequality index R is reduced by 7 percentage points for both the United Kingdom in 1959 and the United States in 1967 after complete redistribution corresponding with a reduction along the trend of about 14 years. The last figure given in Table 6.III.B for the United States will be discussed in Section VII.

VI. SIZE OF HOUSEHOLDS AND FAMILIES

Table 6.IV presents information on an aspect of income distribution that is not often discussed, namely, the changes over time in the size of households and families in higher- and lower-income brackets. Over the period for which figures are available, these changes are

TABLE 6.III.A

INCOME BEFORE (B) AND AFTER (A) COMPLETE REDISTRIBUTION, ASSUMING PUBLIC OVERHEAD EXPENDITURES TO BE OF EQUAL ADVANTAGE TO (a) EACH INCOME RECIPIENT, (b) IN PROPORTION TO INCOME RECEIVED OR (c) EITHER (a) OR (b) DEPENDING ON THE CATEGORY OF PUBLIC EXPENDITURES

Country	DK(R)			NL(H)					S			
Year	1963			1935		1962			1935		1948	
Assumption	B	Aa	Ab	B	Ac	B	Aa	Ab	B	A	B	A
Decile 1						9	21	24				
Quintile 1	52	132	102	59	70	34	60	65			32	35
Decile 9	260	126	151	146	145	153	151	150	166	172	163	161
Decile 10		140	157	366	315	326	267	242	396	370	301	269
Quintile 5	426	266	308	512	460	479	418	392	562	542	464	430
Qu. 5/Qu. 1	8·2	2·0	3·0	8·7	6·6	14·1	7·0	6·0			14·5	12·3
Dec. 10/Dec. 1						36·0	12·7	10·1				
Source:	[21]			[23]		[19]					[3]	

96

Income Distribution in some Western Countries

most pronounced for the Netherlands, where family size in the lower and the upper quintile was approximately equal in 1935-6, but where the size ratio upper/lower had increased to 1·77 by 1962. For deciles the change was from 0·79 to 2·05. For households the 1962 ratios are over 3. These figures reflect demographic changes of various kinds. First, family planning in confessional lower income brackets came late, due to Church resistance. Second, both young and old people today can afford to become or remain independent households, which often they could not in the thirties or twenties.

TABLE 6.III.B
OTHER INEQUALITY INDICATORS, INCOME
BEFORE AND AFTER REDISTRIBUTION

Inequality Index (Concentration ratio of Lorenz curve) R, per cent

Country	GB		USA
Year	1937	1959	1967
Pre redistribution	35	32	42
Post redistribution	27	25	35
Idem, adj. for family size			31

Sources: GB, 1959: Nicholson [18], quoting for 1937 Barna. USA: Lampman [15].

Similar tendencies can be observed, although to a lesser extent, for Germany and Britain but hardly at all for the United States, at least according to Selma Goldsmith [11]. Even so average family size is larger in the upper than in the lower quintile in the United States. For comparison Table 6.IV also lists the figures for India, a developing country with as many inhabitants as Africa and Latin America together. These last figures illustrate the penetration of family planning in the higher income brackets and its virtual absence in the lower income brackets in 1967-8.

VII. INCOME RATIOS FOR PERSONS IN UPPER AND LOWER STRATA

Using Table 6.IV enables us to give a better picture of the trends in income distribution than we have been able to do so far; for, we can

INTERNATIONAL TRADE AND MONEY

TABLE 6.IV
PERSONS (P) OR CONSUMPTION UNITS (U) PER HOUSEHOLD (H) OR FAMILY (F), SELECTED COUNTRIES AND YEARS, IN LOWER AND UPPER DECILES OR QUINTILES

Country H or F P or U	D H P			GB H P		IND H P	
Year	1927–28	1962–3*	1965	1937–39	1957	Rural 1967–8	Urban
Decile 1	3·70	1·81	1·39	3·18	2·00	5·87	6·09
Decile 2	(3·78)	(2·23)	(1·65)			5·72	6·00
Quintile 1	3·74	2·02	1·52			5·80	6·05
Decile 9	(3·95)	(3·30)	(3·13)			4·75	2·89
Decile 10	4·25	3·22	3·13	3·54	4·45	4·20	2·50
Quintile 5	4·10	3·14	3·13			4·48	2·70
Qu. 5 / Qu. 1	1·10	1·55	2·06			0·77	0·45
Dec. 10 / Dec. 1	1·15	1·78	2·25	1·29	2·23	0·71	0·41
Source	[20]	[12]	[26]	[18]		[9]	

Country	NL					USA			
H or F P or U	F U	F U	F P	F P	H P	F P			
Year	1923–4†	1935–6†	1935–6	1962	1962	1903	1935–6	1941	1959
Dec. 1	(3·30)	(3·76)	5·35	2·40	1·21				
Qu. 1	(3·58)	(3·18)	4·50	2·58	1·39	3·48	3·73	3·55	3·24
Dec. 10	(3·20)	(3·36)	4·20	4·99	4·63				
Qu. 5	(3·78)	(3·60)	4·60	4·82	4·50	3·86	3·92	4·00	3·89
Qu. 5 / Qu. 1	(1·05)	(1·13)	1·02	1·77	3·23	1·11	1·05	1·12	1·20
Dec. 10 / Dec. 1	(0·97)	(0·89)	0·79	2·05	3·82				
Source	[2]	[7]	[7]	[19]	[19]	[14]	[11]	[11]	[11]

* Hamburg only.
† Amsterdam only.

Income Distribution in some Western Countries

TABLE 6.V
RATIOS OF INCOME BETWEEN UPPER AND LOWER GROUPS, QUINTILES (Q) OR DECILES (D), PER HOUSEHOLD (H) OR FAMILY (F) COMPARED WITH RATIOS PER PERSON (P), USING ASSUMPTIONS (a), (b) OR (c) ON ADVANTAGE OF PUBLIC EXPENDITURES FOR VARIOUS GROUPS (cf. TABLE III)

A. Highest to Lowest Ratios of Income before Tax

Country	D		NL		USA	
Year	Prewar*	Postwar†	1935–6	1962	1935–6	1959
H or F	H	H	H	H	F	F
Q ratio H or F	17·7	12·0	8·7	10·4	12·6	9·9
Q ratio P	16·1	5·6	8·5	3·2	12·0	8·2
D ratio H or F		34·0		21·0		
D ratio P		15·0		5·5		

Source: Tables 6.I and 6.IV.
* Incomes: 1936; household size: 1927/8.
† Incomes: 1950; household size: 1965.

B. Highest to Lowest Ratio of Income (Quartile or Decile Averages) after Complete Redistribution Per Household (H), Family (F) and Per Person (P)

Country		NL			
Year	1935–6	1962		1962	
H or F	H*	H		F†	
Assumption a, b or c‡	c	a	b	a	b
Q ratio H or F	6·6	7·0	6·0	7·0	6·0
Q ratio P	6·4	2·2	1·9	4·0	3·4
D ratio H or F		12·7	10·1		
D ratio P		3·3	2·6		

Source: Tables 6.III and 6.IV.
* H for incomes, F for family size.
† H for incomes, F for family size.
‡ Cf. Table III.

now calculate ratios of income per capita between high and low family income brackets. It has to be kept in mind that the deciles and quintiles are still based on numbers of households or families and not on numbers of persons in the population. The latter computation could be carried out only with the aid of the raw data.

Part A of Table 6.V shows incomes before tax, Part B incomes after complete redistribution. For recent years the per-capita figures for the few countries where data were available are considerably more favourable than the figures for households or families. In Germany inequality measures are reduced to one-half of their uncorrected value and in the Netherlands to one-third; in the United States the reduction, as expected, is less striking. The quintile ratios that are now obtained for incomes per capita after complete redistribution are comparable to the Danish figures in Table 6.III.A. In

TABLE 6.VI
SOME DATA ON CONSUMPTION EXPENDITURE IN RUPEES PER PERSON PER ANNUM IN LOWER AND UPPER INCOME BRACKETS, 1960/1 AND 1967/8 (CONSTANT 1960/1 PRICES), RURAL (R) AND URBAN (U) AREAS AND RATIOS

Year	1960–1		1967–8	
R or U	R	U	R	U
Decile 1	88·0	113·0	88·4	95·3
Decile 2	100·4	156·1	102·0	145·1
Quintile 1	188·4	269·1	190·4	241·0
Decile 9	382·5	553·5	399·2	580·2
Decile 10	682·0	1061·1	711·7	1054·9
Quintile 5	1064·5	1614·6	1110·9	1635·1
Decile 10/1 ratio	7·8	9·4	8·1	11·0
Quintile 5/1 ratio	5·7	6·0	5·8	6·8

Source: Dandekar and Rath [9].

addition, we may mention that the American figure for R in 1967 given in Table 6.III.B falls in line with those for 1969 given in Table 6.V.A after adjustment for family size.

No figures for Scandinavian countries were found; however, to the extent that the Dutch changes between 1935–6 and 1962 are due to the belated penetration of family planning into lower income groups it can be surmised that changes over the last decades may have been not so pronounced in the Scandinavian countries.

Again for comparison figures have been added for consumption expenditure in India (Table 6.VI). The differences in trends with Western countries are striking and reflect the dramatic problems of developing countries in social matters.

Income Distribution in some Western Countries

VIII. SUMMARY

Although the available material is subject to well-known lacunae and uncertainties, errors in figures concerning changes over time and in the estimation of the effects of redistribution schemes will be less than errors in the absolute figures. Our main findings are:

(i) The trend in income shares of the lowest groups over the past decades has been upward, that of the highest groups downward (Table 6.I.A).

(ii) If the observed percentage reduction of inequality per year were to continue it would take 50 to 85 years in order to reduce existing inequality to one-half (Tables 6.I.B and 6.I.C).

(iii) Taxes have reduced the after-tax income share of the highest decile and raised, after World War II, the share of the lowest decile (Table 6.II.A).

(iv) If the linear trend in inequality indicators for incomes after tax were to continue, halving inequality would take some 25 years or one generation (Table 6.II.B).

(v) Complete redistribution by public finance reduces the ratio of the upper to the lower quintile from 8 to 2·5 in Denmark (1963) and from 14 to 6·5 in the Netherlands (1962) (Table 6.III.A).

(vi) If the trend in R for incomes after complete redistribution were to continue, reduction to one-half of its present value would take 14 years (Section V).

(vii) Demographic factors have equalized income distribution over persons more than over families (Table 6.IV), especially in the Netherlands.

(viii) For the Netherlands in 1962 the ratio of *income per capita* for the upper to the lower family income quintiles is 2 as against 6·5 for *income per household*; in contrast, in 1935-6 there was no difference between this ratio for per capita income and for income per household. Similar, though more moderate, changes took place in Germany and in Britain (Tables 6.IV and 6.V).

(ix) In India the ratios of consumption expenditures per capita of high incomes to low incomes are high and have increased between 1960-1 and 1967-8 (Table 6.VI), illustrating the dramatic social situation.

As a last remark it should be added that, notwithstanding the observed changes in income distribution, it is the author's conviction that further reductions in inequality are called for on general ethical grounds. Some studies on the measures to be taken and their effect have been undertaken and will be published elsewhere.

REFERENCES

1. E. C. Budd, 'Postwar Changes in the Size Distribution of Income in the United States', *American Economic Review, Papers and Proceedings*, Vol. 60, No. 2 (May, 1970), p. 247.
2. Bureau van Statistiek, Amsterdam, Huishoudrekeningen van 212 gezinnen uit verschillende kringen der bevolking, 1923–4, Amsterdam 1927. (Family budgets of 212 families from different population strata in Amsterdam; Dutch.)
3. R. Bentzel, Inkomstfördelningen i Sverige, Uppsala 1953 (Income Distribution in Sweden (diss.) Swedish).
4. Kj. Bjerke, 'Changes in the Danish Income Distribution 1939–52', Income and Wealth Series VI, London, 1956, p. 98.
5. Dorothy Cole and J. E. G. Utting, 'The Distribution of Household and Individual Income', Income and Wealth Series VI, London, 1956, p. 239.
6. Centraal Bureau voor de Statistiek, Inkomensverdeling 1962 en vermogensverdeling 1963, The Hague, 1967, p. 15 (Income Distribution 1962 and Wealth Distribution 1963, Dutch).
7. ——, Huishoudrekeningen van 598 gezinnen 1935–36, The Hague, 1938. (Budgets of 598 families in the Netherlands, 1935–36, Dutch.)
8. ——, Statistische en econometrische onderzoekingen, 1960, p. 51 (Dutch).
9. V. M. Dandekar and Nilakantha Rath, 'Poverty in India', *Economic and Political Weekly*, Vol. 6 (2 Jan. 1971), p. 25, and (9 Jan. 1971), p. 106.
10. S. A. Goldberg and Jenny R. Podoluk, 'Income Size Distribution Statistics in Canada – a Survey and Some Analysis', Income and Wealth Series VI, London, 1956, p. 155.
11. Selma F. Goldsmith, 'Impact of the Income Tax on Socio-Economic Groups of Families in the United States', Income and Wealth Series X, London, 1964, p. 248.
12. Hamburg in Zahlen 1965, p. 270; 1966, p. 149 (Hamburg in Figures, German).
13. P. G. Keat, 'Long-run Changes in Occupational Wage Structure 1900–1956', *Journal of Political Economy*, Vol. 68, No. 6 (Dec. 1960), p. 584.
14. Labor, 18th Report of the Commissioner for ——, 1903. Cost of Living and Retail Prices of Food, Washington 1904, Part I, pp. 582–3.
15. R. J. Lampman, 'Transfer Approaches to Distribution Policy', *American Economic Review, Papers and Proceedings*, Vol. 60, No. 2 (May, 1970), p. 270.
16. H. F. Lydall, 'The Long-Term Trend in the Size Distribution of Income', *Journal of the Royal Statistical Society*, Vol. 122(1) (1959), p. 1.
17. ——, *The Structure of Earnings* (Clarendon Press, Oxford, 1968).
18. J. L. Nicholson, 'Redistribution of Income in the United Kingdom in 1959, 1957 and 1953', Income and Wealth Series X, London, 1964, p. 148.
19. Nota over de inkomensverdeling, Bijlage 15 Miljoenennota 1970, The Hague 1969 (Memorandum on the Income Distribution, Annex 15 to the State budget 1970, Parliamentary Document Session 1969–70, Nr. 10 300, Dutch).

20. Reichsamt, Statistisches, Die Lebenshaltung von 2000 Arbeiter-, Angestellten- und Beamtenhaushaltungen 1927-8, Teil I, Berlin 1932, p. 14. 'The Level of Living of 2000 Worker, Employee and Civil Servant Families 1927/8, German).
21. Råd, Det økonomiske, Formandskabet, Den personlige indkomstfordeling og indkomstudjævningen over de offentlige finanser, Copenhagen 1967 (Presidency of the Economic Council: The personal Income Distribution and Income Redistribution through Public Finance, Danish).
22. L. Soltow, *Toward Income Equality in Norway* (The University of Wisconsin Press, Madison-Milwaukee, 1965), p. 55.
23. H. Vos, Enige kwantitatieve onderzoekingen over de betrekkingen tussen overheidsfinanciën en volkshuishouding, Haarlem 1946, p. 53 (Some Quantitative Investigations on the Relations between Public Finance and the Economy, Dutch).
24. United Nations, *Economic Survey of Europe in 1956*, Geneva, 1957, Chapter IX, p. 6.
25. *Ibid.*, p. 22.
26. Wirtschaft und Statistik 1969, Heft 7, 'Einkommensverhältnisse der Haushalte' (Ergebnis der 1%-Wohnungsstichprobe, 1965), p. 366 (Income Relations of Households; Results of 1 per cent Dwelling Sample 1965; German).

PART III

INTERNATIONAL MONETARY ANALYSIS

7

A Model for the Analysis of Official Intervention in the Foreign Exchange Markets

GIORGIO BASEVI
*University of Louvain
and
University of Bologna*

I. INTRODUCTION

This study has three main objectives. The first is to provide a framework for analysing the internal monetary effects of surpluses and deficits in the balance of a country's international payments. In published models of the foreign exchange markets, both theoretical[2] and empirical,[3] there typically is no link between the determination of exchange rates, on the one hand, and interest rates on the other. Yet, capital movements are described and estimated, in these models, as determined by the joint influence of such variables. This missing link might very well go far toward explaining the weak statistical results that are generally obtained in these models, especially with regard to the sensitivity of capital movements to exchange rates or to covered interest rate differentials. Even in the economy-wide models that have been constructed and estimated for various countries in recent years, the channels through which external surpluses (deficits) inject (absorb) liquidity into (from) the economy is not clarified in a detail sufficient for the analysis of the connections between foreign exchange policy and monetary policy.

The second objective of this study is to provide a framework for analysing the foreign exchange market in all its sections; mainly those determining the spot and forward rates, but in principle also those determining the rates for various maturities of forward ex-

[1] I am grateful to the many friends who commented on a preliminary version of this study. I am particularly indebted to J. A. Bartolomei, who induced me to formalise my ideas on this subject. An earlier version of this paper was published in *Recherches Economiques de Louvain*, No. 3 (October, 1971), pp. 171-91.

[2] See, in particular, Tsiang [22], Sohmen [19], Kenen [9], Frevert [7], Branson [4], and Levin [13].

[3] See, in particular, Stein [20], Stoll [21], Black [2], and Branson [4].

change contracts. In estimated macroeconomic models only the spot exchange rate is endogenous, while forward rates usually are either ignored or exogenous.[4] Moreover, the way the rate is endogenised is through systems of equations for the items in balance of payments statistics. It is the contention of this study that the correct way to endogenise the foreign exchange rates is by setting up a system of equations describing the foreign exchange markets. These equations do not correspond to those based on items of the balance of payments statistics: as shown in this study, these items have to be specifically rearranged in order to approximate, as closely as possible, the transactions actually conducted in the foreign exchange markets.

The third objective of this study is to provide a framework for analysing the policies of the monetary authorities aiming at controlling the money supply while at the same time maintaining external equilibrium through intervention on the spot and forward sections of the foreign exchange market. These policies were already advocated by Keynes as a way out from the dilemma of having to enforce different levels of domestic interest rates according to whether internal or external equilibrium is chosen as the objective of monetary policy.[5] Attempts to enact these policies have been made at times in the UK and, for longer periods, in Germany and in Italy. In these countries the monetary authorities, in the presence of severely limited spot exchange policy and of inefficient or completely unavailable fiscal policy for the purpose of controlling the business cycle, have attempted to use their operations in the forward exchange market as an instrument additional to the control of the money supply or of interest rates.[6] These attempts have been paralleled, especially in the US, by operations aiming at distorting the maturity structure of interest rates so as to maintain, at the same time, short-term interest rates consistent with external equilibrium and long-term interest rates conducive to internal equilibrium and growth. Econometric studies have shown that, at least for the US, the latter type of policy (the so-called 'operation twist') was not particularly effective[7]; in other words, it does not seem that, with well integrated financial

---

[4] For two exceptions see Amano [1], and Helliwell and Maxwell [8].

[5] See Keynes [10], pp. 122–32. This is, of course, a reinterpretation of Keynes in the light of the modern theory of economic policy as developed particularly by Tinbergen and applied to the problems of international payments by Meade, Mundell and many others.

[6] On these experiences, see Bloomfield [3], Brehmen [5], and Masera [14].

[7] See Modigliani and Sutch [16].

markets, the monetary authorities could control separately the short and long term rates of interest. Parallel to this, there is at least a presumption that, with well integrated financial and foreign exchange markets and very elastic capital movements, forward exchange policy along the lines suggested by Keynes and followed by some central banks does not really provide an instrument additional to monetary policy, since the enforcement of a certain level of forward exchange rates reacts on the level of spot rates and on that of interest rates. Thus, the observed surplus (deficit) of the balance of payments that, through forward exchange intervention or special 'swap' contracts, the monetary authorities try to 'sterilise' (finance), might be larger than the surplus (deficit) that would have been observed without the sterilisation or 'recycling' policy. The presumption in fact is that this policy, enacted through forward exchange intervention, has also indirectly affected spot exchange and domestic interest rates in a way contrary to the stated objective of external equilibrium; if so, sterilisation operations would be less effective than might appear superficially, and might not even be effective at all. The inefficacy of sterilisation policies, already pointed out by Mundell[8] in the framework of official intervention limited to the spot exchange market and with perfect capital mobility, would then not be effectively avoided by the adoption of an active forward exchange policy.

To analyse these problems and explore the validity of these presumptions was indeed the initial motivation that induced the author to this study. For this reason, the model is meant to be operational and oriented toward estimation and simulation of actual aggregate behaviour and policies. In particular, it could help to analyse, for a country to which it might be adapted, the effects on interest rates of adopting more flexible exchange systems of the 'crawling peg' or 'sliding parity' variety.

Finally, this study is part of a larger project of research on the foreign and monetary sectors of the Italian economy, which is undertaken within the Project LINK of constructing and estimating interconnected macroeconomic models of various countries and groups of countries in the world.[9]

[8] See Mundell [17].
[9] The Italian model is being constructed by a research group of the Istituto di Scienze Economiche of the University of Bologna, supported by grants from the Consiglio Nazionale delle Ricerche and the Social Science Research Council. The monetary sector of that model, to which this study is closely connected, is described in D'Adda [6].

II. CHARACTERISTICS OF THE MODEL

This study builds upon a model of the spot and forward exchange markets developed by Black [2], but hopefully improves it by correcting a few errors and linking the foreign exchange markets with the market for goods and services on the one hand, and with the money market on the other. It is through these two markets that the model of the foreign exchange market here presented might be connected with an economy-wide macroeconomic model.

To be more precise, four markets are explicitly considered in this model: the market for the national product (for goods and services), the market for spot foreign exchange, the market for forward foreign exchange, and the money market.[10] Four sectors or groups of agents enter these markets: the resident non-banking sector, the foreign (non-resident) sector, the commercial banking sector and the national monetary authorities.

The analysis of the foreign exchange market is based on the distinction of the essential functions that may be performed on it, rather than on that of the operators that perform these functions. The functions are hedging (or covering) and speculation. The first consists in avoiding the risk involved in holding positions of debit or credit denominated in foreign currency, by taking opposite positions in the forward foreign exchange market. The second, on the contrary, consists in deliberately holding open positions in foreign exchange with a view to gaining by closing them in the spot exchange market when payment is due. Thus, while the model shall distinguish between interest arbitrageurs and hedging importers and exporters, it is recognised that both perform the function of covering their risk – which arise from having to receive or make payments of foreign exchange in the future – by contracting to sell or buy forward corresponding amounts of foreign exchange. From this point of view, the only difference between covered interest arbitrage and commercial hedging is in the source of the initial open positions,

---

[10] With additional complications the model could be extended to more than two markets (spot and forward) for foreign exchange, *i.e.* to include forward maturities of one, three, six months, etc. This extension is treated in this model, only through a special hypothesis on the structure of interest and exchange rates. Another possible complication to bring the model closer to reality, is to consider foreign exchange denominated in various currencies, and therefore exchange rates between domestic currency and each of the foreign currencies. For a model that does this, see Frevert [7].

which is the decision to invest short-term capital in one case, and that of granting commercial credit in the other.[11]

The distinction between functions and operators is essential to recognise that in reality a single operation may respond to a mixture of functions – as when speculators take open positions in the spot exchange market – and that a particular operator need not perform always the same function, as when exporters or importers do not cover their open positions. Adherence to this distinction means that actual operations in the foreign exchange market must be decomposed into their essential components, and that as a consequence the foreign exchange market must be artificially reconstructed on the basis of unobserved quantities. This procedure, however, is already well established in the literature, and is essential to isolate elementary behavioural functions.[12]

III. THE MARKET FOR GOODS AND SERVICES

The market for goods and services is analysed only on the demand side, while supply remains exogenous to this model. Let us define

$$Y_t = y_t P_t \tag{1}$$

where Y_t is national money income received during period t, y_t is its real counterpart, and P_t is the GNP implicit price deflator (the 'price level'). National income can also be viewed as the sum of residents' total money expenditure (E_t) plus net money receipts on current and transfer international account (C_t), i.e. for exports minus imports of goods and services and for unrequited income transfers:

$$Y_t = E_t + C_t \tag{2}$$

Identity (2) can alternatively be viewed as an equation expressing the condition of equilibrium in the market for goods and services.

It will be the task of a well developed macroeconomic model to specify functions for the various components of national expenditure. From the point of view of this model it is sufficient to assume a behavioural function for total residents' expenditure dependent on domestic real income, the price level and long-term interest rates, possibly lagged:[13]

$$E_t = E(y_{t-j}, \ldots, P_{t-j}, \ldots, i^d_{t-j,k}); j = 0, 1, \ldots \tag{3}$$

[11] On this see [19], p. 25, [21], p. 61 and [7], pp. 161–2.
[12] This is a device used by most authors. See, for example, [19] and [2].
[13] All functions are here presented in an unspecified form. The same holds true for the length of the lags distribution.

where $i^d_{t-j,k}$ is the domestic interest rate quoted at time $t-j$ on long-term loans (having a typical maturity of k periods).

IV. THE MARKET FOR SPOT FOREIGN EXCHANGE

The condition of equilibrium in the market for spot foreign exchange is:

$$B'_t + K_t + N_t = 0 \qquad (4)$$

In (4) B'_t, if positive, is the excess supply of spot foreign exchange originating from current and transfer account transactions for which there is no lag between the time of commitment and the time at which the payment is due; because of this, there is no foreign exchange risk involved and no question of hedging or speculating by not hedging.[14] On the other hand, the remaining operations on current and transfer account, i.e. all purchases and sales of goods and services for which there is a lag between the time of order and the time when payments are due, do not give rise to any direct demand or supply of spot foreign exchange. In fact, as explained before, all these operations are treated as if they were always and completely covered against exchange risk in the forward market, thus giving rise to an excess supply of forward foreign exchange at time t, to be delivered with a typical delay of one period, e.g. $B''_{t,t+1}$.[15] When the time of payment has come, importers and exporters will simply exchange domestic against foreign currency at rates agreed upon in past forward contracts.[16] K_t, if positive, is the excess supply of spot foreign exchange on account of capital investors, while N_t, if negative, is net official purchases of spot foreign exchange (net accumulation of official liquid international reserves).

[14] In practice it seems that the only type of transactions that might approach the limit of no lag between order and payment due are travel and tourism transactions. This model does not consider the possibility of lags between order and payment due, shorter than the minimum maturity of forward exchange contracts; for a model that does, see [7].

[15] This is not a limiting characteristic of the model, for in so far as traders do not cover, their behaviour will be included in the speculation function.

[16] Failure to recognise this point accounts for an error in Black's model. His equation (2.3′) should not include B_t, which are payments executed in the current period on the basis of forward contracts undertaken by hedging traders in the preceding periods. These payments should not appear in the equation of equilibrium for the spot market, for they involve exchange of currencies at previously fixed forward rates. As such, they do not influence the current spot rate.

It is necessary to identify in detail the components of K_t. These are three. First, there is the excess supply of spot exchange due to investors of short-term capital (interest arbitrageurs) who currently buy and sell spot foreign exchange in order to invest their funds in the most convenient financial market. By definition of pure interest arbitrage, they are supposed to cover their investment in the forward market. Take, for example, a domestic resident who buys today spot foreign exchange in order to purchase foreign short-term assets. At the same time he is supposed to sell forward foreign exchange with a maturity matching that of the asset he has purchased. In this way he covers against the risk of depreciation of the foreign currency, which would reduce the value of his asset in terms of domestic currency. Of course, not all foreign investors do cover against exchange risk; but, insofar as they do not, their behaviour will be considered as speculation and included in the behavioural function that describes it.

Second, there is the excess supply of spot exchange due to investors of long-term capital.[17] Since forward exchange contracts matching long-term investment are not readily available, transaction costs are probably very high for covering long-term investment. Moreover, a change in the exchange rate is proportionately a less important source of losses or gains the longer is the duration of investment. For these reasons, we may assume that exchange risk considerations do not substantially determine long-term investment, so that this involves the spot exchange market only.

Third, the spot market is also entered by speculators when they close open positions previously taken in the forward market. Thus, we define

$$K_t = A_t + I_t + S_t \qquad (5)$$

where A_t, if positive, is the excess supply of spot exchange by arbitrageurs due to net short-term foreign investment in the home country; I_t, if positive, is the excess supply due to long-term investment; and S_t, if positive, is the excess supply of foreign exchange by speculators.

V. ARBITRAGE

It is not evident, at first sight, why S_t should be considered a component of total net supply of spot exchange on account of capital

[17] Following rules-of-thumb generally adopted in balance-of-payments accounting, one-year maturity could be considered as the dividing line between short- and long-term investments.

investments.[18] Consider the outward arbitrageurs who, last period, had sold forward foreign exchange in order to cover the exchange risk on the repatriation of their assets. If, having their asset reached maturity in the present period, they decide to repatriate their funds, this decision should be counted as an inward capital movement. Yet, in order to execute it, they only need deliver the foreign exchange, obtained from the payment of their expired asset, to the counterpart in the forward contract agreed upon last period, and receive domestic currency. Their repatriation of funds, therefore, would not appear directly in the spot market (i.e. not through a positive component of A_t). But it does indirectly, for the counterpart of their forward contract was, in the net and for the moment not considering official intervention, taken up by hedging commercial traders (who in the preceding period had bought forward exchange to cover their net open positions) and by speculators (who, last period, had bought forward exchange in the hope of profiting from its appreciation by selling it in the present period). For the counterpart of forward contracts taken up by commercial traders, the repatriation of arbitrageurs' capital does not pass through the spot exchange market since their funds were directly committed on the forward market to cover the foreign exchange requirements of net importers. For the counterpart taken up by speculators, on the other hand, the repatriation of arbitrageurs' funds does pass through the spot market, since speculators sell in the spot market the foreign exchange obtained from arbitrageurs in fulfilment of their net forward operations, and deliver to them the proceeds of the sale, plus or minus the margin lost or gained.[19]

On the other hand, suppose that last period arbitrageurs decide not to repatriate their funds. They still must honour the forward contracts they had entered into when covering. This they do by buying spot foreign exchange and (in the net and still provisionally excluding official forward intervention) delivering it to hedging commercial traders and to speculators, i.e. to the net counterparts in their forward contracts. Commercial traders will use the foreign exchange thus received to pay their net imports, while speculators will sell it on the spot market. Arbitrageurs' decision not to repatriate

---

[18] Indeed, Black disregards this element in his equation (2.3′).

[19] In practice, repatriating arbitrageurs will probably sell their foreign exchange directly in the spot market, speculators just paying or receiving the difference between forward and spot contracts.

their maturing investments, i.e. to keep their funds abroad, means that they do not give rise to an inflow of capital. Yet, for consistency of the model, A_t (which if positive represents an excess supply of spot exchange on account of short-term capital inflows) must be diminished by the additional purchases of spot exchange by arbitrageurs which are necessary to honour the forward contracts they signed last period to cover their expected (but not realised) repatriation of funds. The additional intervention on the spot market by arbitrageurs, which is necessary to allow them to keep their funds abroad, is partly offset, however, by sales of spot exchange on the part of speculators with whom arbitrageurs had made forward contracts; what is left is that part of arbitrageurs' contracts which, in the net, had been taken up by commercial traders; thus the latters' needs are alimented by the spot market indirectly through arbitrageurs' operations.

Two points should have been cleared by the discussion so far. The first is that supplies and demands coming into the foreign exchange market do not coincide with the credit and debit items of the balance of payments. The second is that, in this model, short-term capital is treated as if it were invested for a length of one period (corresponding to the one-period maturity of forward market) and thus, at the end of each period, either repatriated or reinvested. While this treatment will be justified later, it implies that A_t is really measuring stocks and not flows; in fact, if positive, A_t is the excess supply of spot exchange needed to pay for the stock of net inward investment for one period. If the stock is repatriated at the end of the period, this is the end of the story, for then the repatriation is made through the expiration of forward contracts. If the stock is not repatriated, since the forward sale of domestic currency must be honoured, there is a new sale of spot foreign exchange equal to A_t, which provides the needed domestic currency. The factors determining arbitrageurs' decisions should thus be formulated as referred to stocks rather than flows.

The excess supply of spot exchange, A_t, represents at the same time an excess demand for forward exchange of approximately equal amount,[20] since arbitrageurs by definition cover their positions. Thus,

$$A_t = F^a_{t,\,t+1} \tag{6}$$

[20] The approximation is due to the fact that both principal and interest should be covered, if arbitrage is to exclude all speculative elements. However, contrary to Sohmen's contention ([19], p. 17), it is impossible, at an aggregated level, to

where $F^a_{t,t+1}$ is the arbitrageurs' excess demand for forward exchange at time t for delivery in the following period.

Note that equation (6) implies either that arbitrageurs' capital is always invested in titles having the same maturity (one period) as the maturity of forward contracts, or that, if this is not so, short-term investment is covered by successive forward exchange contracts of one period each. Since clearly the first assumption is not justified by the usual definition of short-term capital, we must explore the meaning of the second assumption.

Consider an investor who has bought a foreign asset with a six months' maturity and suppose that forward exchange markets exist for both three and six months' maturities. He has the choice between covering his investment in the six months' forward market or covering twice successively in the three months' forward market. If he does the first, his present covered value of one unit of foreign exchange is equal to (making 1 period = three months)

$$\frac{r_{t,t+2}}{1+i^d_{t,2}}$$

where $i^d_{t,2}$ is the domestic interest rate at time t on six month loans, expressed as a percentage per six months. If he does the second, he sells three months forward one unit of foreign exchange. In three months' time he will honour the contract by buying spot exchange; he will then cover again by selling three month forward exchange. The expected present value, for this operation, is

$$\frac{r_{t,t+1}}{1+i^d_{t,1}} - \frac{r^{e,t}_{t+1}}{1+i^d_{t,1}} + \frac{r^{e,t}_{t+1,t+2}}{1+i^d_{t,2}}$$

where $i^d_{t,1}$ is the domestic interest rate at time t on three month loans, expressed as a percentage per three months, $r^{e,t}_{t+1}$ is the spot rate expected at time t for time $t+1$, and $r^{e,t}_{t+1,t+2}$ is the forward rate expected at time t for time $t+1$ and maturity $t+2$.

If covering is available in either of these forms, it follows that, disregarding different transaction costs in different maturity sections of the market, equilibrium will lead to equality between the two expressions above. This implies that

$$r_{t,t+2} = (r_{t,t+1} - r^{e,t}_{t+1})\frac{1+i^d_{t,2}}{1+i^d_{t,1}} + r^{e,t}_{t+1,t+2}.$$

specify, in general, the exact correction factor, since the interest rate to be applied depends on whether A_t is positive or negative and on its geographical distribution.

Generalising to all maturities and considering that $r^{e,t}_{t,t+1} = r_{t,t+1}$, we have

$$r_{t,t+j} = \sum_{k=1}^{j-1}(r^{e,t}_{t+k-1,t+k} - r^{e,t}_{t+k})\frac{1+i^d_{t,j}}{1+i^d_{t,k}} + r^{e,t}_{t+j-1,t+j} \quad j = 2, 3, \ldots$$

which shows that, implicit in the maturity structure of interest rates and forward exchange rates, there is a relationship between expected spot and forward exchange rates. Assuming that expectations are indeed as implied by this structure, we can treat arbitrage as if it were covered by successive spot and forward exchange contracts of one-period maturity each, and thus justify equation (6) and the treatment of A_t as a stock variable.

On the basis of the preceding discussion, it is now possible to formulate, albeit in an unspecified form, the behavioural function that determines A_t. Arbitrageurs' net sales of spot exchange are functions of domestic and foreign interest rates and of spot and forward rates of exchange, usually connected in the form of interest rate differentials. Since short-term investment of different maturities are refinanced, in this model, at the end of each forward exchange maturity period, A_t originates from one-period investments made at time t, from two periods investment decided upon at time $t-1$, etc. Thus, covered interest differentials for different maturities determine the function, each, however, lagged by the corresponding periods; i.e. A_t is determined by the one-period covered interest differential observed at time t, by the two-periods covered interest differential observed at time $t-1$, etc. In addition, the size of total (financial) wealth and its riskiness will affect the amount allocated to foreign investment.[21] Finally, given that short-term capital is invested abroad also to provide transactions balances in the financing of foreign trade, exports and imports will be arguments in the function.[22] The considerations already made with respect to interest differentials, suggest that the variables referring to wealth and to the volume of trade should determine A_t also with distributed lags. Thus,

$$A_t = A(d_{t-j,t+1}; W_{t-j}; B'_{t-j}, B''_{t-j,t-j+1}) \quad j = 0, 1, \ldots \quad (7)$$

[21] See on this, Whitman and Miller [15], Lee [12], the papers presented at the N.B.E.R. Conference on International Mobility and Movement of Capital [18], Amano [1], and the survey chapter in Leamer and Stern [11].

[22] While this suggests that imports and exports should determine the function separately, only the net balance on current and transfers account is considered in this provisionally aggregated model, and as such entered as an argument of the function. For a deeper analysis of this point, see Willett [23].

where

$$d_{t-j,t+1} = \frac{1+i^f_{t-j,j+1}}{1+i^d_{t-j,j+1}} - \frac{r_{t-j}}{r_{t-j,t+1}} \quad j=0,1,\ldots \tag{8}$$

are covered interest rate differentials, W_{t-j} are vectors of variables measuring the value and variability of wealth, and the B_{t-j} are values of net commitments on current and transfer account undertaken at periods $t-j$.

VI. SPECULATION

Since speculation is, by definition, always conducted on the forward market, we have

$$S_t = F^s_{t-1,t} \tag{9}$$

where $F^s_{t-1,t}$ is speculators' excess demand for forward exchange in period $t-1$, with a maturity of one period, which is then reversed at time t by a net supply of spot exchange on their part.

In (9), as it was the case for (6), it is implicitly assumed either that speculation is always made with a one-period horizon, or, if made for longer maturities, it is implemented by successive renewals of one-period contracts. Suppose, for example, that both six and three month forward contracts are available, and that a speculator expects the foreign currency to be relatively upvalued in six months' time. He can either buy it six months forward in the hope of selling it spot in six months' time at a higher exchange rate, or he can buy it three months forward, sell it spot in three months' time, buy it again three months forward in three months' time in the hope of selling it spot at a higher price in six months' time. Speculation on the different maturity sections of the market will be in equilibrium when these alternatives are equivalent, i.e. when, in our example, the present expected values from the two operations are equated. The first option has a present expected value equal to

$$(r_{t,t+2} - r^{e,t}_{t+2})/(1+i^d_{t,2})$$

per unit of foreign exchange. The second option has a present expected value equal to

$$(r_{t,t+1} - r^{e,t}_{t+1})/(1+i^d_{t,1}) + (r^{e,t}_{t+1,t+2} - r^{e,t}_{t+2})/(1+i^d_{t,2}).$$

Equating and generalising, we obtain again the condition of Section

V. Assuming that expectations are indeed consistent with this condition on the maturity structures of interest and exchange rates, we can proceed by treating speculation as renewed in each period, according to (9).

The speculators' behavioural function is then supposed to depend on the difference between the forward exchange rate and the rate expected to be quoted in the spot market at the time of maturity of the forward contract. However, as for A_t, the argument above suggests that the speculative positions taken currently in the forward market are determined by the differences between forward and expected spot rates of different maturities, each lagged by the corresponding periods; i.e. F_t^s is determined by the one-period speculative gain expected at time t, $(r_{t,t+1} - r_{t+1}^{e,t})$, by the two periods speculative gain expected at time $t-1$, $(r_{t-1,t+1} - r_{t+1}^{e,t-1})$, and so on. Thus:

$$F_{t,t+1}^s = F^s(r_{t-j,t+1} - r_{t+1}^{e,t-j}) \quad j = 0, 1, \ldots \quad (10)$$

Speculators' expectations are probably formed by an adaptive process determined by a correction of preceding period expectations in the light of the current spot exchange rate. In addition, however, we would like to allow for destabilizing expectations; these may arise when, even in the presence of an unchanged spot rate, it is known that it has been made possible by a given intervention of the exchange authorities in the spot or in the forward market. Moreover, this intervention will be appreciated differently by speculators according to the level of reserves which the authorities hold. In the light of all this, we may write[23]

$$r_{t+1}^{e,t} = R\left(r_t^{e,t-1}, r_t, N_{t-j}, F_{t-j, t-j+1}^n, \sum_{j=1}^{\infty} N_{t-j}\right) \quad = 1, 2, \ldots \quad (11)$$

where $F_{t-j, t-j+1}^n$ is the net supply of one period forward exchange at time $t-j$ by the monetary authorities.

VII. COMMERCIAL HEDGING

The analysis of arbitrage and speculation has already given us, besides the elements that compose the equilibrium condition in the

---

[23] Note that the level of reserves and its change, as well as the official intervention in the forward market, enter function (16) with at least one-period lag, since they are usually published, if at all, with one-period delay.

spot market, two elements that will enter the equilibrium condition in the forward market, namely F_t^a and F_t^s. We must now add the excess supply of forward exchange coming from the surplus of those exports over those imports that involve an exchange risk, i.e. that allow payment with a lag of at least one period. Let us first note that

$$C_t = B''_{t-1,t}\, r_{t-1,t} + B'_t r_t. \tag{12}$$

That is, net receipts of domestic currency by residents on current and transfer account (C_t) are the results of the execution of forward excess sales of foreign exchange agreed upon last period ($B''_{t-1,t}$) as a coverage against the risk on payments due this period, and thus evaluated at last period's forward rate, plus the conversion at the current spot rate of excess supplies of foreign exchange arising from current and transfer account operations not involving exchange risk.

As already recalled in Section II, covered arbitrage and commercial hedging both imply covering a credit or a debit against exchange risk. It is therefore natural that the considerations already made for arbitrage are in order with respect to covered commercial credit. In other words, equation (12) can be justified either on the assumption that there is only and always a one-period lag between the time of import-export orders and the time of payment,[24] or on the assumption that covering is renewed from period to period. This second, more reasonable assumption implies, if accepted, the expectation structure already developed in Section V and found to be implied also by the treatment of speculation. It follows also, from it, that the behavioural function for C_t must depend upon distributed lags of its basic variables. The latter are the determinants of the real import, export and transfer functions. Since it is the object of a larger macroeconomic model to analyse these functions in greater detail, it is enough to suppose, at this level, that they are determined by incomes and the price level (domestic and foreign). In addition, however, they should be determined by forward exchange rates of different maturities, and by the current spot rates for the part of these commercial operations that does not involve delayed payment and therefore exchange risk. For the reasons already explained, the forward rates of different maturities will affect the function with lags equal to the period of maturity, i.e. C_t will be determined by the exchange rate quoted at $t-1$ for one period forward delivery, by the

---

[24] This assumption is made, for example, by Black. See [2], p. 11.

rate quoted at $t-2$ for two-periods forward delivery, and so on, i.e.

$$C_t = C(y_{t-j}, \ldots y^f_{t-j}, \ldots P_{t-j}, \ldots, P^f_{t-j}, \ldots, r_{t-j,t}, \ldots, r_t) \quad j = 1, 2, \ldots \tag{13}$$

VIII. THE MARKET FOR FORWARD FOREIGN EXCHANGE

The one-period forward exchange market is in equilibrium when total demand equals total supply:

$$F^a_{t, t+1} + F^s_{t, t+1} - B''_{t, t+1} - F^n_{t, t+1} \tag{14}$$

where $F^n_{t, t+1}$ (if positive) represents the net supply of forward exchange by the monetary authorities.

IX. THE MONEY MARKET

This market is developed here just enough to clarify the connections with the other markets that are relevant for the objectives of this model. It is left to models specific to the money and financial sectors to go into a greater disaggregation of this market. Thus, the banking system is treated here as an aggregated sector, merging into it the central monetary and exchange authorities with commercial banks. The only consequence of doing this is that we must either suppose that commercial banks do not intervene in the foreign exchange markets (spot and forward) on their own account, or that N_t and $F^n_{t, t+1}$ include commercial banks' operations in the foreign exchange markets.

The demand for the stock of money, following a simple textbook hypothesis, is assumed to be function of money income and the shortest (one-period) domestic interest rate, both with unspecified lags:

$$M_t = M(Y_{t-j}, \ldots, i^d_{t-j, 1}, \ldots) \quad j = 0, 1, \ldots \tag{15}$$

In order to link the short-term rate of interest, which relates to the money market, with the long-term rate of interest, which relates to the expenditure function, and avoid explicit treatment of long-term financial markets, it is expedient to rely on a function for the maturity structure of interest rates:

$$i^d_{t, k} = f(i^d_{t, 1}) \tag{16}$$

The condition of equilibrium in the money market can be obtained in two alternative ways. First, as a condition of equilibrium in the balance sheet of the non-banking sector:

$$E_t - Y_t = (L_t - L_{t-1}) - (M_t - M_{t-1}) + (I_t + A_t)r_t - \\ -F^a_{t-1,t}r_{t-1,t} + S_t(r_t - r_{t-1,t}) \quad (17)$$

This *ex-post* identity says that national expenditure in excess of national income can be supported by an increase in outstanding loans from the banking sector (L_t is the stock of loans at time t), a decumulation of the money stock and a net accumulation of debts (or decumulation of credits) *vis-à-vis* foreign residents. This third source of funds might result from net long-term investment ($I_t r_t$) and the placement of short-term capital by arbitrageurs ($A_t r_t$), minus the net repatriation of last period inward investments by arbitrageurs ($-F^a_{t-1,t}r_{t-1,t}$), plus the net gains of speculators (or their losses if $r_t < r_{t-1,t}$).

Secondly, the equilibrium condition in the money market can be expressed as a condition of equilibrium in the balance sheet of the banking sector. This alternative formulation can, of course, be derived from (17) and the other relationships of the model that describe the conditions of equilibrium in the markets for goods and services, for spot exchange and for forward exchange. In this way, a check is provided that all elements in the model have correctly been considered. Thus, substituting (4) and (5) into (17), we have:

$$E_t - Y_t = (L_t - L_{t-1}) - (M_t - M_{t-1}) - (B'_t + N_t)r_t - \\ -F^a_{t-1,t}r_{t-1,t} - S_t r_{t-1,t}$$

On the other hand, from (2), (9), (12) and (14) we have:

$$E_t - Y_t = -(F^a_{t-1,t} + F^s_{t-1,t} - F^n_{t-1,t})r_{t-1,t} - B'_t r_t$$

Hence

$$M_t - M_{t-1} = L_t - L_{t-1} - N_t r_t - F^n_{t-1,t} r_{t-1,t} \quad (17')$$

which is indeed the condition of equilibrium in the balance sheet of the aggregated banking sector. In fact, condition (17′) shows that an increase in the banking sector's liabilities must be covered by an increase in their assets due to an increase in outstanding loans to the non-banking sector plus an increase in the stock of the banking sector's international reserves. This latter change is composed of two elements. First, a net accumulation of foreign exchange due to

OFFICIAL INTERVENTION IN FOREIGN EXCHANGE MARKETS

net purchases on the spot market in the current period (if N_t is negative), which are converted into domestic currency units at a rate r_t. Second, an additional accumulation due to last period net acquisition of forward exchange (if $F_{t-1, t}^n$ is negative), which must be evaluated at the rate $r_{t-1, t}$ in order to obtain the equivalent addition to domestic money supply. It is interesting to point out that, probably due to the exogenous nature of the forward exchange market in published macroeconomic models, the latter source of liquidity is not explicitly recognised by their authors. Yet its importance is essential to the analysis of the effectiveness of forward exchange policy, for it provides a direct link between official intervention in the forward exchange market and the supply of money.

X. CONSISTENCY OF THE MODEL

The model so far is composed of seventeen basic equations. Considering that lagged variables are predetermined, the variables currently unknown are twenty-seven; Y_t, y_t, P_t, y_t^f, P_t^f, E_t, C_t, B_t', $B_{t, t+1}''$, A_t, S_t, I_t, K_t, N_t, $F_{t, t+1}^a$, $F_{t, t+1}^s$, $F_{t, t+1}^n$, $i_{t, k}^d$, $i_{t, 1}^d$, $i_{t, 1}^f$, r_t, $r_{t, t+1}$, $d_{t, t+1}$, $r_{t+1}^{e, t}$, L_t, M_t, W_t. Some of these are clearly exogenous to the model, namely W_t, which is actually a vector of variables measuring the value and variability of arbitrageurs' wealth, y_t^f, P_t^f, $i_{t, 1}^f$, which are foreign variables, and y_t, since the limited scope of this model does not include the supply side of the national product. Moreover, the model is set up to account for short-run balance-of-payments problems, particularly short-run capital movements. Thus, long-term capital movements, I_t, are left exogenous, although they could be made endogenous, at least in theory, without altering substantially the nature of the analysis. Similar considerations apply to the composition of the current and transfer account, which should be made the object of a deeper analysis in a larger macroeconomic model: here, a behavioural function is considered only for the total, C_t, while the rest of the model endogenises any one of its components, leaving exogenous the other.

There are twenty remaining variables and seventeen equations only. However, an additional equation is added when we consider the institutional arrangements governing the foreign exchange market. Supposing that the country abides with the IMF rules, whereby spot exchange rates are free to move within a lower and an upper bound around the parity, we can write the equation

$$(r_t - \underline{r})(r_t - \bar{r})N_t = 0 \tag{18}$$

where $\underline{r}$ and $\bar{r}$ are respectively the lower and upper bounds around the parity exchange rate. Equation (18) states that, when the exchange rate is either at the lower or the upper bound, the monetary authorities' intervention is determined endogenously by the system of equations (1)–(17), whereas when the exchange rate is within the margins, the monetary authorities do not intervene in the spot exchange market.[25]

The model is now composed of eighteen equations, with twenty variables to be determined. We can either give exogenously two objectives, so that two controlled variables will become endogenous, or set exogenously the level of two controlled variables (policy instruments) and then two policy objectives might assume a determined value. The latter might be, for example, a stable domestic price level and external equilibrium. In the framework of this model, the first objective is represented by a certain value of P_t; as for the second objective, it takes a different connotation depending on whether the exchange rate is at one of the margins or within the band. Suppose the rate is at the ceiling (the floor); then the objective of external equilibrium is represented by a certain value of reserves decumulation (accumulation), i.e. a certain value of N_t. Suppose on the other hand that the exchange rate is strictly within the margins; then the objective of external equilibrium is represented by a certain value of the spot rate, r_t.

The model is framed so as to allow analysis of the joint use of monetary policy and forward exchange policy. Monetary policy can be implemented either by setting the level of the domestic short-term interest rate, $i^d_{t,1}$, or by controlling the total credit supply,[26] L_t. The choice depends on the particular institutional framework to which the model is applied. Similarly, for forward exchange policy the instrument chosen can be either the forward rate, $r_{t,t+1}$, or the volume of intervention, F^n_t.

[25] This is, of course, a simplification of reality in so far as the monetary authorities in fact intervene in the spot exchange market also when the rate is within the band. In any case, the text of this paragraph reflects the institutional arrangements as of before the exchange crisis of spring and summer 1971. Equation (18), which compactly describes the alternating active and passive role of the monetary authorities in the spot exchange market, has been suggested to me by Serge C. Kolm.

[26] If the banking sector is disaggregated into central bank and commercial banks, banks' reserves, rather than total credit supply, could be considered as the policy instrument.

Given the complexity of the model, an analytical solution for the endogenous variables would be extremely difficult. Moreover, it would be useless, in so far as it would probably be impossible, on the basis only of hypotheses on the signs of the parameters, to draw qualitative conclusions on the multipliers of the exogenous variables.

It is thus clear that the system should be solved numerically, on the basis of econometric estimates of the parameters of the functions and through dynamic simulation of the model. To this end, however, the model requires an adequate specification of its behavioural functions and their stochastic characteristics, and a closer adaptation to the institutional framework of the particular economy on the basis of which estimates and simulations are to be obtained.[27]

REFERENCES

1. A. Amano, 'International Capital Movements: Theory and Estimation', Economic Research Institute, Economic Planning Agency, Tokyo, June, 1971 (mimeographed).
2. S. W. Black, 'Theory and Policy Analysis of Short-Term Movements in the Balance of Payments', *Yale Economic Essays*, Vol. 8 (Spring, 1968), pp. 5–78.
3. A. I. Bloomfield, 'Official Intervention in the Forward Exchange Market: Some Recent Experience', Banca Nazionale del Lavoro, *Quarterly Review*, Vol. 49 (March, 1964), pp. 1–42.
4. W. H. Branson, *Financial Capital Flows in the U.S. Balance of Payments*. (North-Holland Publishing Co., Amsterdam, 1968).
5. E. Brehmen, 'Official Forward Exchange Operations: The German Experience', *IMF Staff Papers*, Vol. 11 (November, 1964), pp. 389–413.
6. C. D'Adda, *Base Monetaria, Flussi Finanziari e Domanda Globale* (Società editrice Il Mulino, Bologna, 1971).
7. P. A. Frevert, 'A Theoretical Model of the Forward Exchange', *International Economic Review*, Vol. 8 (June, October, 1967), pp. 153–67, 307–26.
8. J. Helliwell and T. Maxwell, 'Short-Term Capital Flows and the Foreign Exchange Market', Discussion Paper No. 50, Department of Economics, University of British Columbia, Vancouver, April, 1971 (mimeographed).
9. P. B. Kenen, 'Trade, Speculation, and the Forward Exchange Rate', in R. E. Baldwin et al., *Trade, Growth and the Balance of Payments, Essays in Honor of Gottfried Haberler* (Rand McNally & Co., Chicago, 1965), pp. 143–69.
10. J. M. Keynes, *A Tract on Monetary Reform* (Macmillan and Company, London, 1923).
11. E. E. Leamer and R. M. Stern, *Quantitative International Economics* (Allyn and Bacon, Inc., Boston, 1970).
12. C. H. Lee, 'A Stock-Adjustment Analysis of Capital Movements: the United States-Canadian Case', *Journal of Political Economy*, Vol. 77, No. 4 (Part 1) (July/August 1969), pp. 512–23.

[27] Research in this sense is being conducted for the case of West Germany and that of Italy respectively by J. A. Bartolomei and myself.

13. J. H. Levin, *Forward Exchange and Internal-External Equilibrium* (Graduate School of Business Administration, The University of Michigan, Ann Arbor, 1970).
14. F. Masera, 'International Movements of Bank Funds and Monetary Policy, Banca Nazionale del Lavoro,' *Quarterly Review*, Vol. 79 (Dec., 1966), pp. 311–27.
15. N. C. Miller and M. Von Neumann Whitman, 'A Mean-Variance Analysis of United States Long-Term Portfolio Foreign Investment,' *Quarterly Journal of Economics*, Vol. 84, No. 2 (May, 1970), pp. 175–96.
16. F. Modigliani and R. Sutch, 'Debt Management and the Term Structure of Interest Rates: An Empirical Analysis of Recent Experience', *Journal of Political Economy*, Vol. 75, No. 4 (Part II) (August, 1967), pp. 569–89.
17. R. A. Mundell, 'Capital Mobility and Stabilization Policy Under Fixed and Flexible Exchange Rates', *Canadian Journal of Economics and Political Science*, Vol. 29, No. 4 (November, 1963), pp. 475–85.
18. National Bureau of Economic Research, *Conference on International Mobility and Movement of Capital*, January, 1970. (Columbia University Press, New York; forthcoming).
19. E. Sohmen, *The Theory of Forward Exchange* (Department of Economics, International Finance Section, Princeton, 1966).
20. J. L. Stein, 'International Short-Term Capital Movements', *American Economic Review*, Vol. 55, No. 1 (March, 1965), pp. 40–66.
21. H. Stoll, 'An Empirical Study of the Foreign Exchange Market Under Fixed and Flexible Exchange Rate Systems', *Canadian Journal of Economics*, Vol. 1, No. 1 (February, 1968), pp. 55–66.
22. S. C. Tsiang, 'The Theory of Forward Exchange and Effects of Government Intervention on the Forward Exchange Market', *IMF Staff Papers*, Vol. 7 (April, 1959), pp. 75–106.
23. T. D. Willett, 'The Influence of the Trade Balance and Export Financing on International Short-Term Capital Movements: A Theoretical Analysis', *Kyklos*, Vol. 22 (Fasc. 2, 1969), pp. 314–27.

8

Money Supply Process and Monetary Policy in an Open Economy[1]

KARL BRUNNER
University of Rochester
Graduate School of Management

I. INTRODUCTION

A survey of annual reports published by Central Banks or prepared by Council of Experts yields many propositions bearing on the structure or response patterns of monetary systems, or the role and significance of monetary policy. It has been increasingly asserted that the interdependence between credit markets which evolved over the 1960s gradually eroded the power of monetary policy even with respect to short-run movements of monetary aggregates. An expansive policy lowers domestic interest rates and induces consequently an outflow of funds. An attempt at a restrictive policy is similarly doomed to fail. The inflow of funds induced by the rise in interest rates makes it impossible to control the base. Money stock and other monetary aggregates are thus disconnected from domestic monetary policies. These policies are effectively offset by induced capital flows.

It is also argued on other occasions that open economies of the European type helplessly suffer inflations or deflations imported from the United States. This thesis is, however, difficult to reconcile with the thesis of 'offsetting capital flows'. An increase in the base resulting from domestic sources exerts the same effect on interest rates as an increase due to an inflow of international reserves. The occurrence of 'imported inflation' thus denies the existence of offsetting capital flows, and the existence of the latter prevents the emergence of 'imported inflation'. An apologist of official views might, however, reconcile the two positions with the proposition that domestic and international source components of the base affect interest rates and

[1] This paper is based on my project proceeding simultaneously at the University of Konstanz and the University of Rochester. I am as usual deeply indebted to Allan Meltzer. The paper is based on much of our joint work.

monetary aggregates very differently. The resolution of this issue thus requires a somewhat more penetrating analysis of money supply processes than is usually encountered in official documents or textbooks. Such analysis is also required to assess the proposition that European monetary authorities are helplessly exposed to imported inflation and cannot cope with externally imposed variations of money stock or bank credit. This analysis should also clarify the role of monetary authorities, banks and domestic or foreign public in the process shaping money stock, bank credit and interest rates. It is frequently asserted that the behaviour of banks and public dominates the money supply process. The controllability of monetary aggregates by monetary authorities is thus seriously questioned on several grounds.

The issues and propositions surveyed cannot be meaningfully examined in the absence of a coherent analytic framework applicable to money supply processes. Such a framework has been developed and extensively applied in our previous work.[2] It was, however, restricted to economies with comparatively little exposure to balance-of-payments flows and interdependent credit markets. This paper extends the original framework to incorporate major aspects of an open economy. Institutional arrangements encountered in detailed examination of various countries are combined in a generic formulation representing the most important properties of the European environment.

II. THE ANALYTIC FRAMEWORK

The movements of money stock, bank credit and interest rates emerge from the interaction of banks and public on the credit market in response to the behaviour of the monetary authorities. Banks adjust the allocation of earning assets and supply liabilities. The public allocates wealth among the liabilities issued by the monetary system and supplies its own liabilities to banks. The monetary authorities issue base money under two constraints incorporated into the analysis. The balance of payments constrains the joint variations of a Central Bank's international reserves and the bank's net foreign position. The domestic budget constraint links on the other hand

[2] Karl Brunner and Allan H. Meltzer, 'Liquidity Traps for Money, Bank Credit, and Interest Rates', *The Journal of Political Economy*, Vol. 76, No. 1 January/February 1968), pp. 1–37.

the domestic source component of the monetary base with the government sector's budget and financial operations. The analysis will be centered on the adjustment of the credit market and relates the banks' and the public's allocation patterns with the operation of this market. The discussion and presentation of the framework will be organised in four sections.

1. *The monetary base, the balance of payments and the budget relation*
The magnitudes and relations associated with the monetary authorities are effectively expressed by equations describing the monetary base, the balance of payments and the budget relation. Suitable consolidation of balance-sheets of all institutions in the government sector associated with issues of money yields immediately the equation describing the monetary base B

$$B = IR + BA + DB_1 + DB_2, \tag{1}$$

where IR = international reserves held by the government sector; BA = Central Bank advances to banks; DB_1 = domestic sources of base money consisting of government securities and advances to government net of government deposits at the Central Bank; DB_2 = domestic sources of base money independent of the government sector's financial and budgetary position. The above equation reflects the institutional arrangements of a country. It should also be noted that inclusion of such an equation forms a necessary condition of an adequate formulation of money supply processes. In the absence of such an equation it will be impossible to derive propositions about the role of open market operations, about the role of inflationary government finance, the discount mechanism or the impact of international monetary flows on the domestic monetary system. The base equation links the monetary system with the balance of payments and the government's financial position.

The amount of base money directly issued by the government sector is held by the public as currency CB, by the commercial banks as reserves DR and by the postal giro system as reserves PR. This allocation pattern or description of uses of the base is expressed by equation (2)

$$B = DR + PR + CP. \tag{2}$$

This description reflects a specific interpretation of the postal giro system. This system occurs in our account as a banking system separate from the monetary authorities. An alternative view would include the postal giro system with the other accounts of the government sector. The postal giro system's portfolio of securities would thus appear as an additional source component of the base in a modified equation (1), whereas the allocation would also contain the postal deposits held by the public. The choice between the two interpretations of the postal giro system involves some empirical issues bearing on the interrelation between Central Bank and the giro system's asset management. It is quite possible that different European countries require different treatment in this respect.

The allocation components are endogenous entities to be explained by our analysis. A somewhat ambiguous position emerges on the other hand for the source components. The Central Bank's advances to banks are definitely endogenous. The stock of international reserves is also endogenous. The nature of domestic source components on the other hand, particularly DB_1, depends on the Central Bank's policy conceptions. DB_1 is endogenous in all cases of an interest target policy.

We obtain in equation (3) the adjusted monetary base by subtracting the banks' net borrowing from the monetary base. In a closed economy this net borrowing is identical with BA. An open economy offers, however, alternative net borrowing opportunities to the banks. Borrowing from foreign credit markets appears as a substitute to borrowing from the Central Bank. The banks' net foreign position is thus also subtracted from the base together with their liabilities to the Central Bank. Equation (3) expresses the result

$$B^a = B - BA - (FL^1 - FA) - DD^2, \qquad (3)$$

where B^a denotes the adjusted base; FL^1 designates the banks' liabilities to foreigners in foreign currency and stated in home currency equivalents; FA describes the banks' claims against foreigners in foreign currency in home currency equivalents; and DD^2 are the banks' liabilities to foreigners in home currency. The last three terms summarise the banks' net foreign position.

Equation (4) introduces the balance-of-payments constraint where

$$\Delta IR = CAB + \Delta(FL^1 - FA) + \Delta DD^2 - PDNI - GDNI, \qquad (4)$$

CAB denotes the current account balance, $PDNI$ expresses the private direct net investment abroad and $GDNI$ the government's direct net transaction with foreign countries. We obtain by suitable summation the following expression:

$$IR = FB_1 + FB_2 + (FL^1 - FA) + DD^2 \qquad (5)$$

where $FB_1 = \int CABdt - \int GDNIdt$

and $FB_2 = -\int PDNIdt = FLP - FAP$.

The magnitude *FAP* states the public's foreign assets and *FLP* are the public's foreign liabilities (incl. securities issued by domestic corporations and acquired by foreigners). The analysis is somewhat simplified in this paper by assuming that changes in FB_2 involve only investments in fixed coupon securities and do not involve equities.[3]

It is now possible to obtain a new expression of the adjusted monetary base by replacing B^a in (3) by means of (1) and then replacing *IR* by means of (5). The result is equation (6)

$$B^a = DB_1 + DB_2 + FB_1 + FB_2 \qquad (6)$$

i.e. the adjusted base is presented as a magnitude equal to the sum of two domestic and two foreign components. The first foreign component is exogenous relative to the current money supply process, whereas the second component is incorporated as an endogenous entity. It has already been indicated that the state of the domestic components depends on the particular policy procedures applied by a Central Bank.

The statement (6) can be further modified in order to derive an expression which associates the adjusted base with the government's budgetary position. We introduce for this purpose the budget constraint in equation (7)

$$CFD + \Delta DD^{12} + \Delta PD^2 = \Delta S + \Delta DB_1, \qquad (7)$$

where *CFD* denotes the government's money flow deficit, i.e. the difference between actual disbursements and tax receipts. The magnitudes DD^{12} and PD^2 refer to government balances at banks and the postal giro system; *S* is the stock supply of government securities confronting banks, public and the postal giro system. The expression on the left is summarised by CFD^a, the adjusted money flow deficit, i.e. adjusted for changes in the Treasury's balances.

Two parameters are introduced, μ and δ, to characterise the govern-

---

[3] The case will be generalised to include equities in a forthcoming paper on 'The Determination of Interest Rates'.

ment sector's financial policy. These parameters associate S and DB_1 with the evolution of the budgetary position. The parameter μ describes the proportion

$$D\dot{B}_1 = \mu CFD^a + \delta \tag{8}$$

$$\dot{S} = (1-\mu) CFD^a - \delta \tag{9}$$

of the adjusted money flow deficit which is financed by creation of base money via increases in the Central Bank's portfolio of securities or advances in one form or another. The parameter $(1-\mu)$ thus describes the proportion of the money flow deficit financed by issues of new securities. The stock variables are thus defined by suitable integration

$$DB_1 = \int_0^t \mu(\tau) CFD^a(\tau) d\tau + Q \tag{10}$$

$$S = \int_0^t [1-\mu(t)] CFD^a(\tau) d\tau - Q, \tag{11}$$

where Q denotes the integral over δ. The term Q describes the Central Bank's portfolio accumulated by means of open market operations. An open market operation involves an exchange of base money and outstanding securities. It involves thus a change in S and DB_1 which occurs independently of the government's financial requirement expressed by the budget. It should be noted that $\delta = 0$ whenever $0 < \mu < 1$, an open market operation in the sense defined occurs only when μ is either 0 or 1. With μ in the open unit interval, changes in S or DB_1 are completely governed by the budgetary situation. With $CFD^a > 0$ open market purchases (i.e. $\delta > 0$) require that $\mu = 1$, and with $CFD^a < 0$ an open market purchase requires that $\mu = 0$. A similar statement applies to open market sales.

For our subsequent analysis it will be useful to rearrange the definition of S and DB_1 in the following manner:

$$DB_1 = \bar{\mu}(t-1) CCFD^a(t-1) + \hat{\mu} C\hat{F}D^a + Q \tag{12}$$

$$S = [1-\bar{\mu}(t-1)] CCFD^a(t-1) + (1-\hat{\mu}) C\hat{F}D^a - Q, \tag{13}$$

where $\bar{\mu}(t-1)$ denotes the average μ over the interval terminating with $(t-1)$ and $CCFD^a(t-1)$ is the cumulated money flow deficit up to $(t-1)$; ^ is the average μ over the last unit period and CFD^a the deficit over this unit period. The term DB_1 in equation (6) will be replaced in our later analysis by means of the expression in equation (12). Similarly, the term S will be replaced by means of (13).

2. *The commercial banks*

We begin the description of the banks with the balance-sheet statement in equation (14)

$$DR+FR+DEA+FEA = DD^{11}+DD^{12}+DD^2+T+SD+FL+BA, \tag{14}$$

where FR are the banks' foreign currency reserves, DEA are earning assets in domestic currency and FEA earning assets in foreign currency. The term DD^{11} denotes demand deposits in home currency held by domestic residents, T are time deposits, SD are savings deposits, and FL refers to liabilities in foreign currency. It should be noted that DEA denotes earning assets net of capital accounts.

Four behaviour equations characterise the banks' asset allocations relevant for our purposes. The first describes the banks' allocation to reserves in home currency.

$$DR = r^1(DD^{11}+DD^{12}+T+SD)+r^2 DD^2 \tag{15a}$$

$$r^1 = r^1(i,i^e,\bar{p},rr^1); r^2 = r^2(i,i^e,p,rr^2) \tag{b}$$

$$r^1_1<0>r^1_2; r^1_3<0, r^1_4>0, r^2_1<0>r^2_2; r^2_3<0>r^2_4,$$

where r^1 is the average reserve ratio on total domestic deposits and r^2 is the average ratio on foreign held domestic currency deposits. The reserve ratios depend on the internal interest rate i, the external rate i^e, the premium $\bar{p}$ on forward exchange rates offered by Central Banks to commercial banks, and the requirement ratios rr^1 and rr^2. The elasticities of r^1 with respect to the two interest rates depend on the magnitude of the average requirement ratios. In many countries the variable $\bar{p}$ occurs as a policy variable and differs substantially from the premium p determined on the foreign exchange market.

The allocation to foreign reserves and foreign earning assets proceeds according to the following specification:

$$FR = f_1 FL \tag{16a}$$

$$f_1 = f_1(i,i^e,\bar{p},e); f_{11}<0>f_{12}; f_{13}>0<f_{14}, \tag{b}$$

where e is the anticipated change in the exchange rate (domestic currency per unit of foreign currency). Similarly, foreign earning assets are described by (17)

$$FEA = f_2 FL \tag{17a}$$

$$f_2 = f_2(i, i^e, \bar{p}, e); f_{21} < 0 < f_{22}; f_{23} > 0 < f_{24}. \tag{b}$$

The division of total reserves between unborrowed and borrowed reserves is given by equation (18)

$$BA = b(DD^{11} + DD^{12} + T + SD) \tag{18a}$$

$$b = b(i, i^e, \bar{p}); b_1 > 0 < b_2, b_3 > 0. \tag{b}$$

The asset allocations describe essentially the banks' demand behaviour confronting the credit markets. The banks' supply behaviour is introduced in form of price setting functions. Such functions describe the conditions which govern the banks' responses concerning the supply of the various types of liabilities. Corresponding to the five types of liabilities occurring in the balance sheet, five rate of returns are listed: i^{d1} on demand deposits held by the domestic public, i^{d2} on foreign-held (domestic currency) deposits, i^t on time deposits, i^s on savings deposits and i^f on foreign currency deposits. These rates of return may consist entirely of explicit interest payments or at least partly consist of services rendered to the banks' account holders

$$i^{d1} = j^1(i, i^e) \tag{19a}$$

$$i^{d2} = j^2(i, i^e) \tag{b}$$

$$i^t = j^3(i, i^e) \tag{c}$$

$$i^s = j^4(i, i^e) \tag{d}$$

$$i^f = j^5(i, i^e). \tag{e}$$

All five rates of return depend on the internal and external market rate. The dependence may be shaped on occasion by various institutional constraints, most particularly by ceiling rates imposed more or less effectively on the banks by the authorities or voluntarily agreed to by a cartel.

3. *The treasury and the postal giro system*

The treasury already entered the process via the budget constraint. Budgetary decisions bearing on expenditures and taxes affect the monetary system over the stock variables S and DB_1. But the Treasury also manipulates deposit balances at banks, the postal giro and the Central Bank. The last two magnitudes are considered implicitly by our definition of the source component of the base DB_1 and of the postal giro system's earning assets PEA net of Treasury balances at the respective institutions. It follows that variations in Treasury balances at the Central Bank are reflected in DB_1. However, the Treasury's administration of bank balances is explicitly incorporated by means of (20)

$$DD^{12} = gDD^{11}, \tag{20}$$

where g appears in our analysis as a policy parameter.

Two statements describe the aspects of the postal giro system required for our purposes. We introduce first the balance sheet in equation (21)

$$PR + PEA = PD + PT \tag{21}$$

and equation (22) describes the postal banking system's allocation of assets between reserves and securities

$$PR = r^3(PD + PT) \tag{22a}$$

$$r^3 = r^3(i); \quad r_1^3 < 0. \tag{b}$$

The reserve ratio r^3 depends on the market rate reflecting the peculiar institutional constraints imposed by the authorities on the postal giro system. The rates i^{pd} and i^{pt} describe the (possibly implicit) rates of returns offered by the postal banking system to its account customers. It will be assumed that these returns occur as policy parameters manipulated by the monetary or financial authorities.

4. *The public*

The public is confronted with a substantial array of portfolio choices. These choices are scaled with respect to the domestic public's demand deposits. The allocation ratios depend in general on appropriate rates of return associated with the various financial assets and the return on real capital implicitly determined by the asset price-level P of real capital. The real return on real capital r_k is defined by

$$r_k = n\frac{p^o}{P},$$

where n is the expected net real return per unit of real capital, p^o the price level of output and P the market value of real capital. In our present analysis we disregard the interaction between output and asset markets and hold p^o and n constant. Variations in r_k are thus equivalent to (inverse) variations in P. Equations (23) to (30) cover the public's distribution of financial wealth between domestic currency, time deposits, savings deposits, postal deposits, and foreign deposits in domestic and foreign currency.

$$CP = k_1 DD^{11} \qquad (23a)$$

$$k_1 = k_1(i, i^f, i^{d1}, i^t, i^s, i^{pd}, i^{pt}) \qquad (b)$$

$$k_{13} < 0 \geqslant k_{14}; k_{15} < 0 > k_{16}$$

$$PD = k_2 DD^{11} \qquad (24a)$$

$$k_2 = k_2(i, i^f, i^{d1}, i^t, i^s, i^{pd}, i^{pt}) \qquad (b)$$

$$k_{24} < 0 > k_{25}; k_{26} > 0 > k_{27}$$

$$T = t_1 DD^{11} \qquad (25a)$$

$$t_1 = t_1(i, i^f, i^{d1}, i^t, i^s, i^{pd}, i^{pt}, e, P) \qquad (b)$$

$$t_{11} < 0 > t_{12}; t_{13} < 0 < t_{14}; t_{15} < 0 > t_{17}; t_{18} < 0 < t_{19}$$

$$PT = t_2 DD^{11} \qquad (26a)$$

$$t_2 = t_2(i, i^f, i^{d1}, i^t, i^s, i^{pd}, i^{pt}) \qquad (b)$$

$$t_{25} < 0 > t_{26}; t_{27} > 0$$

$$SD = sDD^{11} \qquad (27a)$$

$$s = s(i, i^f, i^{d1}, i^t, i^s, i^{pd}, i^{pt}) \qquad (b)$$

$$s_4 < 0 < s_5; s_6 < 0 > s_7$$

$$DD^2 = q^1 DD^{11} \qquad (28a)$$

$$q^1 = q^1(i, i^f, i^e, i^{d2}, p, e); q_2^1 < 0 < q_4^1; q_5^1 < 0 > q_6^1; q_2^1 < 0 > q_3^1,$$

where e denotes the expected change of the exchange rate and p is the premium on the forward rate of exchange determined by the market.

$$FL = FL^1 + FL^2, \qquad (29)$$

where FL^1 = foreign currency deposits held by foreigners and FL^2 = foreign currency deposits held by domestic residents.

$$FL^1 = q^2 DD^{11} \tag{30a}$$

$$q^2 = q^2(i, i^e, i^f, i^{d1}, i^{d2}, i^t, i^s, e) \tag{b}$$

$$q_1^2 < 0 > q_2^2; q_3^2 > 0 < q_8^2$$

$$FL^2 = q^3 DD^{11} \tag{31a}$$

$$q^3 = q^3(i, i^e, i^f, i^{d1}, i^t, i^s, e, P) \tag{b}$$

$$q_1^3 < 0 > q_2^3; q_3^3 > 0 > q_4^3; q_5^3 < 0 < q_7^3; q_8^2 > 0.$$

Not all rates of return are postulated to exert a significant effect on the various allocation parameters. The expected rate of increase e in the home currency price of foreign currency affects q^1 and t_1 negatively, whereas q^3 is raised by such expectations. Similarly, the return on foreign liabilities FL affects mostly q^2, q^3 and t_1. The conditions on postal deposits influence mostly k_2, t_2, k and s. These responses vary somewhat between countries but we expect to find common patterns in some respects.

Lastly, the patterns concerning the components FB_2 of the adjusted monetary base must be specified. We introduce for this purpose a stock adjustment process

$$FB_{2,t} = hFB^*_{2,t} + (1-h)FB_{2,t-1}$$

where

$$h = \frac{h_1 FLP^*_t - h_2 FAP^*_t}{FLP^*_t - FAP^*_t}$$

provided

$$FLP^*_t \neq FAP^*_t.$$

The desired net stock position FB^*_2 depends on the internal and external interest rate, the forward exchange premium and the expected increase e of the exchange rate. We postulate thus

$$FB^*_2 = FB^*_2(i, i^e, p, e)$$

with

$$FB^*_{21} > 0 > FB^*_{22}; FB^*_{23} < 0 > FB^*_{24}.$$

This formulation reflects the idea that the response of investors to given market conditions is distributed over time. This distribution results from the manner in which information spreads over the system and thus gradually reaches new layers of market participants. The changes in FB_2 are thus viewed to emerge from a portfolio adjustment process involving investors in different countries. It follows that given market conditions do not generate permanent flows continuously changing FB_2. These flows decay over time with unchanged market conditions. Our analysis still requires a description of the public's asset supply σ on the credit market (or the public's 'demand for credit') and also of the domestic public's money demand λ. These behaviour patterns are introduced in the next section.

5. *The asset markets*

Two asset markets are considered in our analysis, the credit market and the Walrasian money market. The market rate i, an index of interest rates formed on bank-oriented credit markets, is proximately determined by the credit-market equation, whereas the asset price P of existing real capital and implicitly the real rate on real capital is determined proximately in the Walrasian money market. The description of the credit market emerges from appropriate aggregation of a loan and a security market. The loan market may be described as

$$\alpha a^1 B^a = L^p,$$

where a^1 is the banks' asset multiplier derived in Appendix I. The product $a^1 B$ thus measures the banks' volume of domestic earning assets denoted by DEA. The parameter α describes the distribution of earning assets between loans and investments. It denotes in particular the proportion of earning assets allocated to the loan portfolio. The left side thus represents the banks' loan portfolio and the right side, i.e. L^p, the public's desired loan liability position. The derivation of the asset multiplier a^1 in Appendix I demonstrates its dependence on the various rates of return introduced into the analysis. An inspection of a^1 shows that it occurs as a rational function of the behaviour parameters characterising the public's and the banks' behaviour. These behaviour parameters depend in turn on the array of rates of return previously discussed. An inspection of these returns reveals that the dependence of the behaviour parameters can eventually be reduced to the internal and external market rates i and i^e, the premia on forward exchange rates $\bar{p}$ and p, the policy variables rr^1, rr^2, r^3, i^{pd}, and i^{pt}. The asset multiplier (and subsequently the monetary multiplier) will thus be expressed as a

Money Supply Process and Monetary Policy

function of these ultimate variables, of which i is endogenous whereas the others occur exogenously.

The securities market juxtaposes the stock supply S of outstanding securities with the portfolio demands of banks, the postal giro system and the public. We obtain thus

$$(1-\alpha)a^1 B^a + PEA + I^p = S,$$

where I^p designates the foreign and domestic public's stock demand function for securities. An explicit recognition of these two components will be useful for the subsequent discussion. We state thus $I^p = I^{pd} + I^{pf}$, with I^{pd} referring to the domestic and I^{pf} to foreign demand. We also note here the connection between I^{pf} and the magnitude FLP occurring as a source component of the base via FB_2 ($=FLP-FAP$). I^{pf} and FLP are identical in our subsequent analysis. This follows from the simplification introduced when discussing FB_2 in a previous section. With changes in FLP constrained to involve securities FLP and I^{pf} are bound to coincide. It is contended that this simplification provides a useful approximation to the actual situation prevailing for many European countries. The marginal costs of information are generally substantially lower for securities than for equities. It follows that the portions of the public's net foreign position immediately relevant for the operation of monetary policy centre on security or credit market transactions.

The two equations can be combined to yield

$$a^1(i, i^e, \bar{p}, p, e, P, rr^1, rr^2, r^3, i^{pd}, i^{pt}) B^a + PEA = \sigma, \tag{31}$$

where the public's (implicit) asset supply to banks and the postal giro system is defined by

$$\sigma = L^p + S - I^p.$$

A behaviour function is thus approximated for an explanation of σ

$$\sigma = \sigma(i, i^e, i^f, P, S, p, e, \pi^d, \pi^f \cdot x) \tag{32}$$
$$\sigma_1 < 0 < \sigma_2; \sigma_3 > 0 > \sigma_4; \sigma_5 = 1;$$
$$\sigma_6 < 0 < \sigma_7; \sigma_8 > 0 < \sigma_9.$$

The new variables π^d and π^f refer to the price level of domestic output and foreign imports. With x denoting the price of foreign currency in terms of domestic currency the magnitude $\pi^f \cdot x$ states the price level of imports in domestic equivalents.

The expression PEA in (31) can also be replaced by the product of an appropriate multiplier a^2 and the adjusted base B^a. The multiplier a^2 is derived in Appendix II. Inspection of its structure reveals that a^2 depends on the same ultimate variables as a^1 but of course in a different manner. We obtain thus in a summary fashion

$$a(i,\ldots)B^a = \sigma(i,\ldots)$$

the description of the credit market as a semi-reduced form of the underlying behaviour specifications. The new multiplier a is the sum of the bank asset and the postal system asset multipliers, i.e. $a = a^1 + a^2$.

The Walrasian money market specifies an equilibrium condition between money stock and money demand, i.e.

$$m(i,P,\ldots)B^a = \lambda(i,i^e,p,i^{d1},i^t,i^s,i^f,i^{pd},i^{pt},P,e,\pi^d,\pi^f.x). \qquad (33)$$

The array of returns on assets in the λ-function can be simplified by replacing some variables by means of their explanations in terms of i and i^e. We obtain thus

$$m(i,i^e,P,\ldots)B^a = \lambda(i,i^e,P,p,e,\pi^d,\pi^f.x).$$

The wealth variable, an important argument in a complete analysis, has been omitted to simplify our account. The reader should note the difference between the present analysis and the standard Keynesian formulation. The latter assigns the proximate determination of interest rates to the 'money market'. The real rate of real capital is on occasion equated with the real rate of interest on financial assets, frequently omitted or implicitly determined with the level of employment in the context of a given production function. Our analysis centers on the joint determination of i and P, or the returns on both financial and real assets. This means that the credit market has to be introduced explicitly into the analysis. Moreover, contrary to an established Keynesian tradition the credit market is not a mirror image of the money market.

III. IMPLICATIONS OF THE MONETARY PROCESS

The analytic framework for the clarification of propositions about the role of monetary policy in an open economy has been constructed. It has been argued that monetary policy cannot be used to control economic activity in an economy enmeshed in the relations of interdependent national credit markets. A necessary condition of monetary impotence in the context of our analysis is a vanishing value of the asset market responses $\varepsilon(i,DB_1)$ and $\varepsilon(P,DB_1)$. Monetary impulses are transmitted to economic activity via the interest rate i and the asset price P of real capital. Aggregate real demand d is modified to the extent that i and P are changed by monetary impulses. These impulses would also remain impotent in case the ratio of asset-market responses matches the ratio of aggregate demand elasticities. The latter condition requires that $\varepsilon(i,DB_1)/\varepsilon(P,DB_1)$ is equal to $-\varepsilon(d,P)/\varepsilon(d,i)$, where $\varepsilon(d,x)$ designates the elasticity of aggregate demand d with respect to x. Inspection of Appendix IV, however, rapidly rules out this particular sufficiency condition of an impotent monetary policy.

The major results will be discussed in the text with appropriate references to the Appendix. Our discussion will be organised in several sections. The first section discusses the influence of relatively autonomous operations on the money supply process. These influences emanate particularly via the balance of payments or the operations of a postal giro system. The next section considers the role of monetary and financial policy. It will be shown that the international interdependence of credit markets does not condemn monetary policy to impotence. In particular, changes of the monetary base in response to the banks' and public's behaviour are neither a necessary nor a sufficient condition of an impotent monetary policy. The instruments available to monetary authorities are not disconnected from the money supply process even by a pronounced endogenous behaviour of the base, or by the banks' ability to move extensively between foreign assets and home currency assets.

1. *The operation of relatively autonomous changes*

An open economy offers opportunities to banks and public to move between foreign and home currency assets with comparatively low transaction and information costs. It has been argued that such substitutions convert the monetary base into a magnitude essentially reflecting the banks' and the public's behaviour. It is further concluded from this endogenous adjustment of the base that monetary policy is impotent and cannot be exploited for stabilisation purposes in an open economy. Our analysis establishes that both the base and the adjusted base are indeed endogenous. But this property, contrary to some impressions in the literature, implies very little. Two distinct aspects should be investigated, the role of autonomous changes operating via the balance of payments and the role of induced reaction patterns associated with the substitutions mentioned above. The latter will be examined in the next section. The role of autonomous changes is considered first.

An inspection of the structure of both asset multiplier a and monetary multiplier m in Appendixes I to III reveals that banks' changing allocations to foreign assets, expressed by changes in $f = f_1 + f_2$ modifies the credit market and the Walrasian money market. A reallocation towards foreign assets (i.e. $\Delta f > 0$) lowers both asset and monetary multiplier and thus depresses the asset price P and raises the domestic interest rate i. The banks' substitution of foreign assets for home currency assets thus exerts a deflationary impulse on domestic economic activity, and a substitution in the direction of home currency assets yields expansive impulses. The banks' portfolio behaviour also affects, however, the volume of base money B and the adjusted base B^a. The latter is influenced via the responses of the public's net foreign position FB_2 to the changes in interest rates and asset price level induced by the portfolio substitutions. A move into foreign assets (i.e. $\Delta f > 0$) raises internal rates and thus expands the net foreign position FB_2 and consequently expands the adjusted base. The public's response induced by the interest mechanism offsets the internal consequences of the banks' (autonomous) portfolio behaviour. The net effect of the banks' portfolio behaviour thus depends on the interest sensitivity of the public's net foreign position. This interest sensitivity moderates the impact of the banks' portfolio shifts on the domestic economy.

Relatively autonomous forces can also operate via the public's allocation parameters $q^j (j = 1,2,3)$. The parameters q^1 and q^2 describe allocations of the foreign public and q^3 behaviour of the domestic public. All three parameters refer to bank liabilities closely related to the balance of payments and the banks' net foreign position. The elasticities of both asset and monetary multiplier with respect to q^2 are proportional to $(1-f)$. It follows that a banking system hedging dominantly via the mutual adjustment of assets and liabilities effectively disconnects q^2 from the internal money supply process. Variations in the foreign public's allocation to the banks' foreign currency liabilities have been effectively disconnected from the domestic economy whenever $f = 1$. The move into a speculative position induced by anticipations of exchange rate movements or the premiums on forward exchanges connects on the other hand variations of q^2 with the internal credit market and money supply process. The responses in case $f \neq 1$ can be determined with the aid of the appropriate multipliers

$$\varepsilon(m,q_2) = \frac{(1-f)q^2}{n^1} \cdot m,$$

where n^1 denotes the numerator of the monetary multiplier, and

$$\varepsilon(a,q_2) = \frac{(1-f)q^2}{n^2}[1+a^1],$$

where n^2 is the numerator of the asset multiplier. A net foreign liability position (i.e. $f<1$) thus yields positive elasticities, whereas a net foreign asset position ($f>1$) yields negative elasticities. The impact of changing allocations by the foreign public with respect to domestic banks' foreign currency liabilities thus depends on the net foreign position of banks. An increase in q^2 is mildly expansive in case banks maintain a net foreign liability position. On the other hand a reduction of q^2 is mildly expansive in case banks maintain a net foreign asset position. The authorities thus possess an opportunity by offering suitable advantages or by imposing appropriate costs on the banks' net foreign position to dissociate the internal process completely from variations of q^2. It is noteworthy that the Italian monetary authorities imposed on occasion the constraint $1 = f$ on their banks.

Variations in the foreign public's allocation q_1 to domestic banks' liabilities expressed in domestic currency are in general less effectively contained. Their effect on the asset and monetary multiplier is proportional to $(1-r^2)$ according to the following expression:

$$\varepsilon(a,q_1) = \frac{q^1(1-r^2)}{n^2}[1+a^1]$$

$$\varepsilon(m,q_1) = \frac{q^1(1-r^2)}{n^1} m.$$

An increase of q^1 thus lowers i and raises P. The expansionary or deflationary impulse emitted by changes in q^1 on the economy are obviously proportional to $(1-r^2)$. This proportionality appears to offer an opportunity to contain changes in q^1. The reserve requirement rr^2 on foreign deposits in domestic currency is a policy parameter available for suitable manipulation by the authorities. With

$rr^2 = 1$ variations in q^1 exert no influence on domestic credit markets. In case autonomous increases in q^1 are typically associated with simultaneous increases of the public's net foreign position FB_2 the resulting rise in the adjusted base would still exert an expansive effect via lower interest rates i and a higher asset price level P. Nevertheless, with $rr^2 = 1$ the operation of the foreign public via the domestic banks would be disconnected from the internal process. Prohibitive requirements on foreign deposits DD^2 induce banks, however, to lower the attractiveness of such deposits to foreign depositors. We expect therefore that substantial amounts of foreign-owned funds will appear in the guise of domestic deposits. The German experience offers some evidence supporting this thesis. It follows that the relevant value of r^2 is really an average of the domestic deposit and foreign deposit requirements with weights dependent on the distribution of foreign-owned deposits between the two accounts. Under the circumstances, it is not possible to contain the effect of changing q^1 simply with the use of reserve requirements on foreign deposits.

The domestic public's allocation to the banks' foreign currency liabilities still remains to be examined. We find a somewhat different situation with respect to the parameter q^3 describing the domestic public's behaviour in this respect. The elasticities of the two multipliers are

$$\varepsilon(a,q^3) = -\frac{q^3 f}{n^2}a^1 + \frac{q_3(1-f)}{n^1}$$

$$\varepsilon(m,q^3) = -\frac{q^3 f}{n^1} \cdot m < 0,$$

where n^2 is the numerator of the asset multiplier and n^1 of the monetary multiplier. It is immediately obvious that even with perfect hedging by mutual adjustments of assets and liabilities (i.e. $f = 1$) both elasticities are negative. It follows that an increase of q^3 raises interest rates i and lowers the asset price level P. Variations in this allocation pattern thus convey expansive or contractive impulses to the domestic economy. The evolution of the Euro-dollar market thus opened a new channel for the public's market responses to be transmitted to credit market and economic activity. Attempts by the authorities to obstruct the domestic public via special costs or constraints on Euro-dollar holdings of domestic residents would only shift the problem. The domestic public would simply invest in other countries, or part of the domestic funds would reappear after a detour abroad in the guise of foreign funds. In either case the public's net foreign position FB_2 is lowered with a corresponding decline of the adjusted base. The response of the adjusted base would essentially replace the response of the multiplier under the circumstances. It should be noted, however, that the occurrence of such responses does not imply either impotence or uselessness of monetary policy. This aspect will be considered in the next section.

Other relatively autonomous operations could still be discussed. The effect of FB_1, however, requires no separate examination. It induces the same response as a change in the domestic source component DB_1 examined in the next section. Similarly, the effect of an increase in the anticipated real return on real capital is not modified essentially in comparison to our previous analysis. The interaction via the balance of payments and the banks' portfolio behaviour probably reinforces somewhat the net expansive effect of the revised anticipations. Only one particular aspect of the process deserves some more attention at this stage. The reader should remember that the analytic framework included the postal giro system. In case the public gradually expands the use of this system in response to favourable conditions offered by the postal authorities the parameters k_2 and t_2 increase. The net effect of such an expansion of the postal giro system depends on the reserve policy pursued by the postal giro. The elasticities of the asset and monetary multiplier with respect to $(k_2 + t_2)$, i.e. the public's allocation to postal deposits reveals the nature of the problem

$$\varepsilon(a,k_2) = -a\frac{r^3,k_2}{n^2} + \frac{(1-r^3)k_2}{n^1}$$

$$\varepsilon(m,k_2) = \frac{k_2}{n^1}[1-r^3 m],$$

where n^1 and n^2 have the usual meaning. For a sufficiently small reserve ratio r^3 the elasticity $\varepsilon(a,k_2)$ is positive and for a sufficiently large value the elasticity turns negative. The sign of $\varepsilon(m,k_2)$ changes in a similar fashion. The situation is compactly summarized in the following argument:

r^3

	small	large
$\varepsilon(a,k_2)$	+	−
$\varepsilon(m,k_2)$	+	−

When these conditions are applied to obtain the asset market responses we obtain

r^3

	small	large
$\varepsilon(i,k_2)$	−	+
$\varepsilon(P,k_2)$	+	−

An increase in k_2 occurring at low or high reserve ratios of the postal giro system thus exerts opposite effects on the economy. Thus, there emerges a range of reserve ratios which minimises the impact of autonomous changes in k_2 on the domestic economy. A similar situation with the same conclusion applies to the case of t_2 in spite of the difference between $\varepsilon(m,k_2)$ and $\varepsilon(m,t_2)$.

2. *The operation of monetary policy*

Recent discussions of monetary policy in an open economy have centered on endogeneity and responsiveness of the volume of base money or the adjusted base. It is usually argued that changes in a country's domestic source component DB_1 induce offsetting changes in the foreign source component FB_2. Monetary policy is thus incapable to modify the monetary base even in the short-run. Policy can only determine the composition of the base between foreign and domestic source components without influencing the total volume. A similar proposition pertaining to the *real* volume of base money and applied to the long-run has been generally accepted since Ricardo–Thornton. But recent discussions have extended the propositions to nominal magnitudes in the short-run.

Money Supply Process and Monetary Policy

These propositions are examined with the aid of the patterns derived from the analytic frame and exhibited in Appendix IV. The reader is reminded that a necessary condition for monetary impulses to exert an influence on aggregate demand and economic activity are non-vanishing responses of interest rates i and asset price level P of real capital on the asset markets. The responses of i and P to changes in the domestic source component DB_1, to changes in the stock supply of government securities S, to the current cash flow deficit of the government sector, to changes in the proportion of the cash flow deficit financed by creation of base money and to open-market operations are listed in Appendix IV, sections 1 to 5, respectively.

We examine first the response of i and P to a change in the domestic source component DB_1. The elasticities are similar in form to the elasticities developed on other occasions for a closed economy. The precise relation between the conditions of a closed economy and the conditions of an open economy are developed in several steps. We redefine first the public's asset supply function σ,

$$\sigma = \sigma^d - I^{pf},$$

where σ^d denotes the domestic component of the implicit asset supply. It corresponds to the conditions of a closed economy once all arguments referring to states of foreign economies are deleted. The second term, I^{pf}, designates the foreign public's stock demand of domestic securities.

We introduce next an important building block in the description of asset market responses. These building blocks are introduced in Appendix IV.1a. They refer to the interest elasticities $\varepsilon(CM,i)$ and $\varepsilon(MM,i)$ or the asset price elasticities $\varepsilon(CM,P)$ and $\varepsilon(MM,P)$ of the excess supply, log aB/σ, on the credit market, and the excess supply, log mB/λ, on the money market. Moreover, we rewrite the asset market conditions as follows:

$$a(\ )B + I^{pf} = \sigma^d$$
$$m(\ )B = \lambda.$$

The elasticities $\varepsilon(i,DB_1)$ and $\varepsilon(P,DB_1)$ listed in Appendix IV can be rearranged somewhat and exhibited as derivations of the reformulated statement. We need for the description of the i response the following expression E_1 (consider Appendix IV.1e):

$$E_1 = \bar{\varepsilon}^d(AM,i) + \varepsilon(I^{pf},i)\left[1 + \frac{\varepsilon^d(MM,P)}{\varepsilon^d(MM,P) - \varepsilon^d(CM,P)}\right]\frac{I^{pf}}{aDB_1} +$$
$$+ \varepsilon(FB_2,i)\frac{FB_2}{DB_1} > 0,$$

where $\bar{\varepsilon}^d(AM,i)$ describes the average interest elasticity of the asset markets of a closed economy (i.e. based on the domestic components of the behaviour structure). Only the first term appears in the analysis of a closed economy. The remaining two terms introduce the interdependence with foreign credit markets. The first term is defined as follows:

$$\bar{\varepsilon}^d(AM,i) = \frac{\varepsilon^d(CM,i)\varepsilon^d(MM,P) - \varepsilon^d(MM,i) \cdot \varepsilon^d(CM,P)}{\varepsilon^d(MM,P) - \varepsilon^d(CM,P)} > 0.$$

The response $\varepsilon(i,DB_1)$ of interest to a change in the base for a closed economy is determined by the negative reciprocal of $\bar{\varepsilon}^d(AM,i)$. The response for an open economy is determined by the negative reciprocal of the whole expression E_1 including the open economy terms. We obtain thus

$$\varepsilon(i,DB_1) = -\frac{1}{E_1} < 0.$$

The reader should note that all three terms of E_1 are positive. It follows that $E_1 > \bar{\varepsilon}^d(AM,i)$ and consequently

$$\varepsilon^d(i,DB_1) < \varepsilon(i,DB_1) < 0.$$

The response of interest rates i to changes in the domestic source component DB_1 are thus lowered numerically by the international interdependence, expressed by elasticity $\varepsilon(FB_2,i)$ and $\varepsilon(I^{pf},i)$. The responsiveness of interest rates to domestic monetary policy actually vanishes as the interest sensitivity of FB_2 and I^{pf} increase monotonically. A hypersensitive response of the public's net foreign position disconnects interest rates from domestic policy and blocks this channel for the transmission of monetary impulses.

The description of the P-response is based on the term E_2 defined as follows:

$$E_2 = \bar{\varepsilon}^d(AM,P) + \left[\varepsilon(FB_2,i)\frac{FB_2}{DB_1} + \varepsilon(I^{pf},i)\frac{I^{pf}}{aDB_1}\right]\frac{\varepsilon^d(MM,P) - \varepsilon^d(CM,P)}{\varepsilon^d(CM,i) - \varepsilon^d(MM,i)}$$
$$+ \varepsilon(I^{pf},i)\frac{I^{pf}}{aDB_1}\frac{\varepsilon^d(MM,P)}{\varepsilon^d(CM,i) - \varepsilon^d(MM,i)} < 0.$$

All three terms of E_2 are negative. The first term describes again the properties of a closed economy based on the domestic components. The term consists of an average asset-price elasticity of asset markets defined as

$$\bar{\varepsilon}^d(AM,P) = \frac{\varepsilon(MM,P)\cdot\varepsilon(CM,i) - \varepsilon(CM,P)\cdot\varepsilon(MM,i)}{\varepsilon(CM,i) - \varepsilon(MM,i)} < 0.$$

The remaining two terms represent the international interdependence effect. The elasticity $\varepsilon(P,DB_1)$ is now defined by expression

$$\varepsilon(P,DB_1) = -\frac{1}{E_2}\cdot\left[1 + \frac{\varepsilon(I^{pf},i)}{\bar{\varepsilon}^d(CM,i) - \varepsilon(MM,i)}\frac{I^{pf}}{\sigma}\right] > 0.$$

An inspection of the P-response reveals an important difference when compared to the i-response. A uniform convergence of $\varepsilon(FB_2,i)$ and $\varepsilon(I^{pf},i)$ to infinity does not determine convergence of $\varepsilon(P,DB_1)$ to zero. The elasticity of P converges actually to the expression

$$\frac{-1}{\left[\frac{FB_2}{DB_1} + \frac{I^{pf}}{aDB_1}\right]\varepsilon^d(MM,P) - \left[\frac{FB_2}{DB_1} + \frac{I^{pf}}{aDB_1}\right]\varepsilon^d(CM,P)} > 0.$$

This channel continues thus to transmit monetary impulses even in the limit of hypersensitive interest responses of the public's net foreign position. Highly interdependent credit markets are thus neither a necessary nor a sufficient condition for impotence of monetary policy. This result depends of course crucially on the fact that monetary impulses are not constrained to the operation of the interest rate i but also involve importantly the asset price level P. It also depends on the approximation which identifies changes in the public's net foreign position FB_2 with transactions on credit markets.

The general results obtained for changes in the domestic source component of the base extend to requirement ratios and discount policy. We note for all policy instruments that the responses in an open economy differ systematically from the responses of a closed economy. But we also note that sensitive interdependence of credit markets does not condemn monetary policy to impotence. One channel remains always in workable condition to transmit the impulses of policy to the domestic economy. This problem requires further examination. It will be argued that a complete blockage of policy expressed by vanishing responses of i and P together with offsetting capital flows cannot occur according to the analysis developed. Consider the structure of the asset markets

$$a[DB_1 + DB_2 + FB_1 + FB_2] = \sigma = \sigma^d - I^{pf}$$
$$mB = \lambda$$

with $I^{pf} = FLP$

and $\sigma^d = L^p + S - I^{pd}$.

The base in the credit-market equation was broken up into its source components. Moreover, the public's asset supply is also partitioned into its components. The reader should note that the public's stock demand for securities is divided into two parts, the domestic and the foreign demand σ^d and I^{pf}. The public's net foreign position FB_2 has also been defined as *FLP-FAP*, the difference between the foreign public's demand for the given economy's liabilities, i.e. *FLP*, and the domestic public's demand for foreign assets, i.e. *FAP*. An offsetting of the changes in DB_1 thus involves changes in *FLP* or *FAP*. Consider now an increase in DB_1 matched by a decrease in FB_2. This decrease is partly accomplished by foreign investors moving out of the economy's liabilities (i.e. reduction in *FLP*) and partly by domestic investors moving out of domestic assets into foreign assets (i.e. an increase in *FAP*). But these changes in *FLP* and *FAP* are necessarily reflected also on the other side of the asset market. *FLP* is the foreign public's stock demand for domestic securities. A reduction of *FLP* necessarily lowers I^{pf} and thus raises σ. Moreover, a substitution of foreign for domestic securities by domestic investors also lowers I^{pd} and raises σ even further. But with an unchanged base σ must be held to its original level. This could only be accomplished by lowering L^p. But the process under examination is initiated by an injection of base money lowering i and raising P to which the public's net foreign position reacts with hypersensitivity. The marginal or potential reduction in i does not lower L^p. And the marginal rise of P would lower L^p only in case firms consider loan financing and equity financing to be almost perfect substitutes. Once we disregard this pattern on empirical grounds, we note that offsetting adjustments of the public's net foreign position to changes in the domestic source component DB_1 are incompatible with vanishing responses of i and P. Vanishing responses of i and P imply that L^p does not change. Moreover, the offsetting capital flows imply $\Delta DB_1 = -\Delta FB_2$ and thus $\Delta B^a = 0$. The money market equation remains undisturbed and satisfied. But the credit-market equation has been disrupted. We have by assumption an unchanged value aB but also a larger σ, as both I^{pf} and I^{pd} fell with FB_2. The responses of the public's net foreign position indeed modify changes in the base induced by policy, but they also induce simultaneously net changes on the supply side of the credit market. The usual arguments overlook that changes in $(FLP-FAP)$ affect immediately both sides of the credit market. They change a source component of the base, but also modify the public's asset supply via the domestic and foreign public's stock demand for domestic securities. It follows therefore, once one grants that loan finance and equity finance are substantially less than perfect substitutes, that offsetting capital flows and vanishing responses of i and P to changes in DB_1 cannot occur simultaneously. The assumption of offsetting capital flows yields an imbalance on the credit market expressed by an unchanged aB confronting a larger σ. This contradiction between offsetting capital flows and vanishing responses of i and P thus forces us to reject at least one of the two theses. Actually, the rejection of either one implies rejection of the other. If i and P continue to respond to DB_1, money demand will be changed by variations in DB_1. It follows that mB^a must change to satisfy the second asset-market equation. This is, however, not achieved by an increasing m. The multiplier is lowered by a lower i and raised by a larger P. The net effect of a smaller i and larger P is substantially less on m than on λ. It follows that B^a must increase. A non-vanishing response of i and P to DB_1 is thus a sufficient condition for short-run changes in DB_1 *not* to be offset by opposite changes in FB_2. On the other hand, suppose that variations in DB_1 are not offset by opposite changes in FB_2. The base is thus modified by changes in DB_1. The left side mB of the money market changes and forces adjustments in i and P to induce values of λ equal to mB. Interest rate and asset price consequently respond, and their response forms a necessary condition for the absence of completely offsetting changes in the public's net foreign position. Our examination thus concludes that monetary policy remains potent for short-run stabilisation purposes even in the context of an open economy.

3. *The operation of financial policy*

Appendix IV also describes the responses to changes in the stock supply of government securities S, the current cash flow deficit CFD^a, the proportion μ of the deficit financed with base money and also to open market operations. All responses are defined in terms of the responses to DB_1 and S. The first has been discussed extensively. The latter can also be expressed in terms of DB_1 responses and asset-market elasticities, as follows:

$$\varepsilon(i,S) = -\varepsilon(i,DB_1)\frac{\varepsilon(MM,P)}{\bar{\varepsilon}(MM,P)-\varepsilon(CM,P)} > 0$$

$$\varepsilon(P,S) = \varepsilon(P,DB_1)\frac{\varepsilon(MM,i)}{\varepsilon(CM,i)-\varepsilon(MM,i)} > 0.$$

It follows that $\varepsilon(i,S) < |\varepsilon(i,DB_1)|$. The corresponding statement for P holds only if $\varepsilon(CM,i) \geqslant 2.\varepsilon(MM,i)$. The reader should note that we impose throughout that $\varepsilon(CM,i) > \varepsilon(MM,i) > 0$.

With the responses to DB_1 and S available, the effect of a cash flow deficit CFD, of open-market operations and of changes in the parameter μ are conveniently expressed by suitable combinations of the two building blocks. We note first the response of i to CFD^a

$$\varepsilon(i,DB_1)\frac{\hat{\mu}CFD^a}{B^a} + \varepsilon(i,S)\frac{(1-\hat{\mu})CFD^a}{B^a}\frac{B^a}{S}.$$

The response of P is defined similarly. The numerical magnitude of the response increases with the deficit and falls algebraically with a rising proportion μ. For some level of μ the deficit does not change interest rates as changes in DB_1 and S just offset each other with respect to i. It is easily established that there exists no value of μ in the unit interval which removes *simultaneously* any effect of a deficit on i and P.

The responses to variations in μ are given by

$$\text{for } i: \frac{\hat{\mu}CFD}{B^a}\left[\varepsilon(i,DB_1)-\varepsilon(i,S)\frac{DB_1}{S}\right] < 0$$

$$\text{for } P: \frac{\hat{\mu}CFD}{B^a}\left[\varepsilon(P,DB_1)-\varepsilon(P,S)\frac{DB_1}{S}\right] > 0.$$

An increase in the proportion of the deficit financed with base money thus lowers i and raises P and exerts consequently an expansionary thrust on the economy.

The effects of open-market operations occur similarly as a combination of a DB_1 and S effect:

$$\text{for } i: \frac{Q}{DB_1}\left[\varepsilon(i,DB_1)-\varepsilon(i,S)\frac{DB_1}{S}\right]<0$$

$$\text{for } P: \frac{Q}{DB_1}\left[\varepsilon(P,DB_1)-\varepsilon(P,S)\frac{DB_1}{S}\right]>0.$$

It should be noted that the S-effect in open market operations reinforces the DB_1 effect on interest rates, but offsets the DB_1 effect on the asset price level. The moderating effect exerted by S on i and P is, however, proportional to DB_1/S which is a small proportion for many countries.

4. *The operation of external influences*

An accelerating inflation in major foreign countries raises the source component FB_1. The results established for DB_1 in section 2 extend naturally to the integral over past current account surpluses. The increase in FB_1 does not induce a matching reduction of FB_2. The resulting increase in the base exerts the same effect on i and P as DB_1. This establishes the inconsistency of the two propositions frequently maintained by monetary authorities, viz. that open economies 'import inflation', and furthermore, that monetary policy is made impotent by offsetting capital flows. Our analysis denies the thesis of completely offsetting capital flows and thus accepts the proposition of 'imported inflation'. Some qualification is necessary, however. Our analysis implies that an increase in FB_1 does induce expansionary influences on the domestic economy. It does not imply that monetary authorities are bound to accept this effect. It implies on the contrary that reductions of DB_1 do effectively offset the influence of FB_1. The real issue of course is the length of time available for such an offsetting policy and whether a Central Bank wishes to exploit the available opportunity. This depends on the magnitude of foreign inflation and the willingness to subsidise foreign countries by exchanging goods for international reserves. A change in the exchange rate would certainly be the more appropriate response to a persistent problem of imported inflation than an offsetting domestic policy.

The domestic effect of such an exchange rate policy deserves some attention. A revaluation of domestic currency (i.e. a lower value of the exchange rate x) lowers the argument $\pi^f x$ in the asset supply σ and money demand λ. Money demand and asset supply thus fall according to the relative importance of imports in the economy under consideration. The revaluation, therefore, lowers interest rates i and raises also P. The effect of a revaluation via the operation of asset markets raises consequently aggregate demand. The total effect of a revaluation consists thus of three components. We note first the expansionary asset-market effect. There occurs secondly the (deflationary) direct substitution between domestic and imported goods induced by the lowering of the relative price of imported goods. Lastly, there emerges the longer-run (relatively deflationary) effect of a lowered rate of increase in FB_1. The asset market and direct substitution effect occur in the shorter-run and tend to offset each other. The major impact of a revaluation appears thus with some delay (see addendum, p. 166).

Variations in foreign interest rates, the premium on forward transactions or the anticipations concerning future exchange rates affect the asset markets and influence the domestic economy. These variations induce probably larger movements on the international capital accounts than the feedbacks to domestic monetary policy. It seems probable that at least portions of those capital flows induced by changes in i^e, $\bar{p}$, p or e have been erroneously attributed to the changes in FB_2 induced by domestic monetary policy by various analysts. The expressions defining $\varepsilon(i,i^e)$ and $\varepsilon(P,i^e)$ in Appendix IV.6 show that an increase of interest rates on foreign credit markets raises interest rates (i) and lowers P on the domestic asset markets. A tightening of foreign credit markets thus emits a deflationary impulse on the domestic economy. This relatively contractive effect is mediated by a reduction in FB_2. Suppose now that the Central Bank moderates the deflationary effect signalled by rising i. It increases DB_1 and thus offsets the reduction of FB_2. This prevents the rise in i and fall in P. But it accelerates the reduction in the public's net foreign position. One is easily misled at this stage to attribute the whole reduction in FB_2 to the increase in DB_1.

The official forward premium $\bar{p}$ granted by Central Banks to commercial banks operates via the monetary and asset multiplier a and m on the asset markets. The expressions in Appendix IV.7 establish that variations of $\bar{p}$ essentially affect only i. An increase in $\bar{p}$ raises domestic interest rates. It can thus be used to counteract the effect of changing interest rates on foreign capital markets. The official forward premium offers in this manner an effective instrument moderating the influence exerted by fluctuations on foreign credit markets.

The forward premium determined on the market operates (in case the authorities offer a more advantageous $\bar{p}$ to banks) via the public's behaviour parameters t_1 and q^3, the public's net foreign position FB_2 and the public's asset supply σ. The net effect via t_1 and q^3 on the monetary multiplier m is probably negligible. The net effect on the asset multiplier depends on the banks' net foreign position f. The effect on the asset multiplier a rises as the banks move into a net foreign liability position (i.e. $f<1$). The patterns for i and P are listed in Appendix IV.8. An increase in the market's forward premium raises domestic interest rates i. Its effect on P depends on the relative interest sensitivity of credit markets, i.e. on $\varepsilon(CM,i)$ relative to $\varepsilon(MM,i)$. If the difference $\varepsilon(CM,i) - \varepsilon(MM,i)$ is of similar order as $\varepsilon(MM,i)$, then P falls with a rise in p. An increase in the market premium thus exerts a deflationary effect mediated dominantly by changes in FB_2 and the components σ^d and I^{pf} of σ. In these circumstances, an interest target policy of the Central Bank would induce offsetting changes in DB_1 which prevent the deflationary spillover from changes in p. It would thus appear that the changes in DB_1 induce the 'offsetting' capital flows which were actually triggered by the forward premium p.

We consider lastly the effect of changing anticipations bearing on the exchange rate. These effects operate dominantly via FB_2 and σ. It should be noted in this context that the exchange rate is defined as domestic currency per unit of foreign currency. A decrease of the anticipated exchange rate lowers i and raises P. The latter result depends again on the interest sensitivity $\varepsilon(CM,i)$ relative to $\varepsilon(MM,i)$. Changing anticipations bearing on the future exchange rate thus unleash deflationary or expansionary effects on the domestic economy. These effects can again be compensated by changes in DB_1. The prevalent attitude of Central Banks, as expressed in pervasive adherence to an interest-target policy, makes such (partial) compensation very probable. It follows that variations in the anticipated exchange rate e induce simultaneously opposite changes in FB_2 and DB_1. Thus, when an interest-rate target is pursued, regressions of ΔFB_2 on ΔDB_1 (and possibly some other variables) which omit the anticipated exchange rate e impound the role of e into the negative coefficient of ΔDB_1. This coefficient is consequently blown up beyond the relevant range measuring the response of FB_2 to an autonomous policy action expressed by DB_1.

IV. CONCLUDING REMARKS

This paper has examined the extension of our previous work on money supply theory to the case of an open economy exposed to highly interdependent credit markets. It has been frequently asserted that such economies cannot effectively apply monetary policy for purposes of shorter-run stabilisation purposes. Offsetting capital flows were asserted to obstruct monetary policy. It has also been asserted that open economies helplessly suffer the inflation imported from major world centres. These two propositions were shown to be inconsistent in the context of our analytic framework. It was further established that completely offsetting capital flows and a vanishing response of the domestic interest rate i and asset price level P to domestic monetary policy cannot occur simultaneously.

It follows that monetary policy remains effective as a short-run stabilisation instrument. There is no doubt, however, that the response patterns of i and P are modified by the interrelation with foreign credit markets. It will require a more extensive analysis to be developed at another occasion to generalise some other results of our analysis to the case of open economies. This applies particularly to the proposition that the relative change of the money stock still yields a good approximation to the *domestic* monetary impulse. It was also shown that a hedging constraint (i.e. $f = 1$) imposed on banks removes all effects on the domestic economy resulting from variations in the parameter q^2, the foreign public's allocation to domestic banks' foreign currency liabilities. Variations in the foreign public's allocation to the domestic banks' domestic currency liabilities (q^1) and of the domestic public to the foreign-currency liabilities (q^3) of the banks, however, continue to modify the monetary and asset multiplier and thus affect the domestic system. Such variations are induced partly by changes in domestic credit market conditions and form in this respect an integral part of the response in i and P. They are also induced, however, by changes in foreign interest rates i^e, the market forward premium p and the anticipated exchange rate e. The magnitude $\bar{p}$ is controllable by policy and the effects of foreign interest rates are modifiable by means of $\bar{p}$ and other instruments of monetary policy. Persistent increases of FB_1 eventually require an adjustment of exchange rates. We established that such a revaluation emits an *expansionary* influence via the adjustment of money demand and asset supply. The magnitude of this influence depends on the degree of openness of an economy. A very open economy may experience a net expansionary effect in the shorter-run from a revaluation, and a net deflationary effect from a devaluation. Lastly, the disruptions caused by changing anticipations of exchange rates pose indeed a severe strain on domestic monetary policy. They induce changes in FB_2 which are quite large relative to DB_1. Such disruptions will continue to occur within an international system combining fixed exchange rates and large or persistent differences in the growth rate of the domestic source component DB_1. In this sense the extensive use of autonomous monetary policy combined with rigid adherence to a fixed exchange rate system yields conditions which severely obstruct the useful application of monetary policy.

List of variables

B	= monetary base
B^a	= adjusted monetary base
BA	= borrowing by commercial banks from Central Bank
CAB	= current account balance
CFD^a	= net cash flow deficit
CP	= currency held by public
DB	= domestic source components of the base
DD^{11}	= domestic demand deposits held domestically by public
DD^{12}	= domestic demand deposits held by the Treasury
DD^2	= demand deposits in home currency held by foreigners
DEA	= domestic earning assets of commercial banks
DR	= domestic reserves of banks
FA	= assets of commercial banks in foreign currency
FAP	= public's foreign assets
FB_1	= autonomous items associated with balance of payment
FB_2	= net foreign position of public
FEA	= foreign earning assets of banks
FL	= bank liabilities stated in foreign currencies
FL^1	= commercial banks' liabilities in foreign currency to foreigners
FLP	= public's foreign liabilities (incl. securities issued by domestic business and held by foreigners)
FR	= foreign reserves of banks
$GDNI$	= government sector's direct net foreign transaction
IR	= international reserves in balance sheet of monetary authorities

I^p	= public's stock demand for domestic securities
I^{pf}	= foreign public's stock demand for domestic securities
I^{pd}	= domestic public's stock demand for domestic securities
L^p	= public's desired loan liability position
PEA	= earning assets of postal checking system, consisting of government securities
PD^1	= postal checking deposits held by public
PD^2	= postal checking deposits held by the Treasury
PR	= reserves of postal checking system
$PDNI$	= private direct net foreign investment
PT	= postal time deposits
S	= stock of government securities outside government sector (including Central Bank and postal checking system)
SD	= savings deposits of banks
T	= time deposits of banks
σ	= public's asset supply on credit market
a	= asset multiplier
m	= monetary multiplier
k_1	= public's currency ratio
t_1	= time deposit ratio
f_1	= banks' allocation to foreign reserves
f_2	= banks' allocation to foreign non-reserve assets
b	= banks' desired borrowing ratio relative to Central Banks
r^3	= reserve ratio of postal giro system
k_2	= public's desired postal checking deposit ratio
t_2	= public's desired postal time deposit ratio
s	= public's desired savings deposit ratio
q^1	= foreign public's allocation to domestic banks' domestic currency liabilities
q^2	= foreign public's allocation to domestic banks' foreign currency liabilities
q^3	= domestic public's allocation to domestic banks' foreign currency liabilities
σ^d	= domestic component of public's asset supply
λ	= money demand
P	= asset price level of real capital
i	= domestic interest rate
i^e	= interest rate on foreign credit markets
p	= premium on forward exchange rate (domestic currency per unit of foreign currency) determined by market

$\bar{p}$ = premium on forward exchange rate offered by Central Banks to commercial banks
e = anticipated change in future exchange rate
x = exchange rate defined as domestic currency per unit of foreign currency
μ = proportion of government sector's cash flow position financed by new base money
δ = pure open-market operation

Appendix I. The monetary multiplier

We begin with equation (3)

$$B^a = B - BA + FA - FL^1 - DD^2$$

and replace first B with the allocation description (2)

$$B^a = DR + PR + CP - BA + FA - FL^1 - DD^2.$$

It should be noted that $FA = FR + FEA$. The terms on the right are replaced seriatim with the aid of the behaviour specifications laid down for banks, public and postal system. The result is

$$B^a = [r^1(1+g+t_1+s) + r^2q^1 + r^3(k_2+t_2) + k_1 - b(1+g+t_1+s) + \\ + (f_1+f_2)(q^2+q^3) - q^2 - q^1] DD^{11}.$$

This expression yields quite immediately

$$DD^{11} = \frac{1}{\Delta} B^a,$$

where the denominator Δ is defined as follows:

$$\Delta = [(r^1-b)(1+g+t_1+s) + k_1] + q^1(r^2-1) + r^3(k_2+t_2) + \\ + [(f_1+f_2)(q^2+q^3) - q^2].$$

This grouping of Δ reveals explicitly the generalisation resulting from incorporating the giro system and the banks' foreign net involvement. The first term on the right is the original expression usually obtained without the generalisation. The second term reflects the effect of foreign held home currency deposits, the third term reflects the effect of the giro system and the last term the banks' foreign currency involvements.

We define the money stock as follows:

$$M = CP + DD^{11} + PD.$$

This implies the formulations

$$M = mB^a$$

with

$$m = \frac{1+k_1+k_2}{\Delta}.$$

Appendix II. The banks' asset multiplier
The magnitude DEA is exhibited as a product:

$$DEA = a^1 B^a.$$

In order to obtain a^1 one begins with the rearranged balance sheet

$$DEA = DD^{11} + DD^{12} + DD^2 + T + SD + FL + BA - DR - FA.$$

Suitable substitution yields

$$DEA = \frac{1}{\Delta}[1+g+q^1+t_1+s+q^2+q^3 - (r^1-b)(1+g+t_1+s) - r^2 q^1 - \\ -(f_1+f_2)(q^2+q^3)]B^a.$$

Suitable rearrangements yields

$$a^1 = \frac{(1+g+t_1+s)[1-(r^1-b)] + q_1(1(-r^2)) + (q^2+q^3)[1-(f_1+f_2)]}{\Delta}.$$

Appendix III. The giro system's asset multiplier
The magnitude PEA is expressed by the product

$$PEA = a^2 B^a.$$

The balance sheet yields

$$PEA = PD + PT - PR$$
$$= (1-r^3)(k_2+t_2)\frac{1}{\Delta}B^a.$$

We obtain thus

$$a^2 = \frac{(1-r^3)(k_2+t_2)}{\Delta}.$$

Appendix IV. The response patterns
1. Response of asset markets to a change in the domestic source component DB_1:

(a) $\varepsilon(P,DB_1) = -\dfrac{\varepsilon(CM,i)-\varepsilon(MM,i)}{\Delta}\dfrac{DB_1}{B^a}$

$\Delta = \varepsilon(CM,i)\varepsilon(MM,P) - \varepsilon(MM,i)\cdot\varepsilon(CM,P)$

$\varepsilon(CM,i) = \varepsilon(a,i) + \varepsilon(FB_2,i)\dfrac{FB_2}{B^a} - \varepsilon(\sigma,i)$

$\varepsilon(MM,i) = \varepsilon(m,i) + \varepsilon(FB_2,i)\dfrac{FB_2}{B^a} - \varepsilon(\lambda,i)$

$\varepsilon(CM,P) = \varepsilon(a,P) - \varepsilon(\sigma,P)$

$\varepsilon(MM,P) = \varepsilon(m,P) - \varepsilon(\lambda,P).$

(b) Definition:

$\varepsilon(FB_2,x) = h_1\varepsilon(FLP^*,x)\dfrac{FLP^*}{aB} - h_2\varepsilon(FAP^*,x)\dfrac{FAP^*}{aB}$

$\varepsilon(a,i) = \varepsilon(a,x)\cdot\varepsilon(x,i)$
$x = r^1, b, t_1, s, f_1+f_2, q_1, q_2, q_3.$

Similar expressions hold for $\varepsilon(a,P)$, $\varepsilon(m,i)$ and $\varepsilon(m,P)$.
Note: The elasticities $\varepsilon(x,i)$ are frequently total elasticities reflecting indirect effects on x (say t_1) exerted by i via i^t, i^s, and other liability conditions.

(c) Interpretation of the building blocks occurring in the response patterns:

$$\varepsilon(CM,i) = \dfrac{d\left(\log\dfrac{aB^a}{\alpha}\right)}{d\log i}.$$

We can interpret aB/σ as an index of the excess supply of bank credit on the credit market CM. The expression $\varepsilon(CM,i)$ thus measures the responsiveness of the credit market's excess supply of bank credit to a change in interest rate. Similarly,

$$\varepsilon(MM,i) = \dfrac{d\left(\log\dfrac{mB^a}{\lambda}\right)}{d\log i}$$

measures the responsiveness of the Walrasian money market's excess supply of money to a change in interest rates.

$$\varepsilon(CM,P) = \frac{d\left(\log\frac{aB^a}{\sigma}\right)}{d\log P}$$

$$\varepsilon(MM,P) = \frac{d\left(\log\frac{mB^a}{\lambda}\right)}{d\log P}$$

The latter two expressions possess a corresponding interpretation.

(d) $$\varepsilon(i,DB_1) = \frac{\varepsilon(MM,P) - \varepsilon(CM,P)}{\Delta} \frac{DB_1}{B^a}$$

(e) The discussion of monetary policy in the text partitions the responses of i and P into terms representing a domestic component and a component reflecting the international interdependence. Our procedure depends crucially on the assumption introduced in the text that $FLP = I^{pf}$ and that changes in FAP reflect opposite changes in I^{pd}. This means that changes in FB_2 involve only investments in securities and do not involve equities. The reader is also reminded that changes in FB_2 are by assumption not reflected in foreign holdings of domestic money. Changes in this foreign demand component are represented by DD^2.

We begin with the lowest level building blocks, the interest and asset price elasticities of the CM and MM market:

$$\varepsilon(CM,i) = \varepsilon^d(CM,i) + \varepsilon^f(CM,i)$$

$$\varepsilon^d(CM,i) = \varepsilon(a,i) - \varepsilon(\sigma^d,i)\frac{\sigma^d}{\sigma} > 0$$

$$\varepsilon^f(CM,i) = \varepsilon(FB_2,i)\frac{FB_2}{B^a} + \varepsilon(I^{pf},i)\frac{I^{pf}}{\sigma} > 0$$

$$\varepsilon(MM,i) = \varepsilon^d(MM,i) + \varepsilon^f(MM,i)$$

$$\varepsilon^d(MM,i) = \varepsilon(m,i) - \varepsilon(\lambda,i)$$

$$\varepsilon^f(MM,i) = \varepsilon(FB_2,i)\frac{FB_2}{B^a}$$

$\varepsilon(CM,P) = \varepsilon^d(CM,P)$

$\varepsilon(MM,P) = \varepsilon^d(MM.P)$.

The response of i can be expressed as follows:

$$\varepsilon(i,DB_1) = -\frac{1}{E^1} < 0,$$

where

$$E_1 = \bar{\varepsilon}^d(AM,i) + \varepsilon(I^{pf},i)\left[1 + \frac{\varepsilon^d(MM,P)}{\varepsilon^d(MM,P) - \varepsilon^d(CM,P)}\right]\frac{I^{pf}}{aDB_1} + \varepsilon(FB_2,i)\frac{FB_2}{DB_1}.$$

The expression E_1 is positive by hypothesis.
The expression $\bar{\varepsilon}^d(AM,i)$ is defined by

$$\bar{\varepsilon}^d(AM,i) = \frac{\varepsilon^d(CM,i) \cdot \varepsilon^d(MM,P) - \varepsilon^d(MM,i)\varepsilon^d(CM,P)}{\varepsilon^d(MM,P) - \varepsilon^d(CM,P)} > 0.$$

This expression can be interpreted as an average of the interest elasticities on the asset markets. The first term of E_1 reflects domestic components and the remaining terms international components.

The response of P to DB_1 can be expressed as follows:

$$\varepsilon(P,DB_1) = -\frac{1}{E_2}\left[1 + \frac{\varepsilon(I^{pf},i)}{\varepsilon^d(CM,i) - \varepsilon^d(MM,i)}\frac{I^{pf}}{\sigma}\right],$$

where

$$E_2 = \bar{\varepsilon}^d(AM,P) + \left[\varepsilon(FB_2,i)\frac{FB_2}{DB_1} + \varepsilon(I^{pf},i)\frac{I^{pf}}{aDB_1}\right].$$

$$\frac{\varepsilon^d(MM,P) - \varepsilon^d(CM,P)}{\varepsilon^d(CM,i) - \varepsilon^d(MM,i)} + \varepsilon(I^{pf},i)\frac{I^{pf}}{aDB_1}.$$

$$\frac{\varepsilon^d(MM,P)}{\varepsilon^d(CM,i) - \varepsilon^d(MM,i)} < 0$$

and

$$\bar{\varepsilon}^d(AM,P) = \frac{\varepsilon^d(CM,i) \cdot \varepsilon^d(MM,P) - \varepsilon^d(MM,i) \cdot \varepsilon^d(CM,P)}{\varepsilon^d(CM,i) - \varepsilon^d(MM,i)} < 0.$$

INTERNATIONAL TRADE AND MONEY

The expression $\bar{\varepsilon}(AM,P)$ can be interpreted as an average of asset price elasticities on the asset market. The reader should note a fundamental order constraint

$$\varepsilon(CM,i) > \varepsilon(MM,i) > 0,$$

i.e. the interest elasticities of the credit market exceed the interest elasticities on the money market.

2. The response to a change in the stock supply S of government securities:

$$\varepsilon(i,S) = \frac{\varepsilon(MM,P)}{\Delta} \frac{S}{aB^a} > 0$$

$$\varepsilon(P,S) = -\frac{\varepsilon(MM,i)}{\Delta} \frac{S}{aB^a} > 0.$$

3. The response to the budget position:

$$\varepsilon(i,CCFD^a) = \varepsilon(i,DB_1)\frac{\hat{\mu}C\hat{F}D^a}{B^a} + \varepsilon(i,S)\frac{(1-\hat{\mu})C\hat{F}D^a}{S}$$

$$= \frac{\hat{\mu}C\hat{F}D^a}{B^a}\left[\varepsilon(i,DB_1) - \varepsilon(i,S)\frac{B^a}{S}\right] + \varepsilon(i,S)\frac{C\hat{F}D^a}{S}$$

$$= \frac{\hat{\mu}C\hat{F}D^a}{B^a}\left[\varepsilon(i,DB_1) - \varepsilon(i,S)\frac{B^a}{S}\right] +$$

$$+ \varepsilon(i,S)\left[\frac{\dot{S}}{S} + \frac{\dot{DB}_1}{DB_1}\frac{DB_1}{S}\right].$$

This elasticity measures the response to a *change* in $CCFD^a$, i.e. to a given *deficit level* CFD^a. The result is obtained by replacing dDB_1 and dS according to $dDB_1 = \hat{\mu}C\hat{F}D^a$, $dS = (1-\hat{\mu})C\hat{F}D^a$ in dDB_1/DB_1 and dS/S.

$$\varepsilon(P,CCFD^a) = \frac{\hat{\mu}CFD^a}{B^a} \cdot \varepsilon(P,DB_1) + \frac{(1-\hat{\mu})C\hat{F}D^a}{S}\varepsilon(P,S).$$

4. The response to a change in the current financial parameter $\hat{\mu}$:

$$\varepsilon(i,\hat{\mu}) = \frac{\hat{\mu}C\hat{F}D^a}{DB_1}\left[\varepsilon(i,DB_1) - \varepsilon(i,S)\frac{DB_1}{S}\right] < 0$$

$$\varepsilon(P,\hat{\mu}) = \frac{\hat{\mu}CFD^a}{DB_1}\left[\varepsilon(P,DB_1) - \varepsilon(P,S)\frac{DB_1}{S}\right].$$

Money Supply Process and Monetary Policy

5. The response to an open market operation:

$$\varepsilon(i,Q) = \frac{Q}{DB_1}\left[\varepsilon(i,DB_1) - \varepsilon(i,S)\frac{DB_1}{S}\right] < 0$$

$$\varepsilon(P,Q) = \frac{Q}{DB_1}\left[\varepsilon(P,DB_1) - \varepsilon(P,S)\frac{DB_1}{S}\right] > 0$$

$$= \frac{Q}{B^a}\frac{\varepsilon(CM,i) - \varepsilon(MM,i)(a-1/a)}{\Delta} > 0.$$

6. The response to a change in the external interest rate i^e:

$$\varepsilon(i,i^e) = \frac{n^1}{\Delta} > 0$$

$$n^1 = [\varepsilon(\sigma,i^e) - \varepsilon(a,i^e)] \cdot \varepsilon(MM,P) - \varepsilon(FB_2,i^e)$$
$$[\varepsilon(MM,P) - \varepsilon(CM,P)]$$

$$\varepsilon(P,i^e) = \frac{n^2}{\Delta} < 0$$

$$n^2 = -[\varepsilon(\sigma,i^e) - \varepsilon(a,i^e)]\varepsilon(MM,i) - \varepsilon(FB_2,i^e)$$
$$[\varepsilon(CM,i) - \varepsilon(MM,i)]$$

Note: This result depends on a vanishing derivative of λ with respect to i^e. A negative derivative lowers both derivatives algebraically.

7. The response to a change in the policy forward premium:

$$\varepsilon(i,\bar{p}) = \frac{-\varepsilon(a,\bar{p}) \cdot \varepsilon(MM,P) + \varepsilon(m,\bar{p}) \cdot \varepsilon(CM,P)}{\Delta} > 0$$

$$\varepsilon(P,\bar{p}) = \frac{-\varepsilon(m,\bar{p}) \cdot \varepsilon(CM,i) + \varepsilon(a,\bar{p}) \cdot \varepsilon(MM,i)}{\Delta} \simeq 0.$$

8. The response to a change in the market forward premium p:

$$\varepsilon(i,p) =$$
$$\frac{-\varepsilon(FB_2,p)[\varepsilon(MM,P) - \varepsilon(CM,P)] + \varepsilon(\sigma,p) \cdot \varepsilon(MM,P)}{\Delta} > 0$$

$$\varepsilon(P,p) =$$
$$\frac{-\varepsilon(FB_2,p)[\varepsilon(CM,i) - \varepsilon(MM,i)] - \varepsilon(\sigma,p) \cdot \varepsilon(MM,i)}{\Delta} < 0.$$

This result is a simplification of the complete response: The net effect of p on the asset and monetary multiplier is of small order and has been neglected consequently.

9. The response to a change in the expected exchange rate.

This operates via $f_1 + f_2$, $q^1, q^2, q^3, t_1, FB_2, \sigma$:

$$0 < \varepsilon(m,e) < \varepsilon(a,e), \varepsilon(FB_2,e) < 0, \varepsilon(\sigma,e) > 0$$

$$\varepsilon(i,e) = \frac{n_1}{\Delta} > 0$$

$$\varepsilon(P,e) = \frac{n_2}{\Delta} \text{ depends crucially on } \varepsilon(FB_2,e)$$

$$n_1 = -\varepsilon(FB_2,e)[\varepsilon(MM,P) - \varepsilon(CM,P)] + \\ + \varepsilon(\sigma,e) \cdot \varepsilon(MM,P) + \varepsilon(m,e) \cdot \varepsilon(CM,P)$$

$$n_2 = -\varepsilon(FB_2,e)[\varepsilon(CM,i) - \varepsilon(MM,i)] - \\ - \varepsilon(\sigma,e) \cdot \varepsilon(MM,i) - \varepsilon(m,e) \cdot \varepsilon(CM,i).$$

ADDENDUM

On the delay noted on p. 154, the reader should also consult the paper by Rudiger Dornbusch "Currency Devaluation, Hoarding and Relative Prices" to be published in the *Journal of Political Economy*.

9

An Analysis of Currency Devaluation in Developing Countries[1]

RICHARD N. COOPER
Yale University

Currency devaluation is one of the most dramatic – even traumatic – measures of economic policy that a government may undertake. It almost always generates cries of outrage and calls for the officials responsible to resign. For these reasons alone, governments are reluctant to devalue their currencies. Yet under the present rules of the international monetary system, laid down in the Articles of Agreement of the International Monetary Fund, devaluation is encouraged whenever a country's international payments position is in 'fundamental disequilibrium', whether that disequilibrium is brought about by factors outside the country or by indigenous developments. Because of the associated trauma, which arises because so many economic adjustments to a discrete change in the exchange rate are crowded into a relatively short period, currency devaluation has come to be regarded as a measure of last resort, with countless partial substitutes adopted before devaluation is finally undertaken. Despite this procrastination, over 200 devaluations in fact occurred between the inauguration of the IMF in 1947 and the end of 1970; to be sure, some were small and many took place in the years of postwar readjustment, especially 1949. In addition, there were five upvaluations, or revaluations, of currencies before the significant revaluations of 1971.

By convention, changes in the value of a currency are measured against the American dollar, so a devaluation means a reduction in the dollar price of a unit of foreign currency or, what is the same thing, an increase in the number of units of foreign currency that can be purchased for a dollar. (The numerical measure of the extent of

[1] Parts of this paper draw extensively on my *Currency Devaluation in Developing Countries*, Princeton Essays in International Finance, No. 86, June, 1971. I wish to thank the Princeton International Finance Section for permission to reproduce certain sections of this paper.

devaluation will always be higher with the latter measure than with the former; for example, the 1967 devaluation of the British pound from $2·80 to $2·40 was 14·3 per cent and 16·7 per cent on the two measures, respectively.) By law, changes in currency parities are against gold, but since the official dollar price of gold was unchanged from 1934 to 1971, these changes normally come to the same thing. Except when many currencies are devalued at the same time – as they were in September, 1949, to a lesser extent in November, 1967 (when over a dozen countries devalued with the pound), in August, 1969 (when fourteen French African countries devalued their currencies along with the French franc), and in December 1971, (when over fifty countries devalued along with the US dollar with respect to the currencies of other industrial countries) – a currency devaluation against the dollar is also against the rest of the global payments system, that is, against all other currencies.

Largely because they are so numerous, but partly also because they devalue on average somewhat more often than the developed countries do, less developed countries account for most currency devaluations. Yet the standard analysis of currency devaluation, which has advanced substantially during this period and is still being transformed and further refined, fails to take into account many of the features that are typical of developing countries today, and which influence substantially the impact of currency devaluation on their economies and on their payments positions.

This essay attempts to do two things. First, it suggests how the standard analysis of currency devaluation has to be modified to take into account the diverse purposes to which the foreign exchange system is put in many less developed countries, and the extent to which these diverse purposes influence the nature of devaluation and its effects on the economy. Second, it draws on postwar experience with about two dozen devaluations to see to what extent the anxieties of government officials, bankers, and traders, and even some economists, about devaluation and its effects are justified, and interprets some of this experience in light of the earlier theoretical discussion.

I. AN ANALYSIS OF DEVALUATION FOR MOST DEVELOPING COUNTRIES

The foreign-exchange system of a country can be used to pursue

Currency Devaluation in Developing Countries

many objectives other than clearance of the foreign-exchange market. Faced with inadequate instruments of policy to achieve the many objectives expected of them, the governments of many less developed countries have called upon it to do so. These functions range from fostering industrialisation, improving the terms of trade, and raising revenue to redistributing income among broad classes and even doling out favours to political supporters. A practice used frequently to accomplish all three of the first objectives, and also to redistribute income, is to give primary export products a rate of conversion into local currency lower than the rate that importers must pay to purchase foreign exchange (and that exporters of non-traditional products receive). Import-substituting investment is stimulated by the unfavourable rate on imports, foreign export prices are higher than they otherwise would be in the rare event that the country can influence world prices for its products, and the government gains revenue from the often substantial difference between the buying and selling prices of foreign exchange. Similarly, imported consumer goods are often charged a rate much higher than imported investment goods, in an effort to stimulate investment in manufacturing (and with the undesirable side-effect of encouraging modes of production that use relatively more capital and relatively more imported ingredients or components). Finally, and not least, the exchange system can be used to redistribute income between broad classes, as for example, in Argentina when the exchange rate applied to traditional exports, meat and wheat, was deliberately kept low for a number of years with a view to keeping down the cost of living for urban workers.

All of these functions involve multiple exchange rates of some kind, either explicit or implicit, that is, charging different exchange rates according to the commodity or service, the origin or destination, or the persons involved in the transaction. As such, they inevitably invite arbitrage and require policing – but so of course do taxes, which they often replace in function.

Moreover, politicians have learned that an objective achieved indirectly is frequently socially acceptable when direct action would not be. This is not always because of an imperfect understanding of the indirect means in contrast to the direct means, although that plays an important role. It is much easier for an interest group to mobilize successfully against an export tax than it is to mobilise against an over-valued currency supplemented by high import tariffs and possibly accompanied by some export subsidies, even though the two systems might have precisely the same effects. As Fritz Machlup has said (in connection with Special Drawing Rights):

> We have often seen how disagreements among scholars were resolved when ambiguous language was replaced by clear formulations not permitting different interpretations. The opposite is true in politics. Disagreements on political matters, national or international, can be resolved only if excessively clear language is avoided, so that each negotiating party can put its own interpretation on the provisions proposed and may claim victory in having its own point of view prevail in the final agreement.[2]

Machlup was speaking of language, but the same is true of action; a roundabout way of accomplishing a controversial objective will often succeed where direct action would fail, because it obscures, perhaps even from the policy-makers themselves, who is really benefiting and who is being hurt.

The difficulty is that the pursuit of these diverse objectives too often leads to neglect of the function of the exchange rate in allocating the supply of foreign exchange. When balance-of-payments pressures develop (sometimes as a result of inflationary policies, which in the short run are often also a successfully ambiguous way to reconcile conflicting social objectives), officials engage in a series of patchwork efforts and marginal adjustments to make the problem go away (raising tariffs here, prohibiting payments there), which may disturb the original objectives as well as coping only inadequately with the payments difficulty. When devaluation finally occurs, in consequence, the occasion is also taken (sometimes under pressures from the IMF or from foreign-aid donors) to sweep away many of the *ad hoc* measures that have been instituted to avoid the necessity for devaluation.

This fact makes currency devaluation in many developing countries (and some developed ones) a good deal more complex than a simple adjustment of the exchange rate, and the analysis must be modified to take these other adjustments into account. Broadly speaking, one can distinguish four types of devaluation 'packages': (1) straight devaluation (involving a discrete change in the principal exchange rate, as opposed to a freely depreciating rate or an ad-

---

[2] Fritz Machlup, *Remaking the International Monetary System* (The Johns Hopkins Press, Baltimore, 1968), p. 7.

ministered 'slide' in the rate, such as was adopted by Brazil, Chile, and Colombia in the late sixties, whereby the rate was depreciated by a small amount every two to eight weeks); (2) devaluation with a *stabilisation* programme of contractionary monetary and fiscal policy aimed at reducing the level of aggregate demand, or at least the rate of increase of demand; (3) devaluation accompanied by *liberalisation*, whereby imports and other international payments that were previously prohibited or subject to quota are allowed to take place freely under much less restraint than before the devaluation; and (4) devaluation accompanied by partial or full *unification* of exchange rates, whereby a pre-existing diversity of exchange rates is collapsed into a single, unified rate, or at most two rates, the lower one applying to traditional exports of primary products and in effect amounting to a tax on these exports.

It is obvious that these categories are not mutually exclusive. Devaluation may involve simultaneously a stabilisation programme, liberalisation, and exchange-rate unification, and in fact at least some elements of all are often present in devaluation in developing countries. For example, of 24 devaluations studied in some detail (and which will provide the basis for evidence cited below), ten involved a fairly substantial degree of trade liberalisation, ten (partially overlapping) involved a major consolidation of rates, and virtually all were accompanied by at least token measures of stabilisation.

These various simultaneous adjustments must be taken into account in analysing the economic effects of devaluation. In particular, it is necessary to distinguish between devaluation from a position of open payments deficit and devaluation from a position in which a latent deficit is suppressed by import controls and related measures, which are removed upon devaluation. An additional complication is that less developed countries are more likely at the time of devaluation to be generating new money demand at a rate greater than can be accommodated by total domestic output plus foreign assistance and other long-term capital inflows from abroad; in short, they are pursuing inflationary policies, as opposed merely to having costs that have gotten out of line in the course of *past* inflation.

In fact, most devaluing countries have some combination of an open payments deficit and a suppressed one. But for clarity of exposition, and to bring out the contrast with the standard analysis most clearly, we will consider devaluation from a position in which the payments deficit is fully suppressed by other measures, and where the devaluation is accompanied by liberalisation and/or unification of the exchange system involving the removal of special taxes, subsidies, and prohibitions that have been installed earlier. In addition, we will suppose that the country is not pursuing inflationary policies at the time of devaluation.

Low elasticities

The first point to note is that the elasticity of demand for imports is likely to be low when imports are concentrated on raw materials, semi-fabricated products, and capital goods, a structure prevalent in less developed countries. With import substitution in an advanced stage, all the easy substitutions having already been made in the pursuit of industrialisation, imports depend largely on output rather than income and are not very sensitive to relative price changes. There is more room for substituting home production for imports of foodstuffs, although it will usually take a season or longer to bring this about. Moreover, import liberalisation and exchange-rate unification will actually result in a *reduction* of the prices of those imports most tightly restrained before the devaluation, so consumption of them will be encouraged.

There is greater diversity of experience with regard to exports. Some countries – producers of oil, copper, and cocoa, for instance – have virtually no domestic consumption of the export goods. In others, exports include the major wage good – beef in Argentina and fish in Iceland, for instance. In the former countries, increasing exports require enlarged output and development of new export products, and neither of these courses may be easy in the short run, although tree crops can sometimes be more intensively harvested. In the latter countries, there is more room for immediate increases in exports permitted by reductions in domestic consumption of the export products, but this gain is brought about only by courting a wage-price spiral, on which more will be said below. In developed countries, by contrast, there are many domestically consumed goods that are actual or potential exports, and hence there is much room for short-term increases in export supply by diverting output from the home to the foreign market.

When it comes to incentives to enlarge output and expand capacity, the principal reallocation here is between import-competing goods and exports, rather than between home goods and all foreign-trade goods, as in the case of some developed economies. This is because by assumption imports have already been stringently limited by high tariffs, disadvantageous exchange rates, and quantitative restrictions, all of which create a strong price incentive for domestic production. Some exports may also have been subsidised and, where this is so, devaluation accompanied by removal of the subsidy may leave no new incentive to increase production for export. But generally speaking exports are heavily penalised under the regimes we are considering, and devaluation has the effect of reducing the premium for producing import-competing goods for the home market and increasing the premium for production for export, with the principal shift in incentives coming between these two sectors rather than with respect to the home goods sector (although of course there will also be some incentive to shift resources into that sector from the import-competing sector and out of it to the export sector).

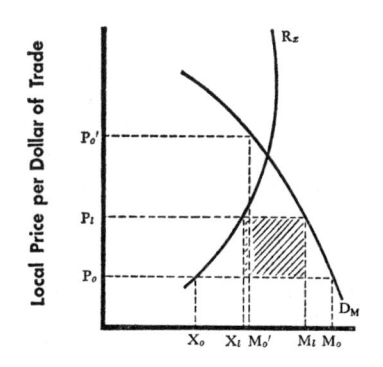

FIGURE 9.1

These points can be shown in Figure 9.1, which depicts a devaluing country's demand for imports, D_m and a schedule of its receipts for exports, R_x. On the factually reasonable assumption that the foreign prices of their imports are beyond their influence, the import schedule reflects both quantities and foreign exchange expenditure on imports; the export schedule, in contrast, reflects only foreign currency receipts, this being a combination of quantity supplied for export and the foreign currency price that any given quantity can fetch. It thus reflects both domestic supply conditions and foreign demand conditions.

We assume initially an exchange rate that leads to a domestic price P_o per dollar of exports; this is also the price that importers pay for each dollar of foreign exchange. It results in export receipts X_o and imports M_o, leaving a large trade deficit. The authorities may find it necessary to ration the foreign exchange to hold imports to M_o', a level that is sustainable with X_o in export receipts and $M_o'-X_o$ in capital inflow, say under a foreign aid programme loan. Under these circumstances, the domestic market price of imported goods will rise to P_o' and importers will earn a scarcity rent of $P_o'-P_o$ per dollar of imports, brought about by the rationing system. (Auctioning the import licences would of course capture these rents in the absence of collusion among the importers, but auctioning in fact is rare.) Payments are in balance, taking into account the capital inflow.

Devaluation of the currency can supplant the rationing system by increasing the price of foreign currency to P_1. Export receipts will rise to X_1, and as a result of the more favourable exchange rate production of export goods will increase. If the rationing system is retained, the country will now find itself in payments surplus; but abandonment of the system will lead the local price of imports to *fall* to P_1 and imports will rise to M_1, preserving payments balance after allowing for the foreign assistance ($= M_o' - X_o = M_1 - X_1$). Thus local production of import-competing goods will be discouraged by lower prices and a greater volume of imports. This marks a sharp contrast with straight devaluation from a position of open deficit, where production of import-competing as well as export goods is encouraged, since the local prices of both are raised relative to non-traded goods.

New investment in the capacity to export will require that investors expect the improvement in their position to last, i.e., that the devaluation and associated policies will establish a new regime that will not simply slide back into the old configuration of policies. Establishing these expectations is one of the most difficult tasks of those carrying out the reform. The same problem exists in principle in devaluation from open deficit too, but developing countries that have not relied on restriction of imports for payments reasons stand a better chance of success, because investors will expect any emerging disequilibrium to be corrected, rather than suppressed by controls.

Furthermore, the required investment may differ in character from that in developed countries. Where manufactures can be competitively exported under the new regime, conversion from domestic manufacturing may be relatively easy; but opening up export markets for manufactured goods for the first time is a drawn-out process, requiring the establishment of new marketing channels. The shift from domestic to export crops in agriculture – or the opening of new lands – is generally easier; but for livestock and for tree crops the required gestation period may be several years.

For all these reasons, some pessimism with regard to price elasticities would be quite justified for many developing countries, at least in the short run, but as we will see below, it does not usually go far enough to prevent devaluation from improving the trade balance.

Effects on aggregate demand

The absorption approach to devaluation suggests that a devaluation that merely substitutes for other measures, leading to no net improvement in the balance of goods and services, requires no cut in aggregate expenditure or increase in total output to 'make room' for an improvement. But it is still worth asking what pressure devaluation in these circumstances might put on aggregate expenditure and output, since this will give some guide to the possible need for compensatory macro-economic policy.

To provide a framework for discussion, one that captures several of the key elements even though it does not do justice to them all, consider the following simple macro-economic model:

$$Y = E+D \quad\quad i = i(Y,p,L)$$
$$E = E(Y,i,r) \quad L = H+R$$
$$D = D(Y,r) \quad\quad \Delta R = D+K$$

Here Y is the level of output and income in the devaluing country, E is total domestic expenditure, D is the balance on goods and services, L is the money supply, H is domestic credit, R is international reserves, and K is capital inflow, all measured in domestic currency. In addition, r is the exchange rate measured as the dollar cost of a unit of local currency, i is the interest rate on financial assets other than money, and p is the domestic price level. We assume here that the local price of all domestic production, including production for export, is held constant – e.g. by the availability of unemployed resources at fixed money wages – so the only variation in p comes about through a devaluation-induced rise in local-currency import prices. Foreign prices of imports are assumed unchanged, so devaluation on these assumptions implies an equivalent worsening in the terms of trade. The function determining interest rates in turn reflects the equality of demand for real money balances with the supply.

In order to discover the impact effect on output, Y, we must ask what will be the effects of devaluation on its two components, the level of domestic expenditure and the external balance measured in domestic currency. The impact on output will in turn affect incomes, expenditure, imports, and output again in a multiplier process. But the impact effect will tell us the impetus to this multiplier process, and in particular whether it is expansionary or deflationary. Total differentiation of the model above and re-arrangement of terms yields:

$$dY = \frac{1}{s+m-E_i i_y}[D_r dr + E_r dr + E_i(i_L dL + i_p dp)],$$

where the subscripts indicate partial differentiation with respect to the indicated variable, $s = 1-E_y$, and $m = -D_y$. Thus the change in income, dY, is seen to depend upon a devaluation-induced change in the trade balance, a devaluation-induced shift in the level of expenditure, and a money-supply and price-induced shift in the level of expenditure, all augmented by an income multiplier. Let us consider the three terms within the brackets in turn, for these determine whether output will be increased or reduced as a result of devaluation.

To take the external balance first, for the reasons given above this might actually worsen in the period immediately following devaluation, when measured in foreign currency, and this by itself would have a deflationary impact upon the economy. The worsening would occur if import liberalisation takes effect immediately, giving rise to an increase in imports, while the stimulus to exports occurs only with a lag. In time, of course, the stimulus to exports will also stimulate the domestic economy; but the immediate impact would be a deflationary one. Furthermore, any discrepancy between the local-currency value of a dollar's worth of imports and a dollar's worth of exports, for example due to tariffs, means that even a parallel expansion of imports and exports will be deflationary, provided the government does not spend the additional revenue at once.

Moreover, devaluation is deflationary to the extent that import quotas are replaced in their import-restricting effects by the depreciated exchange rate. Scarcity rents that went to privileged importers before the devaluation would now accrue to the central bank as it sells foreign exchange. In effect, price rationing will have replaced quantitative rationing, with no ultimate effect on the *final* market price, but with a higher domestic currency price to the importer or firm enjoying the licence.

Finally, the inelasticity of demand for imports suggests that a sharp rise in their local-currency price will lead to an increase in *expenditure* upon them, even if the quantity and foreign-exchange value of imports fall. In this respect devaluation is like an efficient revenue-oriented excise tax, increasing the price far more than it reduces the quantity purchased. Since imports will generally exceed exports due to inflows of foreign grants and capital, sometimes by a substantial margin, exports will have to expand a great deal before the increased local currency income from their sale exceeds the increased local currency expenditure on imports. Thus in Figure 1, which is drawn on the assumption that exports and imports increase by the same amount in terms of foreign currency, total local currency expenditure on imports increases by $P_1 M_1 - P_0 M'_0$, while local currency receipts rise by only the L-shaped area $P_1 X_1 - P_0 X_0$. The difference is the shaded rectangle, representing the increased local currency value of the capital inflow, which if the government does not spend it promptly represents a deflationary force, like additional tax receipts. A greater devaluation would have led to imports lower than M_1, but an inelastic demand for imports would lead to a still further increase in total domestic expenditure on them. Thus even though the trade balance would have improved in terms of foreign currency, the devaluation would have had a deflationary impact on this account; for some (possibly excessive) degree of devaluation, however, increased receipts from exports would overtake the increased expenditures on imports, and the conventional assumption that successful devaluation is expansionary will prevail.

The exact conditions under which the trade balance effect of devaluation will be deflationary have been set down elsewhere,[3] but they may be summarised briefly by noting that $B = rD$, where B is the trade balance measured in foreign currency. Taking differentials yields

$$dB = r(1+k)dD + kB,$$

where k is the proportionate devaluation, and is negative. Thus for an initial trade deficit the second term on the right is positive,

---

[3] See my 'Devaluation and Aggregate Demand in Aid-Receiving Countries', in J. Bhagwati *et al.*, *Trade, Balance of Payments, and Growth* (North-Holland Publishing Co., Amsterdam, 1971), pp. 355–76.

giving rise to the possibility that dD is negative even when the trade balance in foreign currency has improved. This will in fact happen provided the elasticity of demand for imports (ε_m) is below unity and the foreign elasticity of demand for exports (ε_x) is sufficiently low, though it may be above unity.

The point can be made geometrically in terms of demand elasticities, indicating whether the balance improves or deteriorates in domestic and foreign currency. This is shown in Figure 9.2, where $dB = 0$ and $dD = 0$ result in two boundaries marking off three regions. Between the boundaries, which are influenced also by the initial trade imbalance (X/M) and by the elasticity of supply of ex-

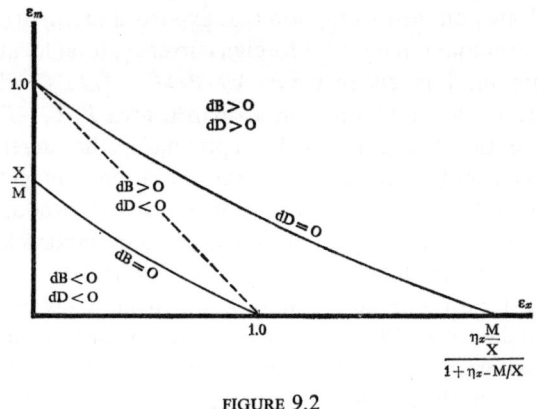

FIGURE 9.2

ports (η_x, which determines the curvature of the boundaries, they being straight lines if domestic costs are constant, as in the model above), the trade balance will improve in terms of foreign currency and deteriorate in terms of domestic currency, thereby exerting deflationary pressure on the economy. If trade is initially in balance, the two boundaries will coincide and a devaluation that improves the balance will also be expansionary. (The dashed straight line joining the unity positions on each axis represents the celebrated Marshall–Lerner condition, under which for infinite supply elasticities devaluation will improve the trade balance – and be expansionary in its domestic effects – if the sum of the two demand elasticities exceeds unity.) But many less developing countries meet the conditions for falling into the middle region, with continuing aid-financed trade deficits, low elasticities of demand for imports, and moderate foreign elasticities of demand for their exports, at least in the short run that is relevant for considering the impact effect on income. Therefore, the foreign sector may well exert a deflationary impact on the economy following devaluation – and indeed did so in 14 of the 24 devaluations examined below.

The external sector, however, is only one component of demand. It is necessary also to ask how devaluation may affect the level of total domestic expenditure, E. Refined analysis is required to discuss the possible effects satisfactorily, but here it will be sufficient to identify six effects that are likely to be important in developing countries, some arising directly from the change in exchange rate, others from monetary effects induced by the devaluation.

(1) There is first the *speculative effect*, which is also important in devaluations from open deficits. If devaluation has been anticipated and is expected to lead to a general increase in prices, there will be anticipatory buying before the devaluation. The post-devaluation period will therefore commence with larger-than-usual holdings of goods. Total expenditure by the public may therefore drop in the period immediately following devaluation, until these inventories are worked off. (This effect would also lead to a rise in imports before and a drop after the devaluation, insofar as this is permitted by the system of licensing or other controls.) Though the speculative effect will normally lead to a drop in expenditure, it may also lead to an increase if the price increases following devaluation are expected to lead to general inflation, or if another devaluation is in prospect.

(2) Devaluation will generally lead to a redistribution of income, and this *distributive effect*, while present for any devaluation, is likely to be especially important in developing countries with heavy reliance on primary products for export. Unless checked by special export taxes, a devaluation will lead to a sharp increase in rewards to those in the export industry, who are often landowners. Whether large or small, landowners are likely to have different saving and consumption patterns from urban dwellers, generally saving more out of marginal changes in income, at least in the short run. Thus, a redistribution of real income from workers to businessmen and from urban to rural dwellers is likely, in the first instance, to lead to a drop in total expenditure out of a given aggregate income, and this drop will be deflationary. But of course the redistributional effect could also go the other way, if as a result of devaluation the real income of those with a low marginal propensity to save is increased at the ex-

pense of others. The redistributional effect will also affect the level of imports out of a given total income, since the consumption pattern of those who gain may differ from that of losers. But this effect is likely to be less marked than the total expenditure effect, partly because much of the import bill of developing countries represents inputs into domestically produced goods and services, so they are somewhat more widely diffused throughout the economy than would be the case for direct imports of manufactured consumer goods. Diaz-Alejandro has documented well the dominating importance of the redistributive effect following the Argentine devaluation of 1959, where the shift of income to the landowners led to a sharp drop in domestic spending and therefore to a secondary drop in imports.[4]

(3) A devaluation will lead to a rise in the domestic costs of servicing *external debt* denominated in foreign currency. These are implicitly included in our calculation of *dD* above. But where the liabilities are those of businessmen who do not benefit much from the devaluation, it may lead to bankruptcy, even when businesses are otherwise sound, and to an attendant decline in business spending, both by the bankrupt firms and by others affected adversely or merely made anxious. This factor allegedly figured in the decline in investment following the Argentine devaluation of 1962. Even where the debt is held officially, the problem of raising the local-currency counterpart of external servicing charges often poses a serious problem, and sometimes represents a serious inhibition to devaluation.

Indeed (to digress for a moment), these 'accounting' relationships, usually ignored by economists, often preoccupy officials and bankers. Local development banks that have borrowed abroad (for instance, from the World Bank or IDA) in foreign currencies and re-lent to local business in domestic currency have accepted an exchange risk that has occasionally provided the major barrier to devaluation: to allow its development bank to fail might psychologically undermine the government's development plans. But if the bank is to be saved, who is to absorb the devaluation loss, and how? (The obvious retrospective answer is that local borrowers should be charged interest rates sufficiently above what the development bank pays on its foreign debt to cover the exchange risk – with the added advantage that such rates will more closely approximate the true cost of capital

---

[4] Carlos F. Diaz-Alejandro, *Exchange Rate Devaluation in a Semi-Industrialized Country* (M.I.T. Press, Cambridge, 1965).

in the developing country. But development banks have often failed to do this. Or, if they have done it, they have failed to set aside a sufficiently large reserve out of the difference in rates.)

A similar problem arises for net *creditors* when the value of their foreign claims is reduced in terms of local currency by devaluation abroad or revaluation of the home currency. Thus, Hong Kong inadvisedly devalued its currency following the 1967 devaluation of sterling, apparently because the commercial banks in Hong Kong held large sterling assets against their local-currency deposits, and the banking system would have been threatened if the relationship between sterling and Hong Kong dollars had not been preserved. But the government thought better of this decision and revalued again four days later, in the meantime having worked out a way to indemnify the banks out of official reserves. By the same token, the German Bundesbank showed substantial paper losses (in marks) on its assets held in gold and dollars following the revaluations of 1961 and 1969. The 1961 revaluation was delayed until the German government would agree to indemnify the bank for its 'losses' (which were entirely paper losses arising from double-entry bookkeeping conventions) out of the budget over a period of seven years. Where private parties have incurred foreign debt, of course, the loss is real to the firm or bank, and that may have undesirable consequences for the economy as a whole. But a thorough discussion of this important issue is beyond the scope of the present essay.

(4) When the balance of goods and services has turned adverse in terms of domestic currency – as we have seen above may frequently be expected – then in the absence of countervailing monetary action a domestic *credit squeeze* may result, since importers and others will be paying more into the central bank for foreign exchange than exporters are receiving.[5] This credit stringency in turn may lead to higher interest rates and a reduction in domestic expenditure.

---

[5] It might be mentioned in passing that in most developing countries the distinction between monetary and fiscal policy does not have the same meaning it has in more advanced countries. Since capital markets are little developed and access to foreign capital markets is limited, budget deficits, after allowing for foreign assistance, must be financed by the banking system, which results directly or indirectly in monetary expansion. Thus, the usual focus on eliminating government deficits is merely an indirect way to limit the rate of monetary expansion, provided, of course, that bank credit to the private sector is also kept under control. Similarly, increased government receipts from the local sale of foreign aid funds or goods will lead to repayment of the central bank and a resulting contraction in the money supply.

(5) In addition to affecting the money stock, devaluation may also influence the *demand for real money balances*. By raising the local prices of imports and (in general, outside our formal framework) of export products, devaluation will reduce the real value of a given money stock. Indeed, a monetary interpretation of balance-of-payments difficulties and their correction focuses on the excess of money holdings as a source of the deficit, and on the devaluation-induced reduction in real balances as the corrective, leading to a reduction in spending. In the case of devaluation from a suppressed deficit, however, this money demand effect is more complicated, and may not be present at all. A devaluation that simply displaces other instruments of policy, with no effect on domestic prices, will not alter the real value of money balances. If, as is more typically the case, devaluation displaces restraints on imports but also raises the local prices of exports, the effect on the real value of money holdings will depend upon the importance of export products in local expenditure. When export products are extensively purchased by residents, the monetary effect will tend to reduce domestic spending. Import liberalisation, on the other hand, cuts the other way insofar as import prices actually fall.[6]

(6) In the long run another factor comes into play: to the extent that devaluation displaces measures that led to a less efficient use of resources, the devaluation package will lead (after the necessary reallocation of resources has taken place) to an increase in real income, and this *resource efficiency effect* in turn will require a supporting increase in real money holdings. Unless it is supplied by the monetary authorities, this demand for money balances will depress expenditure relative to potential income.[7]

The upshot of these various considerations is that devaluation in developing countries is likely to be deflationary in the first instance,

[6] Murray Kemp has argued that a small currency devaluation from equilibrium will have *no* net effects on expenditure levels, apart from the effect on the trade balance, with the real money balance effect just offsetting any other tendencies, and in particular offsetting the Laursen–Metzler effect, whereby a reduction in real income arising from a devaluation-induced deterioration in the terms of trade will give rise to an upward shift in money expenditure out of a given money income. But Kemp's finding derives from a model at a higher level of generalisation than is being considered here, and it therefore leaves no room for most of the influences identified in the text. See his *The Pure Theory of International Trade* (Prentice-Hall, Englewood Cliffs, N.J., 1964), pp. 277–80.

[7] This source of deflationary pressure has been emphasized by Egon Sohmen in 'The Effect of Devaluation on the Price Level', *Quarterly Journal of Economics*, Vol. 72, No. 2 (May, 1958), pp. 273–83.

and thus may 'make room' for any improvement in the balance on goods and services, without active reinforcement from monetary and fiscal policy. Indeed, for reasons given below, it may sometimes be desirable to accompany devaluation with modestly *expansionary* policies. Frequently, however, the devaluation will take place against a background of excessively expansionary policies. In this case the devaluation-induced deflation will be helpful in bringing the economy under control, but these effects must be taken into account if the government is to avoid overshooting the target with deliberately contractionary measures.

In short, unless the devaluation is very successful in stimulating exports or in stimulating investment, the absorption approach to devaluation is of less relevance to devaluation in developing countries except in manifestly inflationary situations – the real problem will often be getting adequate capacity in the export sector, not in releasing resources overall.

Before turning to the actual experience of devaluations in developing countries, it should be noted that a devaluation will have powerful short-run distributive effects (alluded to above in the discussion of the impact of devaluation on expenditure). When tariffs are reduced (unless they are offset by a reduction in subsidies), the government loses revenue; when quotas are eliminated, quota-holders lose the quasi-rents they enjoyed by getting scarce resource (the right to import) at a price below its social value. When prices rise, all those on fixed money incomes suffer. Petty officials responsible for licensing or tariff collection may also lose the 'fees' they can collect by virtue of their position of control. The gainers are those in the actual and potential export industries and, where a quota system is replaced by a dual exchange-rate system (the lower rate usually applying to traditional exports), the government. These prospective gains and losses influence sectional attitudes toward devaluation and their willingness to help make it succeed.

II. SOME EVIDENCE ON THE IMPACT OF DEVALUATION

Having set out how the conventional analysis of devaluation may have to be adapted to devaluations in developing countries, we turn now to the actual experience of these countries with devaluation. As noted in the introduction, currency devaluations have occurred with some frequency in the last 25 years despite widespread reluctance to engage in them. Many of these were small, or were by countries with inadequate statistics, or were by developed countries, or were part of a larger movement of exchange rates of one block of countries as against another – the last kind of devaluation raising rather different issues for analysis than have been considered above. The evidence drawn on here derives from a study of 23 devaluations occurring over the period 1953–66 and including most of major devaluations in developing countries in the early 1960s.[8]

There are many questions that one can ask about the consequences of devaluation and its associated package of policies, which may have profound effects upon the allocation of resources, growth, and the distribution of income in developing economies. We are not concerned with these ultimate effects – although empirical work on them is all too rare – but, rather, with the immediate, impact effects of devaluation. These start the transition to the longer-term effects, if they are given a chance to work themselves out. The reason for focusing on impact effects is that they often determine whether the longer-term effects will be given a chance to work themselves out. Officials have notoriously short planning horizons, and their anxieties about the impact effects of devaluation often lead to a postponement of devaluation and the substitution in its place of numerous *ad hoc* measures, imposing substantial costs by impeding the efficient operation of the economy.

The reluctance of officials arises in large measure from the considerations adduced in the introduction: devaluation will disturb an implicit social contract among different segments of society – or at least will jar some groups out of their acquiescence in the existing state of affairs, with its numerous implicit compromises – and officials are understandably anxious about rocking an overloaded and delicately balanced boat. But sooner or later the decision may be forced upon them, when for external or internal reasons the external disequilibrium deepens and a suppressed deficit becomes an open deficit which can be corrected only by disturbing the social equilibrium anyway.

More specific anxieties are also expressed about the consequences of devaluation, however, and they can be grouped under four headings:

---

[8] A more complete description and analysis of these cases is found in Chapter 13 of G. Ranis, ed., *Government and Economic Development* (Yale University Press, New Haven, 1971).

Currency Devaluation in Developing Countries

(i) Devaluation, it is feared, will not achieve the desired improvement in the balance of payments, because neither imports nor exports are sufficiently sensitive to relative price changes within the acceptable range of such changes – in a phrase, elasticity pessimism.

(ii) Devaluation will worsen the terms of trade of the country and thus will impose real costs on it.

(iii) By raising domestic prices, devaluation will set in motion a wage-price spiral that will rapidly undercut the improved competitiveness that the devaluation is designed to achieve.

(iv) Whatever its economic effects, it is thought that devaluation will be politically disastrous for those officials responsible for it.

Let us see to what extent these fears are justified by experience, adopting the short-run (one year, say) perspective of the official.

Impact on trade and payments

In nearly two-thirds of the two-dozen devaluations examined (see Table 9.I) the balance on goods and services, measured in foreign currency (as is appropriate for balance-of-payments analysis, although a number of countries record their payments positions in domestic currency), improved in the year following devaluation. In over 80 per cent of the cases either this or the overall monetary balance (often both) improved in the year following devaluation. Of the four countries that showed a worsening on both counts, two involved important import liberalisation resulting in a rise in imports.

Of course, these actual improvements could have taken place for reasons quite independent of the devaluation, for example an increase in world demand for the country's products or a drop in domestic expenditure due to a crop failure. Adjustment of the trade data to allow for movements in world demand and for changes in the level of domestic activity reveals a slight increase in the number of countries that improve their trade balance following devaluation.

These improvements occurred despite good reasons for being an elasticity pessimist about developing countries, for the reasons already given above. No doubt some part of the improvement both in trade and in overall payments can be explained by the speculative considerations already mentioned – a reversal of flows after the devaluation occurred. But not all of it can be explained in this way,

TABLE 9.1
SELECTED CURRENCY DEVALUATIONS, 1953–66

Country	Time of devaluation	Nominal devaluation[a] (per cent change in dollars per unit of local currency)	Effective devaluation for imports[b]	Change in balance on goods and services from previous year $ million	Monetary balance in following year $ million	Per cent change in real wages in manufacturing in the following 12 months
Argentina	Jan. 1959	66	61	270	119	−25
Brazil	Sept. 1964	66[c]	61[c]	159	458	−3
Colombia	Nov. 1962	26	23	30	−29	−3
Colombia	Sept. 1965	33	25	−253	−39	−5
Costa Rica	Sept. 1961	15	6	−2	7	8
Ecuador	July 1961	17	16	18	12	5
Greece	Apr. 1953	50	41	60	56	n.a.
Iceland	Feb. 1960	57	41	2	6	n.a.
Iceland	Aug. 1961	12	11	3	20	n.a.
India	June 1966	37	30	−35	−10	n.a.
Israel	Feb. 1962	40	26	−33	164	1
Korea	Feb. 1960	25	34	−34	1	2
Korea	Feb. 1961	50	36	64	47	8
Korea	May 1964	49	50	112	−30	5
Mexico	Apr. 1954	31	31	98	−40	−1
Morocco	Oct. 1959	17	12	−94	65	−1
Pakistan	July 1955	30	28	−21	18	0
Peru	Jan. 1958–					
	Apr. 1959	31	31	78	18	−12
Philippines	Jan. 1962	40	16	99	36	3
Philippines	Nov. 1965	10	0	46	−29	−3
Spain	July 1959	30	26	404	465	n.a.
Tunisia	Sept. 1964	20	17	−56	−3	n.a.
Turkey	Aug. 1958	56	39	−31	−2	−8

[a] Parity or principal import rate. [b] Excluding the effects of relaxation of import quotas. [c] During calendar year 1964.
Note: For definitions, explanations, and qualifications, see source: R. N. Cooper, 'An Assessment of Currency Devaluation in Developing Countries', in Gustav Ranis (ed.), *Government and Economic Development*, New Haven, Yale University Press, 1971.

for the second year following devaluation usually showed a preservation of, and sometimes a substantial increase in, the gains. The fact that supply elasticities are low in the short run helps in theory to assure that there is little or no loss in export receipts such as would arise if supply could be increased rapidly at unchanged *domestic* prices. A steadiness in export earnings combined with some reduction in imports will assure some improvement in the trade balance, but only a modest one. In only three of the cases examined did the improvement in the trade balance exceed the initial trade deficit, thereby swinging the country into trade surplus – a fact that should not be surprising for countries that normally import capital from the rest of the world.

Interestingly enough, most of the countries that liberalised imports experienced a reduction in the volume of imports in the year following devaluation – partly because of a decline in activity and a switching away from imports to domestic sources of supply, but even more because import liberalisation was often delayed from three to nine months following the devaluation, apparently reflecting a wait-and-see attitude on the part of the authorities toward the devaluation. In delaying, however, they increased the risk of a wage-price spiral.

Impact on the terms of trade
Many countries do not have even reasonably comprehensive data on the prices they pay for imports and receive for their exports, hence on their terms of trade. Among those that do, somewhat under one-half showed a deterioration in the terms of trade following devaluation. But some of these deteriorations were independent of the devaluation, and in any case all were small relative to the size of the devaluation – one or two per cent, compared with nominal devaluations ranging from ten to nearly seventy per cent.

The negligible deterioration observed in the terms of trade may of course have been due to preventive measures taken by the devaluing countries. Most of them imposed special taxes (or a disadvantageous exchange rate, lower than the new principal rate) on certain exports of primary products. But usually these taxes were imposed for distributive or revenue reasons and not to prevent a deterioration in the terms of trade through a fall in foreign-currency prices of exports. A standard pattern, for example, is to impose a tax roughly equivalent to the amount of devaluation on exports out of the current harvest, on the ground that the quantity of such exports can be increased only marginally (unless domestic consumption is substantial) and there is no reason to pass windfall gains on to the farmers. The new exchange rate is applied to subsequent harvests. In other instances the tax has been imposed to prevent an immediate rise in the domestic price of an export product important in local consumption, such as olive oil in Greece. In both cases it is a rise in domestic prices, not a fall in foreign ones, that the authorities are guarding against. Where only one or two foreign marketing organisations dominate a country's exports sales, however, these buyers may retain their pre-devaluation buying price for domestic produce, which of course implies a decline in the price in terms of foreign currency. Thus, existing institutional arrangements may permit foreign buyers, in the short run, to improve their terms of trade at the expense of the devaluing country, and a tax will help to prevent this. In the long run, competition from potential foreign buyers will also prevent it, but by that time domestic supplies may also have increased. Finally, there are some commodities – such as hazel nuts in Turkey, jute in Pakistan, cocoa in Ghana – where one country does have a dominant position in the world market, and in these cases too the imposition of an export tax or its equivalent will prevent a deterioration in the terms of trade.

But preoccupation with the terms-of-trade effects of devaluation in fact reflects a misunderstanding of the purposes of devaluation, or at best confuses devaluation theory with optimal-tariff theory. A country that dominates world markets in one or more of its export products can increase its welfare by imposing a tax on those exports up to the point at which the additional gains from further increases in the foreign-currency price (arising from the willingness of foreign buyers to pay part of the tax) just compensate for the additional welfare losses arising from the tax-induced reduction in trade. If the devaluing country has already imposed such optimising export tariffs – import tariffs alone will not do here, because in equilibrium they also discourage manufactured exports, on which the optimal export tax is surely zero for developing countries – then devaluation will not require their alteration unless the cause of the payments imbalance also happens to have altered the optimum export tax. A pre-devaluation rise in domestic costs and prices, leading indeed to the need for devaluation, will have improved the country's terms of trade beyond the optimal point. The objective should be to maximise net returns on exporting, not merely to prevent a deterioration in the terms of trade, and in these circumstances some lowering of export prices in terms of foreign currency will be desirable to stimulate foreign purchases.

Impact on wages and prices

Assessing the impact of devaluation on domestic prices and wages is exceptionally difficult, and only partly because price and wage data are sparse and of dubious quality for most developing countries. It is difficult also because exogenous events, expectational patterns based on the same history that led to the devaluation, and policies associated with but sometimes also at variance with the devaluation may all have important influences on both wages and prices.

It is useful first of all to distinguish between demand-induced and cost-induced increases in prices and wages. By conventional analysis, both should be present following a successful devaluation, for the improved trade balance will increase the claims on domestic output, and the devaluation will lead directly to an increase in the local prices of imports and other foreign-trade goods. We have seen, however, that devaluation may lead to a decline rather than an increase in demand for domestic output, and this alone would tend to depress prices. The extent to which devaluing countries have taken the advice normally tendered to pursue deflationary monetary and fiscal policies will reinforce these devaluation-induced pressures. There is of course no contradiction between deflationary pressures and observed price increases; the devaluation here is very much like an excise tax, which reduces demand by withdrawing purchasing power from circulation, but also raises prices. Where the devaluation merely substitutes for other measures to restrict imports, such as quotas or special tariffs, there need, of course, be no rise in these prices following devaluation, for under competitive conditions the local market prices will have already risen to reflect scarcity values.

In fact, some depression in economic activity is frequently found following devaluation in developing countries, sometimes lasting only a few months, not infrequently lasting more than a year. While it is impossible to disentangle the deflationary effects of devaluation from those of autonomous policy measures designed to facilitate success of the devaluation, there is much circumstantial evidence to suggest that the extent of depression is a surprise to the authorities in the devaluing countries, that they have not adequately taken into account the depressing effects of the devaluation itself, or that they have exaggerated its expansionary impetus. In too many cases, of course, the need to devalue arises from pre-devaluation inflation that has not been brought fully under control even after devaluation, and these cases reinforce the views of those who insist on strongly deflationary measures to accompany devaluation; in those cases further deflation is necessary to make the devaluation work. But in other cases further deflation is not necessary, and on the contrary may aggravate the difficulties of the authorities in keeping the situation under control just as exports are expanding most rapidly. We return to this possibility below.

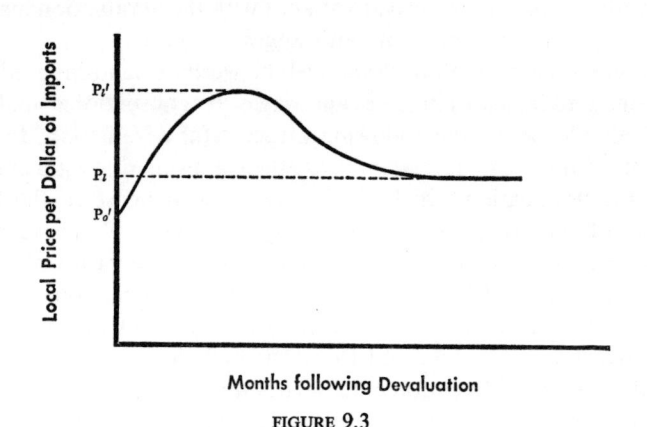

FIGURE 9.3

Despite the theoretical argument that under some circumstances domestic prices need not rise following devaluation, in fact they invariably do. This is partly because there is normally some effective devaluation for imports and export products, even when export subsidies are removed and imports are liberalised, and partly because the instinctive reaction of importers is to pass along to their customers any increase in costs that they have incurred. If they are already charging what the market will bear, however, as shown earlier in Figure 9.1, these higher prices are not sustainable in a given monetary environment, and in the course of time competition among importers will result in a subsequent drop in prices – not to below the pre-devaluation level, but toward it to an extent governed by the degree to which devaluation substitutes for import quotas as a restraint on imports. Such a pattern can be observed for about half of the few countries for which adequate monthly data on local prices of imports are available: prices rise sharply following devaluation, reach a peak three or four months later, and then gradually drop back, sometimes substantially as depicted in Figure 9.3. In an inflationary monetary environment, of course, one does not observe a post-devaluation decline in prices, but the rate of increase is reduced temporarily.

Higher prices will raise costs directly (especially since most imports are intermediate products and capital goods) and they will also stimulate demands for higher money incomes by local factors of production, especially wage and salary employees. But the cycle of wage and price increases should be self-limiting, unless *all* parties (including the government) attempt to maintain their real incomes in the face of rising import prices, or unless the devaluation stimulates price increases that are quite unrelated to increases in costs. In addition, for either case the monetary authorities must support the increase in money incomes with domestic credit expansion, if domestic prices and incomes are to rise by the full amount of the devaluation without generating unemployment.

An open deficit will reflect both a level of expenditure and a distribution of income that is not sustainable at the existing level of output and with the existing structure of taxation and expenditures insofar as they affect distribution. Devaluation requires that some real incomes go down and that total expenditure go down, even though aggregate income need not drop. If, however, those who benefited from the initial disequilibrium insist on retaining the same level of real income, and if they have the market power through administered prices or through wage bargaining to stake out that claim in monetary terms, then the devaluation cannot succeed without general deflation leading to unemployment – unless, of course, there is some unutilised capacity and the tax system can be so altered as to assure that enough of the increased output will go to the powerful factors in the post-devaluation period. Even this will not work if these factors insist on maintaining their pre-devaluation *share* of income.

Second, the devaluation may stimulate price increases that were overdue in any case, but for reasons of law, custom, fear of public opprobrium, or simply inertia were not made earlier – the liquidation of unliquidated monopoly gains, to use Galbraith's term. This problem arises especially with public utilities subjected to an inflationary environment in the past. Being highly visible to the public, electric companies and bus companies do not readily raise their rates, and they are frequently under substantial government pressure not to do so. A currency devaluation, being little understood by the public, presents a natural occasion to raise such prices and lay responsibility on the devaluation. Several devaluations have led to rioting in the streets – as well as larger wage claims – when an economically unrelated but psychologically related increase in urban bus fares occurred shortly afterward.

In either case the monetary authorities are confronted with a dilemma; it is here that management of a devaluation is trickiest. Economists have been too little interested in these matters of management, even though they affect the final result (that is, the path is important for determining the equilibrium, or indeed, whether equilibrium is achieved). For if the authorities do not allow some monetary expansion, unemployment and under-utilisation will result; and if they do allow it, the effects of the devaluation will be weakened and perhaps undermined. That various groups attempt to maintain their pre-devaluation income poses a more acute problem in the case of devaluation from open deficit than devaluation from suppressed deficit, since in the latter case much of the adjustment toward equilibrium income distribution will already have been made, except insofar as some firms and individuals are profiting from quantitative restrictions. Since developing countries generally do rely on quantitative restrictions before devaluation, and since they also generally have some open deficit in spite of their *ad hoc* adjustments, the problem remains a practical one.

In the event, price-wage spiralling does not generally get out of control, at least within the year or so following devaluation. Twelve months after devaluation, wholesale prices of imported goods will generally have risen, but by less than the devaluation (after having fallen from a peak reached three or four months after devaluation, as noted earlier), general wholesale prices will have risen less than this, consumer prices will have risen by about the same as wholesale prices and, except where devaluations are small, manufacturing wages will have risen by less than consumer prices, showing a decline in real wages following the devaluation (see the last column of Table 9.I, which shows a decline in real wages for half the countries for which data are available, and negligible increases in several others, despite continued growth in output). Thus nonwage incomes of employed factors – mostly profits and rents – show an increase in real terms a year later, and it is this increase that provides the incentive for the necessary reallocation of resources, which reallocation may ultimately restore and even raise real wages, depending on the relative factor intensities in the export industries as opposed to the protected industries.

Thus, to sum up briefly the experience following devaluations in less developed countries, it seems that official anxieties concerning the economic effects are exaggerated. The firmest generalisation that can be made is that country experiences are highly diverse, which of course may be unsettling to cautious officials. But, for a hypothetical 'representative' country, devaluation seems to improve both the trade balance and the payments position within the first year; it does not seem to lead to deterioration in the terms of trade of any consequence; it does lead to price increases, but not by amounts great enough to undermine the devaluation; price increases of imports are substantially less than the devaluation, suggesting that importer margins have been reduced; real wages fall; and there is a slump in economic activity following the devaluation.

The political impact
The fourth apprehension concerns the political fate of those responsible for the decision to devalue, and here the experience is not nearly so encouraging. A naive test is whether the government fell within a year of the devaluation. In nearly 30 per cent of the cases examined it did. Some of these changes in government were clearly unrelated to the devaluation – Costa Rica and Colombia each happened to have elections within the year, for example, and both countries have quite regularly voted out the incumbent government in recent history, devaluation or not. But in other cases the devaluation and associated policies for managing the economy were the main issue on which the government fell. And there were near misses in both Israel (1962) and India (1966), where the ruling government came under severe criticism for its decision to devalue, but survived the crisis for more than a year.

A check was provided by examining a random control group of similar countries that did not devalue; and governments changed within the year in only 14 per cent of the control sample. Thus it appears that devaluation – or the policies that led to the need for devaluation or the policies that followed it – roughly doubles the chance that a ruling group will be removed from power. But the test will have to be refined considerably before it can be regarded as anything more than suggestive, in particular by selecting a control group from countries that seem to be in some balance-of-payments difficulty, either of an open or a suppressed type, rather than just from all developing countries.

Ministers of finance fared much worse. Nearly 60 per cent of them lost their jobs in the year following devaluation – half of them of course when their governments fell – compared with a turnover in a control group of only 18 per cent. So the chances of ouster for the official immediately responsible seems to increase by a factor of three as a result of devaluation. Again the test should be refined. And, in any case, losing one's job as finance minister does not necessarily end a political career; James Callaghan of Britain felt obliged to resign after devaluing sterling, but was immediately made Home Secretary.

III. CONCLUSIONS

Managing a devaluation through the transition phase to final success requires both judgment and delicacy in handling. Consider first the problem of aggregate demand. As we noted, this frequently falls following a devaluation, and unless the economy was badly overheated beforehand it may lead to a drop in profits and employment. If the slump is sufficiently severe and prolonged, it will evoke calls for expansionary action by the government, for few governments these days can escape responsibility for developments in their economies. If the government then yields to these pressures, the expansionary policies may come when devaluation-induced export expansion is also taking hold with a lag, and thereby increase demand pressures on the economy at just the wrong time. The better course of action, on these grounds, would be to mitigate the slump – that is, to take some modest *expansionary* action with or immediately following the devaluation, contrary to the usual advice – and then to draw back with monetary and fiscal policy when new export demand is becoming important. Properly timed, this would reduce the social and economic costs of the slump and would prevent belated expansionary action, in response to political pressure, from undermining the effects of the devaluations on the trade balance.

On the other hand, we have also seen that there is often a sharp increase in prices in the period immediately following devaluation,

CURRENCY DEVALUATION IN DEVELOPING COUNTRIES

as importers attempt to pass on to their customers all or most of the increased cost of foreign goods. To the extent that these price increases, some of which are not otherwise sustainable, get built into wages and other local costs, they will undermine the devaluation. Timing here becomes crucial. The authorities should do what they can to reduce the temporary increase in prices (lest it become permanent), to make sure that it comes quickly and is brief, and to delay any wage settlements or administered price increases until after the peak of import prices has been reached and they are falling.

The size of the temporary increase in prices can be influenced by the speed and extent of import liberalisation, and this argues for liberalising imports at once with devaluation (or even before, if that can be done without signalling the intention to devalue), instead of waiting for several months as most countries have done. With respect to the promptness with which prices of imported goods begin to fall after their initial rise, the slump in total demand reinforces the desired outcome, and this factor cuts against the suggestion above that the slump should be mitigated. The timing of prospective wage settlements should if possible be taken into account in choosing the time to devalue, the aim being to allow a considerable lapse of time between devaluation and major wage settlements. Necessary increases in administered prices, such as those of public utilities or of industries in the public sector, should also be delayed until the temporary rise is past and some prices are falling. Finally, seasonality of food prices should also be taken into account; devaluations immediately after a good harvest are more likely to achieve prolonged success than are devaluations after a poor harvest or before the new harvest is in, when food stocks are low and food prices are rising. Bad harvests, in particular, have greatly weakened the impact of several devaluations, notably those of India in 1966 and Colombia in 1962.

New investment in the export sector will take place only if investors believe that the change in relative prices achieved through devaluation is a reasonably durable one. Thus, in terms of the timing of export response, *expectations* about the capacity and the will of the authorities to keep the economy under control are as important as their actual success in doing so. Here history lives in the present. A country with a poor record of monetary and fiscal management, and with a history of inflation, is likely to have greater difficulty in bringing about the required reallocation of resources than one with more favourable experience in these respects. A slump, deep if not prolonged, may (regrettably) be necessary in such a country in order to establish a new pattern of expectations.

Thus there is a dilemma with respect to macroeconomic management in the period immediately following a devaluation, and in the end the authorities must inevitably tailor their policies to the particular requirements of the country, to some extent even playing by ear. Short-term economic management of this type remains very much an art.

At the same time, the apparent political consequences of devaluation – an increased probability that governments will lose their positions and ministers their jobs – is unsettling. For it means that there may be a sharp conflict between the personal interests of those in authority and the interests of the country, a conflict that has to be resolved by those same persons, and which too often may be resolved at the expense of the country. This conflict perhaps plays an even greater role than the 'social contract' considerations outlined earlier in leading to procrastination over devaluation and an attempt to substitute *ad hoc* restrictions and subventions.

It would thus be desirable to depoliticise the whole question of devaluation by making it less traumatic both for the officials and for the public. This suggests another reason, in addition to the economic ones, for moving toward greater flexibility of exchange rates, along the lines of the gliding parity, as Brazil and Colombia have done. Gradual changes in exchange rates would not only eliminate the political jolt and major economic dislocations following a large discrete devaluation, with its sharp alteration of relative prices and hence of factor incomes, but would also avoid the major misallocation of resources that takes place as a disequilibrium builds up under a fixed exchange rate. Taking exchange-rate changes in small, frequent steps would also help to resolve the dilemma posed above: a slump would not be necessary to redirect resources into export industries.

10

Some Misconceptions on the Sharing of the Burden of Adjustment between Deficit and Surplus Countries

JACQUES L'HUILLIER
Graduate Institute of International Studies

The idea that the burden of balance-of-payments adjustment falls more heavily on deficit than on surplus countries is commonly found in economic literature. Those who condemn this sharing of the burden of adjustment as inequitable usually see as its source the limited supply of international liquidity. Under a system of fixed exchange rates, disequilibrium results in a shift of international liquidity from deficit to surplus countries; the former would then be compelled to re-establish equilibrium under the menace of a run on reserves while the latter could ignore their reserve surplus since they are not subjected to such a menace.

This injustice, however, is not inevitable, it is said. It does not arise under a system of completely flexible exchange rates. And it need not arise even under a fixed exchange-rate system. It was absent from the classical adjustment mechanism because the change in relative price levels came about through the simultaneous rise of prices in the surplus countries and fall of prices in deficit countries. It is argued, however, that the classical mechanism no longer functions and that under today's fixed exchange-rate system international co-operation is required to distribute the burden of adjustment equitably between deficit and surplus countries.

Yet, this view is highly questionable, in spite of its apparent simplicity, for it is based on several misconceptions. First, the concept of the burden of adjustment is not clearly defined. Secondly, no mention is made of the burden of disequilibrium. Finally, countries' responsibilities for creating the disequilibrium are not taken into consideration.

Classical theory will serve as a point of departure. I will try to show that it is incorrect to cite classical writers as authority for making the reabsorption of imbalances in international payments an obligation of surplus countries. Classical theory can also help eliminate misconceptions concerning the purported need to modify the distribution of the burden of readjustment.

Finally, I will look at the problem as it arises today and attempt to destroy the myth that deficit countries are the martyrs of the international economy.

I. THE CLASSICAL CONCEPTS OF DISEQUILIBRIUM AND ADJUSTMENT IN INTERNATIONAL PAYMENTS

1. *Equilibrium*

I will begin with the meaning of equilibrium for the classical writers.

Let us assume that only trade in goods and services takes place and that capital transactions are excluded.

Comparative costs are determined by factor endowments in various countries and by technology. Differences in comparative costs from one economy to another are the source of the gains from international trade.

In a monetary economy, the existence of distinct national monetary units among which exchange rates are fixed must be taken into account. Costs and prices (which are equal to costs under the assumption of competition) of goods and services in different countries can be compared through exchange rates. Comparative costs are thus translated into comparative advantage. Reciprocal demand reacts to these price differentials giving rise to trade flows. Suppose that trade, and thus payments, are in equilibrium at existing exchange rates. There are then clear gains from international trade since each country pays for its imports entirely with exports and is assured that the goods it imports are obtained more cheaply through exports than through home production.

In this state of equilibrium all economies are in full employment. Full employment output is equal to income which, in turn, is entirely spent. Part of this income is spent on foreign goods and services. Conversely, a portion of the rest of the world's income is spent on the output of each country. As the imports and exports of each country are equal by assumption, world demand for goods and services is distributed among countries in proportion to national contributions to world production.

Sharing of the Burden of Adjustment

2. Disequilibrium and adjustment

According to classical theorists, disequilibrium arises only as a consequence of real changes, or, more precisely, from structural transformations in the economy; that is modification of comparative costs following a change in factor endowments or in technology, or a change in tastes. Countries develop deficits if the relative cost of their goods increases thus leading to a fall in foreign demand, if the taste of residents for foreign goods grows, or if foreign preferences for home goods diminish. In all cases aggregate demand for domestic output decreases by the amount of the deficit, and under-employment of the same magnitude sets in.

However, compensatory gold financing lowers the price level in deficit countries relative to that in surplus countries by shrinking the money supply of the former and expanding that of the latter. This fall in relative prices brings about a new set of comparative advantages that re-establishes trade equilibrium. Once adjustment is complete, (former) deficit countries are again in a state of full employment.

3. The problem of sharing the burden of adjustment

This problem did not exist for classical economists.

(i) The terms of trade of deficit countries do indeed deteriorate and those of surplus countries improve. But this phenomenon is not a consequence of the adjustment process. It is the consequence of the structural changes that have taken place in the economy. Changes in the relative price levels serve only to establish the new pattern of comparative advantage that corresponds to the structural changes.

(ii) A worsening of the terms of trade of deficit countries implies that for each quantity of imports these countries must supply a greater quantity of exports than before. The under-employment that accompanies disequilibrium in deficit countries helps to provide the spare production capacity needed to cope with the alteration in terms of trade necessary to establish the new equilibrium position. Under-employment is short-lived.

(iii) Deficit countries do not risk an exhaustion of their international reserves, nor are surplus countries threatened with excessive accumulation of international liquidity. For, national money supplies and international liquidity are in perfect osmosis. This is obvious if money is metallic. If money supplies are fiduciary and if the currency principle is observed, money is, in effect, constituted of gold certificates.

According to the strict interpretation of the quantity theory of money, the size of national product and the need for money are exactly proportional. The change in the terms of trade mentioned above modifies the relative importance of nominal national products and consequently the relative needs for money of the countries involved. The compensatory financing that occurred during disequilibrium brought about a redistribution of the world money supply corresponding to these new money needs.

4. *Capital flows*

The classical conclusions above remain valid when capital movements are taken into account.

In each country all current saving is available for investment and is actually used entirely to finance investment. Globally, world savings can be distributed among national capital markets according to differences in the marginal efficiency of capital in a pattern different from that of original saving formation.

Starting from equilibrium an increase in the marginal efficiency of capital in one country relative to the rest of the world will attract savings from abroad. That country will develop a surplus and the rest of the world a deficit. Temporary under-employment will emerge in the deficit countries because investment can take place only in an amount equal to available saving within these countries, in other words in a lesser amount than domestic saving formation.

Adjustment then occurs through flows of goods and services, under the same conditions as described above.

II. THE 'BURDEN' OF ADJUSTMENT AND OF DISEQUILIBRIUM IN THE CONTEMPORARY WORLD

1. *Internal equilibrium*

If costs and prices are rigid downward, the decrease in demand that falls on production in the deficit countries will be amplified through the multiplier effect. It is no longer only a matter, as in the classical mechanism, of creating the spare production capacity needed to cope with the changed terms of trade.

Adjustment is nevertheless possible, since a decrease in income produces a fall in imports; however, the fall in income and product is a multiple of the fall in imports. The depression that accompanies adjustment in deficit countries may be intolerable.

On the other hand, we have also learned since the time of the classical economists that an economy does not automatically remain in a state of full employment even if payments are in equilibrium. It can undergo a depression, either spontaneously or because of unwise monetary or fiscal policies. When under-employment hits some countries, they tend to develop an external surplus and their depression spreads to other countries, which in turn tend to develop deficits. By not combating depression at home the former are responsible for creating a disequilibrium and impose a burden on the latter during the period of disequilibrium. In other words, international payments disequilibrium arises not only from structural change but also from national policy.

Under such conditions deficit countries can rightly consider themselves victims. This was often the case in the 1930s. The regrettable circumstances of the inter-war period have greatly contributed to the creation of a bias in favour of deficit countries, an attitude that has survived the radically changed conditions of the post-war period.

Since World War II, to the extent that national policies have affected international payments equilibrium, the typical case has been that of countries letting inflation rather than depression take hold of their economies. They develop a deficit and inflation spreads to surplus countries. If the deficit country's authorities give the inflationary pressures free rein, no adjustment is possible since domestic demand continuously exceeds domestic output, or, equivalently the flow of loanable funds exceeds that of domestic saving. In this disequilibrium situation the surplus countries are contaminated by inflation; and it is only by adopting a deliberate policy of accelerating inflation at home that they can hope to see their misfortune at least contribute to the restoration of payments equilibrium.

2. *The qualitative deterioration of international transactions and the distortion of the terms of trade*

In these changed post-war circumstances, it is not surprising to find persistent disequilibria instead of the temporary ones contemplated by classical economists.

In such circumstances, comparative advantage ratios become biased. The terms of trade of deficit countries improve and those of surplus countries deteriorate unjustifiably in comparison to the terms of trade that would rule under payments equilibrium. Moreover, the nature of international capital movements also changes; for, interest-rate differentials are now governed more by divergences in national monetary policies than by variations in the flow of saving and in the expected rate of return on capital. Because of the close link between short- and long-term capital markets, these distortions affect long-term as well as short-term interest rates.

Both deficit and surplus countries suffer from this qualitative deterioration in trade and capital movements. But the fact remains that the inflationary policy of deficit countries is the basic cause of these disorders and that the terms of trade of surplus countries deteriorate unjustly.

When deficit countries try to implement adjustment policies, they frequently experience great difficulties because they have waited too long. On the one hand, even if surplus countries have paid their price in the form of a dose of inflation, the inflation that deficit countries have inflicted upon themselves is such that their general cost and price level is now seriously out of line in relation to that of surplus countries with the result that a deflationary policy on the part of the deficit countries brings on a serious recession yet without succeeding in re-establishing external equilibrium. Past inflation also diminishes the effectiveness of restrictive monetary policy by generating expectations of future price rises.

This is how cases of 'difficult' adjustment problems multiply, where deficit countries suffer from recession and surplus countries from inflation, 'dilemma' situations that can be remedied only by adjustment of currency parities. Yet, deficit countries too often interpret the change in the exchange rate as the freedom to return immediately to an outright expansionary policy, even before the inflationary reflexes of the public have subsided.

During the adjustment period when the change in exchange rates helps to restore equilibrium, the trend in the terms of trade reverses itself: the terms of deficit countries deteriorate and those of surplus countries improve. The deficit countries have the impression of being on the losing side, forgetting that they benefited from artificially generous terms of trade during the disequilibrium period.

3. *International liquidity and the problem of the burden of adjustment*
During the last decade the question of a possible shortage of international liquidity has often been discussed. It was once thought that the amount of liquidity necessary for continuity in international

payments under a fixed exchange-rate system could be determined objectively. The criterion most often proposed was an increase in international liquidity proportional to the growth of international trade in visibles. Unfortunately, these attempts at determining an objective criterion have not been successful if only because they imply that it is possible to find a period of reference when the 'need' for liquidity was equal to the existing stock.

The role of international liquidity is to permit stabilisation of exchange rates until adjustment policies – monetary or fiscal – have taken hold. This grace period must be long enough for deficit countries not to be forced, under pressure, to establish exchange controls or to resort prematurely to parity changes.

This role, however, is distorted if countries in disequilibrium do not take appropriate corrective measures. We have argued above that the responsibility for the emergence of disequilibria since the last war rests primarily with the deficit countries. The indifference many of them have shown toward their external balance explains the extraordinary persistence of these disequilibria.

Under these conditions, one can no longer speak of the need for liquidity on an aggregate world level, for deficit and surplus countries experience this need in extremely different degrees.

For the deficit countries, international liquidity is always insufficient since the excessive duration of their deficits exposes them to the exhaustion of their reserves.

The United States is in a special position because the rest of the world's demand for dollar reserves gave Americans the power to create international liquidity. Strictly speaking, the external balance of the United States was not in deficit, for the accumulation of dollar holdings by non-residents, governmental or private, could be interpreted as a continuous inflow of short-term capital offsetting the negative entries in other parts of the external accounts. It was only when non-residents became less eager to hold dollar balances that the United States was faced with serious difficulties. A real payments 'deficit' appeared from the moment it became necessary to revive non-residents' waning enthusiasm by such devices as tight monetary policy or exchange guarantees.

The point of view of surplus countries is quite different. For them, the contemporary world suffers from an over-abundance rather than a shortage of international liquidity. It is precisely because it seems senseless to invest such an important part of their resources in reserves that they are led to initiate measures to correct disequilibrium, even though they are not responsible for it, by yielding to inflation or revaluing their currency.

Not only do surplus countries feel drowned in international liquidity; they also object to the composition of this liquidity. They find the emphasis on paper money exaggerated. The preference several of these countries have for gold is not as irrational as it may seem. These are not primitive beings attracted to a barbaric relic. Instead they reason, quite simply, that gold, unlike other forms of liquidity, would retain its value as a commodity even if it was demoted from its monetary function. When surplus countries accumulate other forms of international liquidity, they feel that after a certain point they no longer receive payment for their surplus but only provide credit for deficit countries. It should be noted that this impression is not related to the source of the liquidity. This reaction does not occur because liquidity is created by credit operations as in the case, for example, of dollar holdings created by swap agreements. It could also occur in the case of metal if metal were no longer desired.

Finally, one must take into account the consequences of a revaluation for the real value of the reserves of surplus countries and compare them to those of a devaluation of deficit countries' currencies, including the dollar.

As far as dollar reserves are concerned, it does not matter whether deficit countries devalue or surplus countries revalue; in either case the purchasing power of the dollars does not change in the United States and the other deficit countries. If dollar holders benefit from an exchange-rate guarantee in relation to their own currency (as is the case for dollars acquired through swap agreements or for Roosa bonds) there is no difference either, since this guarantee applies if the debtor's currency is devalued as well as if the holder's currency is revalued.

The effects are different with respect to gold reserves and forms of liquidity whose value is defined in terms of gold such as super gold tranches at the IMF or SDRs. If deficit countries devalue, the purchasing power of these forms of liquidity held by surplus countries rises immediately in deficit countries and remains unchanged in surplus countries. If surplus countries revalue, the purchasing power of the reserves in question remains the same in deficit countries but falls in surplus countries.

Sharing of the Burden of Adjustment

In this brief note I have tried to show that the surplus countries are not the villains of the play as the deficit countries sometimes make them out to be. There is reason to believe that the misunderstandings that surround this issue are not foreign to the malaise which is currently eroding the international monetary system.

11

The Monetary Approach to Balance-of-Payments Theory

HARRY G. JOHNSON
*London School of Economics
and Political Science and the
University of Chicago*

My purpose in this essay is to present the main outline of a new approach to the theory of the balance of payments and of balance-of-payments adjustment (including devaluation and revaluation) that has been emerging in recent years from several sources. Concretely, this new approach is to be found, on the one hand, in the change in policy orientation adopted by the British Government under pressure from the International Monetary Fund after the failure of the devaluation of 1967 to produce the expected improvement in the British balance of payments, the theoretical basis for this new orientation being traceable to the work of the Dutch economist, J. J. Koopmans. On the other hand this new approach finds its origins in the theoretical work of my colleagues at the University of Chicago – R. A. Mundell and his students – though it is only fair to note that economists elsewhere have been working along similar lines. Its essence is to put at the forefront of analysis the monetary rather than the relative price aspects of international adjustment.

To put the new approach in perspective, it is helpful to go back to the origins of balance-of-payments theory in the work of David Hume, and specifically his contribution of the analysis of the price-specie-flow mechanism. Hume was concerned to refute the concentration of the mercantilists on the objective of accumulating precious metals within the country, and their consequent recommendation of policies designed to bring about a surplus on the balance of payments. His analysis, couched in terms relevant to the emerging new approach to balance-of-payments theory, showed that the amount of money in a country would be adjusted automatically to the demand for it, through surpluses or deficits in the balance of payments, induced by the effects on relative national money price levels of excess supplies of or excess demands for money. Hence the mercantilist desire to accumulate 'treasure' was in conflict with the basic mechanism of international monetary adjustment and could only be *ephemerally* successful.

Three points are worth noting about the price-specie-flow mechanism at this stage. First, in contemporary terminology, it assumes (in line with the stylised facts of that time) that all money is 'outside' money (precious metals). That is, there is no commercial or central banking system capable of creating money not backed by international reserves, domestic money and international reserves being the same thing. Second, the mechanism of adjustment focuses on international transactions in goods, as distinguished from securities, a characteristic that has remained dominant in balance-of-payments theory. Third, in the detailed analysis of the mechanism there is a rather awkward compromise between the assumption of a closed and of an open economy, in which it is assumed that domestic prices can vary from purchasing-power-parity under the influence of imbalances between money demand and money supply, but that such variations give rise to changes in trade flows which alter the balance of payments and hence the domestic stock of money in the longer run. As we shall see, the new approach to balance-of-payments theory, while basically Humean in spirit, places the emphasis not on relative price changes but on the direct influence of excess demand for or supply of money on the balance between income and expenditure, or more generally between total acquisition and disposal of funds whether through production and consumption or through borrowing and lending, and therefore on the overall balance of payments.

Hume's analysis ran in terms of an automatic mechanism of international adjustment motivated by money flows and consequential changes in national money price levels. The subsequent elaboration of the theory, up to and partly through the 1930s, retained the general notion of automaticity while adding in the complications required by the existence of credit money provided by commercial banks and of central banking based on partial international reserve holdings, and by the possibility of attraction or otherwise of international short-term capital movements through international interest-rate differentials. In addition, Cassel contributed the purchasing-power-parity theory of the equilibrium determination of the values of floating exchange rates.

In the 1930s under the stimulus on the one hand of the collapse of the international regime of fixed exchange rates and the emergence of mass unemployment as a major economic problem, and on the other hand of the Keynesian revolution – which altered the basic assumptions of theory from wage and price flexibility with full employment to wage rigidity with normal mass unemployment – a new approach to balance-of-payments theory emerged which viewed international adjustment not as an automatic process but as a policy problem for governments. The key problem, the classic article on which is Joan Robinson's essay on the foreign exchanges, was the conditions under which a devaluation would improve a country's balance of payments. Under Keynesian assumptions of wage rigidity, a devaluation would change the real prices of domestic goods relative to foreign goods in the foreign and domestic markets and thereby promote substitutions in production and consumption. Again, under Keynesian assumptions of mass unemployment, any repercussions of these substitutions on the demand for domestic output could be assumed to be met by variations in output and employment, and repercussions of such variations onto the balance of payments could be regarded as secondary. Finally, if the same assumptions are combined with the general Keynesian denigration of the influence of money on the economy and concentration on the short run, the connections between the balance of payments and the money supply, and between the money supply and aggregate demand, could be disregarded. Attention was therefore concentrated on the 'elasticity conditions' required for the impact effect of a devaluation – that is, of the associated change in relative real prices – to be an improvement in the balance of payments. These conditions were, for a simple model with perfectly elastic supplies and initially balanced trade, that the sum of the elasticities of home and foreign demand for imports should exceed unity (the so-called 'Marshall–Lerner condition'); for more complex models, assuming independent elasticities of demands for imports and supplies of exports, a fearfully complex algebraic expression, cumbersome but challenging to derive and explore. (Much of the interest in this body of work lay in the related questions of whether a devaluation that improved the balance of payments would necessarily turn a country's terms of trade against it and increase domestic employment.)

The so-called 'elasticity approach' to devaluation proved demonstrably unsatisfactory in the immediate postwar period of full and over-full employment, owing to its implicit assumption of the existence of unemployed resources that could be mobilised to produce the additional exports and import-substitutes required to satisfy a favorable impact-effect. Recognition of this by the profession came in three versions. One version was carping at the irrelevance of 'orthodox theory' (which the elasticity approach really was not), and was generally associated with the recommendation of exchange controls and quantitative import restrictions as an alternative to devaluation. The second was S. S. Alexander's 'absorption approach', which argued essentially that a favourable effect from devaluation alone, in a fully employed economy, depends not on elasticities but requires that the inflation resulting from the devaluation in these conditions produce a reduction in aggregate absorption relative to aggregate productive capacity. One part of the mechanism that might bring this about in Alexander's analysis is worth mentioning as foreshadowing the new approach to be discussed below; the 'real balance effect', by which the rise in prices consequent on the excess demand generated by devaluation deflates the real value of the domestic money supply and so induces a reduction in spending out of income.

The presentation of the 'absorption approach' as an alternative to the 'elasticity approach' led to considerable controversy and extensive efforts to reconcile the two. The truth lies, however, in the recognition that a fully employed economy cannot use devaluation alone as a policy instrument for correcting a balance-of-payments deficit. It must use a combination of devaluation – to obtain an allocation of foreign and domestic demand among domestic and foreign output consistent with balance-of-payments equilibrium – and deflation – to match aggregate domestic demand with aggregate domestic supply. More generally, it must use a proper combination of what I have elsewhere called 'expenditure-reducing' and 'expenditure-switching' policies. This general principle is developed at length in James Meade's classic book on *The Theory of International Economic Policy: The Balance of Payments*, though it was known before. It constitutes the third, and most useful, version of the recognition of the inadequacies of the 'elasticity approach' and also provides a synthesis between that approach and the 'absorption approach' that is logically satisfactory (though not economically satisfactory from the point of view of the new monetary approach). Unfortunately, Meade presented his analysis in terms of a short-run equilibrium analysis and on the assumption that the policy-makers understood the theory as well as he did, both of which characteristics made the book extremely inaccessible to policy-makers and may help to account for the bumbling of British demand-management policy after the devaluation of 1967. Also, following the tradition of British central banking and monetary theory, Meade identified monetary policy with the fixing of the level of interest rates, a procedure that automatically excludes consideration of the monetary consequences of devaluation by assuming them to be absorbed by the monetary authorities (this is the reason for the economic objection to the Meade synthesis mentioned above).

Subsequent to the work of Meade and others in the 1950s, the main development in conventional balance-of-payments theory has been the development of the theory of the fiscal-monetary policy mix following the pioneering contributions of R. A. Mundell. In the general logic of the Meade system, a country has to have two policy instruments if it is to achieve simultaneously internal and external balance (full employment and balance-of-payments equilibrium). In Meade's system, the instruments are demand management by fiscal and/or monetary policy, and the exchange rate (or controls, or wage-price flexibility). What if wages are rigid, and controls and exchange-rate changes are ruled out by national and international political considerations? A solution can still be found, at least in principle, if capital is internationally mobile in response to interest rate differentials. Fiscal expansion and monetary expansion then have the same effects on the current account, increasing imports and possibly decreasing exports, but opposite effects on the capital account: fiscal expansion increases domestic interest rates and attracts a capital inflow while monetary expansion has the opposite effect; it follows that the two policies can be 'mixed' so as to achieve a capital account surplus or deficit equal to the current account deficit or surplus at the level of full employment of the economy. This extension of the Meade approach has lent itself to almost infinite mathematical product differentiation, with little significant improvement in quality of economic product, and will not concern us further except to note that theoretical investigation of the model led naturally into the question of what would happen if capital were perfectly mobile, and more specifically into the implications of this assumption for the ability of the monetary authority to control the domestic money supply.

To recapitulate, the essential structure of what may be termed the standard model of balance-of-payments theory is a Keynesian model of income determination in which flows of consumption and investment expenditure are determined by aggregate income and demand-management policy variables (taxes and expenditures, and interest rates), and where the level of exports and the division of total expenditure between domestic and foreign goods (imports) are determined by the exchange rate which fixes the relative real prices of exports relative to foreign prices and of imports relative to domestic prices. By showing a proper mix of demand-management policies and the exchange rate, the authorities can obtain full employment consistently with any current-account surplus or deficit. The net current-account surplus (or deficit) is equal to the excess (or deficiency) of the economy's flow of production over its flow of absorption, or to the excess (or deficiency) of its exports over its imports, or to the net excess (deficiency) of the flow of savings in relation to the flow of investment. By convention, but by no means necessarily, the current-account surplus or deficit is identified with the overall balance-of-payments position; it is easy enough to incorporate in the analysis the determination of the balance on capital account by the differential between domestic and foreign interest rates, as is in fact done in the theory of the fiscal-monetary policy mix.

The basic assumption on which this system of balance-of-payments analysis rests, and which forms the point of departure of the new 'monetary' approach to balance-of-payments theory, is that the monetary consequences of balance-of-payments surpluses or deficits can be and are absorbed (sterilised) by the monetary authorities so that a surplus or deficit can be treated as a flow equilibrium. The new approach assumes – in some cases, asserts – that these monetary inflows or outflows associated with surpluses or deficits are not sterilised – or cannot be, within a period relevant to policy analysis – but instead influence the domestic money supply. Since the demand for money is a demand for a stock and not a flow, variation of the supply of money relative to the demand for it associated with deficit or surplus must work towards an equilibrium between money demand and money supply with a corresponding equilibration of the balance of payments. Deficits and surpluses represent phases of stock adjustment in the money market and not equilibrium flows, and should not be treated within an analytical framework that treats them as equilibrium phenomena.

It should be noted, however, that this criticism applies to the use of the standard model for the analysis and policy prescription of situations involving deficits or surpluses; where the standard model is used for the analysis of the policies required to secure balance-of-payments equilibrium, it is generally not subject to this criticism because by assumption the domestic money market will be in equilibrium. But even in this case the fiscal-monetary mix version of it is open to criticism for confusing stock-adjustment in the market for securities, in response to a change in interest-rate differentials between national capital markets, with a flow equilibrium.

In order to obtain flow equilibrium deficits or surpluses on the basis of stock adjustments in the money market (and also possibly the securities market), it is necessary to construct a model in which the need for stock adjustments is being continuously re-created by economic change – in other words, to analyse an economy, or an international economy, in which economic growth is going on. This is one of the important technical differences between the new 'monetary' models of the balance of payments and the standard Keynesian model – and a potent source of difficulty in comparing the results of the two types of analysis.

A further difference between the two types of models is that the 'monetary' models almost invariably assume – in contrast to the emphasis of the standard model on the influence of relative prices on trade flows – that a country's price level is pegged to the world price level and must move rigidly in line with it. One justification for this assumption is that, at least among the advanced industrial countries, industrial competition is so pervasive that elasticities of substitution among the industrial products of the various countries approximate more closely to infinity than to the relatively low numbers implicit in the standard model. Another and more sophisticated justification is derivable from the general framework of the monetarist approach, namely that changes in relative national price levels can only be transitory concomitants of the process of stock-adjustment to monetary disequilibrium and that in the longer-run analysis of balance-of-payments phenomena among growing economies attention should be focused on long-run equilibrium price relationships – which for simplicity can most easily be taken as constant.

This point has sometimes been put in terms of the positive charge that the standard model rests on 'money illusion', in the sense that it assumes that workers will accept a reduction in their real standard of living brought about by a devaluation which they would not accept in the form of a forced reduction of domestic money wages. An alternative version of this charge is that the standard model assumes that workers can be cheated out of their real marginal product by devaluation. The charge, however, is incorrect: if rectification of a balance-of-payments deficit requires that the domestic marginal product of labour in terms of foreign goods falls, because the price of domestic goods relative to foreign goods must be reduced in the foreign and home markets to induce substitution between these goods favourable to the balance of payments, it requires no money illusion but only economic realism for the workers to accept this fact. Applications of the standard model to the case of devaluation, however, do require the assumption of money illusion if the elasticities of substitution between domestic and foreign goods are in fact high (approximately infinite), and it is nevertheless assumed that wages will remain unchanged in terms of domestic currency. For in this case it is being expected that workers will be content to accept wages below the international value of their marginal product, and that employers will not be driven by competition for labour in the face of this disequilibrium to bid wages up to their marginal productivity levels. The issue therefore is not one of the standard model wrongly assuming the presence of money illusion on the part of the workers, but of its possibly wrongly assuming low elasticities of substitution between domestic and foreign goods – which is an error in empirical assumptions rather than in model construction.

One further difference between the two types of model of balance-of-payments theory is worth noting. Whereas the Keynesian model assumes that employment and output are variable at (relatively) constant prices and wages, the monetary models assume that output and employment tend to full employment levels, with reactions to changes taking the form of price and wage adjustments. This difference mirrors a broader difference between the Keynesian and quantity theory approaches to monetary theory for the closed economy. The assumption of full employment in the monetary balance-of-payments models can be defended on the grounds that these models are concerned with the longer run, and that for this perspective the assumption of full employment is more appropriate than the assumption of general mass unemployment for the actual world economy since the end of World War II.

I now turn from the discussion of theoretical issues in model-construction to an exposition of some monetarist models of balance-of-payments behaviour in a growing world economy. The models to be constructed are extremely simple, inasmuch as they concentrate on the overall balance of the balance of payments, i.e. on the trend of international reserve acquisition or loss, and ignore the composition of the balance of payments as between current account, capital account, and overall balance, as well as the question of changes in the structure of the balance-of-payments accounts that may occur as a country passes through various stages of economic growth. Nevertheless they will, I hope, provide some interesting insights into balance-of-payments phenomena.

To begin with, it is useful to develop some general expressions relating the growth rates of economic aggregates to the growth rates of their components or of the independent variables to which they are functionally related. These can be established by elementary calculus, and are merely stated here. In the formulas, g is the growth rate per unit of time of a subscripted aggregate or variable, A and B are components of an aggregate, $f(A,B)$ is a function of A and B, and η denotes the elasticity of the aggregate defined by the function with respect to the subscripted variable. Then we have

$$g_{A+B} = \frac{A}{A+B}g_A + \frac{B}{A+B}g_B$$

$$g_{A-B} = \frac{A}{A-B}g_A - \frac{B}{A-B}g_B$$

$$g_{AB} = g_A + g_B$$

$$g_{A/B} = g_A - g_B$$

$$g_{f(A,B)} = \eta_A g_A + \eta_B g_B$$

(where η denotes an elasticity).

I begin with a discussion of monetary equilibrium in a single country, maintaining a fixed exchange rate with the rest of the world, assumed to be growing over time, and small enough and diversified enough in relation to the world economy for its price level to be the world price level, and its interest rate the world interest rate. (Differentials between domestic and foreign prices indices, or between domestic and foreign interest rates, could readily be allowed for, provided they are assumed fixed by economic conditions.) In addition, it is assumed that the supply of money is instantaneously adjusted to the demand for it, because the residents of the country can get rid of or acquire money either through the international market for commodities or through the international securities market. Which mechanism of adjustment of money supply to money demand prevails will determine the way in which monetary policy affects the composition of the balance of payments, but that is a question not pursued in the present analysis.

The consequence of these assumptions is that domestic monetary policy does not determine the domestic money supply but instead determines only the division of the backing of the money supply the public demands, between international reserves and domestic credit. Monetary policy, in other words, controls the volume of domestic credit and not the money supply; and control over domestic credit controls the balance of payments and thus the behaviour of the country's international reserves.

The demand for money may be simply specified as

$$M_d = pf(y,i)$$

where M_d is the nominal quantity of domestic money demanded, y is real output, i is the interest rate or alternative opportunity cost of holding money, p is the foreign and therefore domestic price level, and multiplication of the demand for real balances $f(y,i)$ by p assumes the standard homogeneity postulate of monetary theory. The supply of money is

$$M_s = R + D$$

where R is the international reserve and D the domestic credit or domestic assets backing of the money supply. Since by assumption M_s must be equal to M_d,

$$R = M_d - D$$

and

$$g_R = \frac{1}{R}B(t) = \frac{M_d}{R}g_{M_d} - \frac{D}{R}g_D,$$

where $B(t) = \dfrac{dR}{dt}$ is the current overall balance of payments. Letting $r = \dfrac{R}{M_s} = \dfrac{R}{M_d}$, the initial international reserve ratio, and substituting for g_{M_d},

$$g_R = \frac{1}{r}(g_p + \eta_y g_y + \eta_i g_i) - \frac{1-r}{r} g_D.$$

Simplifying by assuming constant world prices and interest rates,

$$g_R = \frac{1}{r}\eta_y g_y - \frac{1-r}{r} g_D,$$

that is reserve growth and the balance of payments are positively related to domestic economic growth and the income elasticity of demand for money, and negatively related to the rate of domestic credit expansion. Simplifying still further by assuming no domestic growth ($g_y = 0$)

$$g_R = -\frac{1-r}{r} g_D,$$

that is, reserve growth and the balance of payments are inversely related to the rate of domestic credit expansion.

These results are to be contrasted with various Keynesian theories about the relation between economic growth and the balance of payments. According to one such theory derived from the multiplier analysis, economic growth must worsen the balance of payments through increasing imports relative to exports; this theory neglects the influence of the demand for money on export supply and import demand and on the international flow of securities. According to another and more sophisticated theory, domestic credit expansion will tend to improve the balance of payments by stimulating investment and productivity increase and so lowering domestic prices in relation to foreign prices and improving the current account through the resulting substitutions of domestic for foreign goods in the foreign and domestic markets. This theory begs a number of questions even in naive Keynesian terms; in terms of the present approach it commits the error of attempting to deduce the consequences of domestic credit expansion from its presumed relative price effects without reference to the monetary aspect of balance-of-payments surpluses and deficits.

Henceforth the analysis will be simplified by assuming that world interest rates are constant, so that the growth of demand for real balances depends only on the growth of real output (the growth of demand for nominal money balances depends of course also on the rate of change of the price level). This assumption can be justified on the grounds that real rates of return on investment are relatively stable, and that money rates of interest in a longer-run growth context will be equal to real rates of return plus the (actual and expected) rate of world price inflation or minus the (actual and expected) rate of world price deflation.

The foregoing model was concerned with one small country in a large world economy. The next model considers monetary equilibrium in the world system as a whole. For initial simplicity it is assumed that there is a single world money, i.e. no national credit money supplementing international reserves. This assumption does considerable violence to reality, but it can be rationalised on the assumption that each national economy's domestic banking system can be compressed into a functional relation between its real output and its demand for real international reserves. The essential difference between this model and the preceding one is that the world price level becomes endogenous instead of exogenous, determined by the relation between the growth rates of demand for and supply of international reserves.

For the world economy, the growth rate of demand for international money, assuming the homogeneity postulate as before, is

$$g_{M_d} = \sum_i w_i \eta_{y_i} g_{y_i} + g_p,$$

where the w_i are initial country shares in the world money supply. Equilibrium requires $g_{M_d} = g_{M_s}$, where g_{M_s} is the growth rate of the world money supply. This requirement determines the rate of change of world prices:

$$g_p = g_{M_s} - \sum_i w_i \eta_{y_i} g_{y_i}.$$

The growth rate of an individual country's holdings of international money (which is also its balance-of-payments surplus, or deficit if negative, as a proportion of its initial reserves) is

$$\begin{aligned} g_{M_j} &= \eta_{y_j} g_{y_j} + g_p \\ &= \eta_{y_j} g_{y_j} + g_{M_s} - \sum_i w_i \eta_{y_i} g_{y_i} \\ &= g_{M_s} + (1 - w_j)\left(\eta_{y_j} g_{y_j} - \sum_{i \neq j} \frac{w_i}{1 - w_j} \eta_{y_i} g_{y_i} \right) \\ &= g_{M_s} + (1 - w_j)(\eta_{y_j} g_{y_j} - \overline{\eta_{y_i} g_{y_i}}), \end{aligned}$$

where the bar denotes the average product of income elasticity of demand for real balances and rate of growth of real income in the rest of the world, or

$$g_{M_j} = g_{M_s} + \eta_{y_j}g_{y_j} - \overline{\eta_y g_y},$$

when the bar denotes the average product of the two terms for the whole world economy.

A country will acquire world money (through a balance-of-payments surplus) faster or slower than the rate of world monetary expansion depending on whether the product of its income elasticity of demand for real balances and its growth rate of output exceeds or falls short of either this average product for the rest of the world or this average product for the whole world including itself. In the latter event it may lose international reserves even though total world reserves are growing.

If for further simplification it is assumed that the growth rate of world reserves is zero, the condition just stated determines whether the country has a surplus or a deficit. If for further simplification the income-elasticity of demand for real balances is assumed to be everywhere unity, the expression reduces to

$$g_{M_j} = (1-w_j)(g_{y_j} - \overline{g_{y_i}}) = g_{y_j} - \overline{g_y},$$

the bars successively denoting the average growth rate in the rest of the world and the average growth rate of the world as a whole. The country gains or loses reserves depending on whether its real growth rate is greater or smaller than the world average.

The preceding model aggregated national monetary systems into a demand for international money derived from real output. I now turn to a model in which the world economy possesses an international reserve money, but in which the residents of the various countries demand national monies which are based partly on international money reserves and partly on domestic credit. In the model, the total money supply for the world economy is

$$M = R + \sum_i D_i$$
$$= \sum_i w_i r_i M + \sum_i w_i(1-r_i)M,$$

where R is total international reserve money, D_i is domestic credit in country i; w_i is country i's share in the total world stock of money and r_i is country i's ratio of international reserve money to its domestic money supply.

BALANCE-OF-PAYMENTS THEORY

As before, the rate of growth of world demand for money is

$$g_{M_d} = \sum_i w_i \eta_{y_i} g_{y_i} + g_p.$$

The rate of growth of the world money supply is

$$g_{M_s} = \sum_i w_i r_i g_R + \sum_i w_i (1-r_i) g_{D_i}.$$

These two equations determine the rate of change of world prices, through the requirement that $g_{M_d} = g_{M_s}$:

$$g_p = \sum_i w_i r_i g_R + \sum_i w_i (1-r_i) g_{D_i} - \sum_i w_i \eta_{y_i} g_{y_i}.$$

From previous results, the growth rate of an individual country's reserves is

$$g_{r_j} = \frac{1}{r_j}(g_p + \eta_{y_j} g_{y_j}) - \frac{1-r_j}{r_j} g_{D_j}$$

$$= \frac{1}{r_j}\sum_i w_i r_i g_R + \frac{1}{r_j}\sum_i w_i (1-r_i) g_{D_i} + \frac{1}{r_j} \eta_{y_j} g_{y_j} -$$

$$- \frac{1}{r_j}\sum_i w_i \eta_{y_i} g_{y_i} - \frac{1-r_j}{r_j} g_{D_j}$$

$$= \frac{1}{r_j}\left\{\sum_i w_i r_i g_R + (\eta_{y_j} g_{y_j} - \overline{\eta_y g_y}) - [(1-r_j) g_{D_j} - \overline{(1-r) g_D}]\right\},$$

where the bars again indicate the average product of the barred terms for the world economy.

This expression indicates that a country's reserves will grow faster the lower its initial reserve ratio, the faster the growth of total world reserves, the higher its income elasticity of demand for money and its real growth rate relative to other countries, and the lower its international reserve ratio and rate of domestic credit expansion relative to other countries.

Simplifying by assuming that income elasticities of demand for money are everywhere unity, and that international reserve ratios are also the same everywhere, we obtain

$$g_{R_j} = g_R + \frac{1}{r}(g_{y_j} - \overline{g_y}) - \frac{1-r}{r}(g_{D_j} - \overline{g_D})$$

which shows that the growth rate of a country's reserves will on these assumptions tend to be faster than the world average if its real growth rate is greater than the world average, and slower than the world average if its rate of credit expansion is greater than the world average, and vice versa.

An alternative approach in this model is to formulate the money supply for the world in terms of the ratio of international reserves to total money stock r, initial shares in international reserves s_i, and initial ratios of domestic credit to reserves d_i. (Note that $r = 1/1+d$, where d is the ratio of credit to reserves.) Then

$$M = \sum_i s_i R + \sum_i d_i s_i R$$

$$g_{M_d} = \sum_i s_i(1+d_i)\eta_{y_i}g_{y_i} + g_p$$

$$g_{M_s} = r(g_R + \sum_i d_i s_i g_{D_i})$$

$$g_p = r(g_R + \sum_i d_i s_i g_{D_i}) - \sum_i s_i(1+d_i)\eta_{y_i}g_{y_i}$$

$$g_{R_j} = (1+d_j)(g_p + \eta_{y_j}g_{y_j}) - d_j g_{D_j}$$
$$= (1+d_j)rg_R + [(1+d_j)\eta_{y_j}g_{y_j} - \sum_i s_i(1+d_i)\eta_{y_i}g_{y_i}] -$$
$$- [d_j g_{D_j} - (1+d_j)r\sum_i d_i s_i g_{D_i}]$$
$$= (1+d_j)rg_R + [(1+d_j)\eta_{y_j}g_{y_j} - \sum_i s_i(1+d_i)\eta_{y_i}g_{y_i}] -$$
$$- \left(d_j g_{D_j} - \frac{1+d_j}{1+d}\sum_i d_i s_i g_{D_i}\right).$$

This alternative formulation, which will not be explored further here, naturally produces the same qualitative results as the one presented above.

The next stage in making the 'monetary' model of balance-of-payments behaviour more realistic is to introduce a reserve currency country whose currency is held as a substitute for the basic international money. The interesting problem in this case is the behaviour of the reserves of the reserve currency country. The total world money supply is as before the sum of reserves and domestic credit created by the individual countries; but the reserve currency role enables the reserve currency country to induce other countries to hold its domestic money, backed by its own domestic credit, instead of or in addition to providing their own money by domestic credit creation.

BALANCE-OF-PAYMENTS THEORY

As before we have

$$g_{M_s} = \sum_i w_i r_i g_R + \sum_i w_i(1-r_i)g_{D_i}$$

$$g_p = \sum_i w_i r_i g_R + \sum_i w_i(1-r_i)g_{D_i} - \sum_i w_i \eta_{y_i} g_{y_i}.$$

But now the behaviour of the reserve currency country's reserves is determined by the relation between the growth of both foreign and domestic demand for its money, and its domestic credit expansion. Still assuming homogeneity in money demand, we have

$$g_{R_j} = \frac{1}{r_j}[g_p + h\eta_{y_j} + g_{y_j} + (1-h)g_f] - \frac{1-r_j}{r_j}g_{D_j},$$

where h is the proportion of the reserve currency country's currency held by residents and g_f is the rate of growth of foreign demand for its money as a reserve currency, in real terms. This can be rewritten as

$$g_{R_j} = \frac{1}{r_j}[(1-h)g_f + \sum_i w_i r_i g_R + (h\eta_{y_j} g_{y_j} - \overline{\eta_y g_y})] - \\ - [(1-r_j)g_{D_j} - \overline{(1-r)g_D})].$$

If the real foreign demand for the reserve country's currency is assumed to be a constant proportion of the foreign money supply, the expression simplifies to

$$g_{R_j} = \frac{1}{r_j}\left\{\sum_i w_i r_i g_R + h(\eta_{y_j} g_{y_j} - \overline{\eta_y g_y}) - [(1-r_j)g_{D_j} - \overline{(1-r)g_D})]\right\}.$$

Assuming unitary income-elasticities of demand for real balances everywhere and the same initial ratios of international reserves to domestic money, it simplifies further to

$$g_{R_j} = g_R + \frac{h}{r}(g_{y_j} - \overline{g_y}) - \frac{1-r}{r}(g_{D_j} - \overline{g_D}).$$

That is, the reserve currency country will gain reserves faster than the rate of growth of total reserves if its real growth rate exceeds the world average or its rate of domestic credit expansion is below the world average, and vice versa.

An alternative formulation of the problem, using the same two assumptions for simplicity, is to ask what rate of growth of foreign holdings of the reserve currency is necessary to enable the reserve currency country's reserves to grow at the world rate. The answer is

$$g_f = \frac{1}{1-h}[(1-r)(g_{D_j}-\overline{g_D})-(hg_{y_j}-\overline{g_y})].$$

That is, foreign demand for the reserve currency must grow faster, the larger the reserve currency country's rate of domestic credit expansion relative to the rate of credit expansion abroad and the lower its real rate of growth relative to the real world growth rate.

Finally, I apply the general class of monetary models of the balance of payments developed above to the problem of the effects of a devaluation of a currency. The application is not entirely satisfactory theoretically, since the mathematics employed relate to continuous change whereas a devaluation is a once-over affair. Still, the results are suggestive.

For this problem, retain the assumption that domestic prices must keep in line with foreign prices, but introduce an exchange rate that can be changed, and represent devaluation by an instantaneous rate of change of the exchange rate. The demand for money now becomes

$$M_d = \rho \, p_f(y,i)$$

where p_f is the foreign price level and ρ is the price of foreign currency in terms of domestic currency. The rate of growth of reserves then becomes

$$g_R = \frac{1}{r}(g_\rho + g_{p_f} + \eta_y g_y + \eta_i g_i) - \frac{1-r}{r}g_D.$$

(Note that this formula re-introduces the interest rate as a determinant of the demand for money; for analysis, g_i may be interpreted as an expected rate of change of the money interest rate.)

There are several points to notice about the formula, with specific reference to the British devaluation of the pound in 1967 and the initial failure of that devaluation to improve the balance of payments.

First, aside from the scale factor $(1-r)$, devaluation is equivalent to domestic credit contraction; its function is to deflate domestic real balances and thereby to cause domestic residents to attempt to restore their real balances through the international commodity and security markets.

Second, since devaluation is a one-shot affair, it can be only a transitory factor for improvement in the balance of payments. Lasting improvement can only be achieved via a decrease in the rate of domestic credit expansion.

Third, the beneficial transitory effects of devaluation on reserves and the balance of payments can be offset or neutralised by any one or more of the following developments: (i) an increase in the rate of domestic credit expansion, which the authorities may allow either unwittingly or as a consequence of efforts to hold down interest rates on government debt; (ii) a fall in the growth rate (though this requires modifying the model to allow unemployment, which may be induced by deflationary official policies or by lags in the adjustment of production to demand); (iii) a rise in interest rates inducing a fall in the demand for real balances relative to income: here interest rates have to be interpreted to include the expected money rate of return on holdings of goods, which may be expected to rise temporarily as a consequence of devaluation and the inflationary expectations generated by it.

It may be noted in passing that the equation for devaluation can be converted into an equation for the motion of a freely floating exchange rate as a function of policy variables, as follows:

$$g_\rho = rg_R + (1-r)g_D - g_{p_f} - \eta_y g_y - \eta_i g_i.$$

The monetary models of the balance of payments surveyed in this paper are long-run models, inasmuch as they assume full employment of resources and the necessity for domestic price levels to keep in line with the world price level. The Keynesian model with which they have been contrasted applies to a shorter run in which these assumptions do not necessarily, or commonly, hold. The Keynesian model has become the basis for policy thinking and policy formulation. The monetary models suggest that it may be very misleading to rely on the Keynesian model as a guide to policy making over a succession of short periods within each of which the Keynesian model may appear to be a reasonable approximation to reality.

Appendix

The formulae presented in the text can be applied to a number of other problems than those mentioned, simply by rearranging terms. Thus, if a small country in an open international economy wishes to maintain a certain balance-of-payments surplus (growth-rate of reserves), it must control the growth rate of domestic credit according to the formula:

$$g_o = \frac{1}{1-r}(g_p + \eta_y g_y + \eta_i g_i - rg_R^*)$$

where g_R^* is the desired growth rate of reserves.

Similarly, in a world economy without a reserve currency country, if there is an international monetary authority that has control over the growth of world reserves, and it seeks to maintain world price stability, the formula it must follow (assuming stability of interest rates) is

$$g^*_{MS} = \sum_i w_i \eta_{yi} g_{yi}.$$

Note that this formula will not imply a constant growth rate of world reserves over time, if income elasticities of demand for money, or growth rates of real output, vary among countries.

The formula is still more complex if the fractional reserve character of domestic money supplies is allowed for, being

$$g^*_R = \frac{\sum_i w_i \eta_{yi} g_{yi} - \sum_i w_i (1-r_i) g_{Di}}{\sum_i w_i Y_i}.$$

Note that the presence of a reserve currency country does not affect this formula; however, it affects its empirical value indirectly through the effects of reserve currency status on the willingness of the reserve currency country to expand domestic credit, and the possible desires of other countries to expand domestic credit in order to avoid accumulating excess stocks of the reserve currency.

Finally, for a country on a floating exchange rate, the movement of the exchange rate over time is related to domestic credit expansion and to exchange market intervention intended to alter (or having the effect of altering) the country's international reserves and is given by the formula:

$$g_\rho = r g^*_R + (1-r) g^*_D - g_{p_f} - \eta_y g_y - \eta_i g_i,$$

(where the last term should probably be dropped, as a transitional factor).

12

Adjustment, Policy, and Monetary Equilibrium in a Two-Country Model[1]

ALEXANDER K. SWOBODA
Graduate Institute of International Studies

and

RUDIGER DORNBUSCH
University of Rochester

I. INTRODUCTION

Aggregative models focusing on the interdependence of the national incomes of underemployed economies were first developed by Lloyd Metzler in his analysis of the transfer problem and in the foreign-trade multiplier literature.[2] Equilibrium in these models is characterised simply by the equality of domestic output with total expenditure on domestic goods; although highly suggestive, these formulations postulate no forces making for complete balance-of-payments adjustment, neglect monetary equilibrium, and ignore other than autonomous capital movements.[3] Subsequent work, particularly that of James Meade, Harry Johnson, and Robert Mundell has done much to incorporate monetary equilibrium and induced capital

[1] This is a revised version of a (somewhat more extended) paper written in August, 1969. We have benefited from the comments of the members of the Harvard International Trade Seminar (in particular those of Michael B. Connolly and Gottfried Haberler) where the earlier version was presented in December, 1969. We are also deeply indebted to Harry G. Johnson and Robert A. Mundell for their helpful comments.

[2] Metzler's initial analysis of the two-country case is contained in L. A. Metzler, 'The Transfer Problem Reconsidered', *Journal of Political Economy*, Vol. 50 (June, 1942), pp. 397–414, and is extended to the *n*-country case in his 'A Multiple-Country Theory of Income Transfers', *Journal of Political Economy*, Vol. 61 (February, 1951), pp. 14–29. Examples of the early work on international trade multipliers are L. A. Metzler, 'Underemployment Equilibrium in International Trade', *Econometrica*, Vol. 10 (April, 1942), pp. 97–112 and Fritz Machlup, *International Trade and the National Income Multiplier* (Blakiston Co. Philadelphia, 1943).

[3] The authors cited in the preceding footnote were well aware of these limitations.

P

movements in the analysis of international adjustment.[4] This analysis has mostly been carried out for the case of the single country, a country assumed to be sufficiently 'small' to allow neglect of foreign repercussions (though Meade does take foreign repercussions into detailed account but under rather special monetary assumptions). Mundell's two-country model of adjustment in the special case of perfect capital mobility is a notable exception.[5]

This paper attempts to integrate and extend, for the case of fixed exchange rates and unemployment, two broad classes of comparative-statics propositions that have been developed in the literature mentioned above. The first class concerns the small, open economy; the other allows for foreign repercussions. Assuming monetary policy to consist of once-and-for-all changes in the stock of domestic assets of the banking system (no neutralisation operations are undertaken nor do monetary authorities follow Meade's 'neutral monetary policy' of pegging the interest rate) and fiscal policy to consist of changes in government expenditure on home-produced goods, the following propositions hold for the case of the small, unemployed, and open economy: (1) Monetary policy has no lasting effect on the equilibrium values of income or the rate of interest whatever the degree of capital mobility.[6] (2) The effectiveness of fiscal policy depends directly on the degree of capital mobility. (3) When capital movements are responsive to interest-rate differentials, internal and external balance can be reached simultaneously through an appropriate use of monetary and fiscal policy. (4) In the absence of neutralisation operations, balance-of-payments adjustment is complete and automatic, albeit sometimes having undesirable repercussions on internal balance.

Foreign-trade multiplier models on the other hand, do allow for foreign repercussions through the trade balance but neglect monetary

[4] See J. E. Meade, *The Balance of Payments* (Oxford University Press, London, 1951) and *The Balance of Payments Mathematical Supplement* (Oxford University Press, London, 1951), various articles by Mundell as collected in R. A. Mundell, *International Economics* (The Macmillan Co., New York, 1968), and H. G. Johnson, 'Towards a General Theory of the Balance of Payments', in *International Trade and Economic Growth* (George Allen and Unwin Ltd., London, 1958).

[5] See R. A. Mundell, 'A Reply: Capital Mobility and Size', *Canadian Journal of Economics and Political Science*, Vol. 30 (August, 1964), pp. 421–31, reprinted in his *International Economics, op. cit.*, pp. 262–71.

[6] This conclusion has not always been fully perceived in the literature. For an explicit statement, see A. K. Swoboda, 'Equilibrium, Quasi-Equilibrium, and Macroeconomic Policy under Fixed Exchange Rates', *Quarterly Journal of Economics*, Vol. 86 (February, 1972).

considerations (or resort to the equivalent devices of assuming either that the interest elasticity of the demand for money is infinite in all countries or that authorities peg interest rates). These models lead to the conclusion that fiscal expansion in one country leads to real income gains in both countries and to a residual payments deficit for the expanding country. Furthermore, an income transfer raises the income level of the recipient country, lowers that of the donor, and, under certain restrictive assumptions, will be under-effected. Presumably, price changes are required to eliminate the balance-of-payments disequilibria that subsist even after income levels have adjusted to the impact of fiscal expansion or transfers. That neglect of monetary considerations may seriously vitiate these conclusions is brought out by Mundell's two-country model under perfect capital mobility which demonstrates that, contrary to expectation, fiscal expansion may have beggar-my-neighbour repercussions on the rest of the world; moreover, Mundell shows that the effectiveness of monetary policy under fixed exchange rates is inversely related to the size of the country relative to the rest of the world.[7]

These two classes of propositions leave three issues unanswered: first, the validity of conclusions based on the monetary model of the small open economy when foreign repercussions are allowed for; second, the consequence of introducing a financial sector for the results derived from trade-multiplier models concerning income transfers and business-cycle transmission (though we do have partial answers to these first two questions for the special case of perfect capital mobility); third, the sensitivity of Mundell's two-country model to the assumption of perfect capital mobility. Some of the answers suggested in this paper can be outlined here. First, the extension of most of the small-country results to the foreign-repercussions case is straightforward. Second, the requirement of monetary equilibrium substantially alters conclusions reached on the basis of pure-income models: for instance, adjustment is always complete and, in a special case, the impact of income transfers depends solely on monetary parameters. Third, money-supply disturbances affect income levels lastingly only insofar as they increase or decrease the *world* stock of money. This implies that, for given real parameters, the impact of a money supply change (except on the distribution of reserves) is independent of its national origin; put another way, a

[7] See R. A. Mundell, 'A Reply: Capital Mobility and Size', *op. cit.*

given 'natural distribution of specie' – or rather of money supplies – tends to be (re-)established automatically through the monetary mechanism of adjustment. Furthermore, the preceding result is independent of the degree of capital mobility: the comparative statics – though not the speed – of adjustment to monetary disturbances are impervious to the degree of capital mobility.

To derive these and other conclusions, we develop a simple – and, we hope, heuristically appealing – graphical technique that can be applied to a wide variety of problems. This technique enables us to analyse equilibrium, adjustment, and the impact of macroeconomic policy in a two-country underemployment world – under fixed exchange rates and different assumptions about available asset choices and the interest elasticity of capital flows. Varying these assumptions makes it possible to test the sensitivity of the conclusions to alternative formulations of the demand-for-money equations and to the degree of capital mobility. In section II money is demanded for transactions purposes only and capital is immobile internationally: the 'quantity theory of money' is added to the Keynesian trade-multiplier models and the consequences for transfer theory examined. Section III adds bond markets and rates of interest and presents the two-country version of the IS-LM variety of macroeconomic models under capital immobility. Section IV generalises the analysis by allowing for various degrees of capital mobility. It should perhaps be stressed at the outset that our models are essentially 'Keynesian' and share these models' limitations. In particular, the net value of assets does not enter expenditure functions, growth deriving from net current investment is neglected, and changes in debt service due to open-market operations are implicitly assumed not to affect disposable income (i.e. the necessary re-distribution policy is assumed to be undertaken).

Throughout sections II-IV our concern is twofold: to analyse the nature of general equilibrium in our two-country world and to develop the comparative statics of various policy measures.[8] The latter fall under two main headings: (1) *monetary policies,* for instance, changes in a country's money supply, redistributions of the world money stock, or international reserve creation (e.g. gold dis-

---

[8] In an earlier draft of this paper (referred to as 'Preliminary Draft' below), we also investigated in slightly more detail the stability of the models we use. This draft is available from the authors on request. For the sake of brevity, we only refer in passing to stability in the body of the present paper.

Adjustment, Policy, and Monetary Equilibrium

coveries and SDR distributions); and (2) *fiscal policies* such as government expenditure changes, income transfers, or expenditure-switching policies. Yet another type of policy, namely, global policies, is taken up in section V.

II. A Simple Monetary Model Under Capital Immobility

Consider a first model in which we have goods and money but no bonds. The system is described by equations (1)–(5) below and illustrated in Figure 12.1 and Figure 12.2.

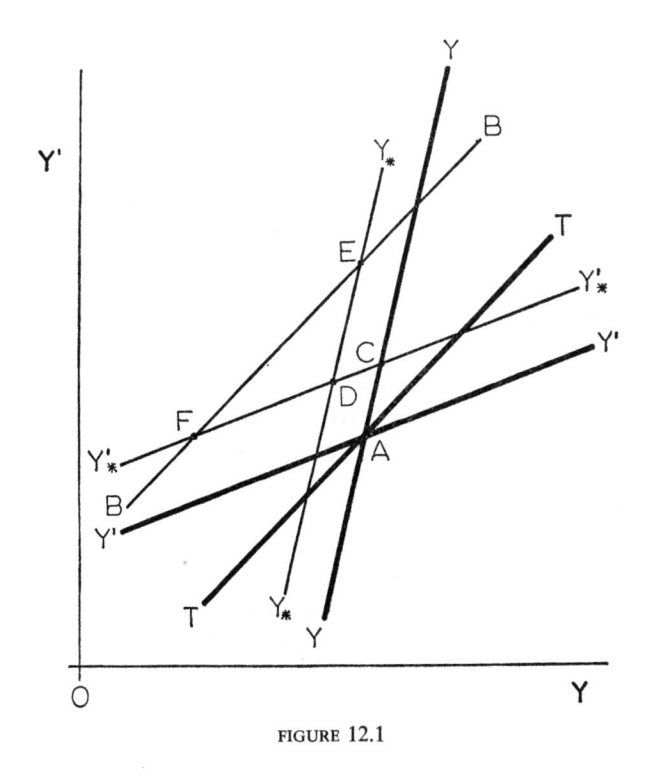

FIGURE 12.1

It will prove convenient to consider, first and separately, the goods and services markets. Equilibrium in these markets requires the equality of output with expenditure on home-produced goods in countries 1 and 2 simultaneously. These conditions are expressed algebraically by equations (1) and (2) below:

$$Y = E'(Y) + T(Y, Y') \qquad (1)$$

$$Y' = E'(Y') - T(Y, Y') \qquad (2)$$

where the exchange rate is set equal to 1 through an appropriate choice of units of measurement.[9] Unprimed variables refer to the first country, primed variables to the second. Y represents national output, E domestic expenditure, and T the balance of trade. The two-country trade-multiplier model formed by equations (1) and (2) is depicted in Figure 12.1. Equations (1) and (2) are represented by lines YY and $Y'Y'$, respectively, while the line TT traces out those income combinations which ensure balance-of-trade equilibrium ($T = 0$). For convenience (and for convenience only), autonomous expenditure levels have been chosen so as to yield a zero trade balance at the initial equilibrium point, A. Let m and s denote marginal propensities to import and save, respectively. The slopes of YY, TT, and $Y'Y'$ are $(s+m)/m'$, m/m', and $m/(s'+m')$, respectively, from which it follows that TT is steeper than $Y'Y'$, that it lies between YY and $Y'Y'$, and that all three lines slope upward. Excess demand for the first country's goods prevails above YY, excess demand for the second country's goods below $Y'Y'$, and country 1 experiences a balance-of-trade deficit below and to the right of TT.

The two main conclusions derived from two-country pure income models can be illustrated with the help of Figure 12.1. First, increased expenditure by, say, country 2 worsens that country's balance of payments and leads to increased income in both countries: graphically, $Y'Y'$ shifts to $Y'_*Y'_*$ and equilibrium from point A to C, the latter point lying above TT. Second, an income transfer from country 1 to country 2, financed and disposed of by an equal increase in expenditure *on home-produced goods* in country 2 and decrease in country 1, decreases the income of the transferring country, increases that of the recipient, and improves the balance of trade but worsens the balance of payments of the transferring country (i.e. the transfer is under-effected). Graphically, YY and $Y'Y'$ shift so as to intersect at point D; D must lie above TT but below BB, the locus of income

[9] The graphical technique used to depict equations (1) and (2) was first developed in R. Robinson, 'A Graphical Analysis of the Foreign Trade Multiplier', *The Economic Journal*, Vol. 62 (September, 1952), pp. 546–64.

combinations that yield equilibrium in the balance of payments inclusive of the transfer.[10] As emphasised by Harry Johnson, this 'Metzler-Machlup' result depends crucially on the assumption that the financing and disposal of the transfer can be assimilated to a tax and subsidy falling entirely on expenditure for home-produced goods; under different assumptions, the transfer could be over-effected as well as under-effected.[11] As our main interest is in the 'secondary' mechanism of monetary adjustment we adopt the 'Metzler–Machlup' case for simplicity.

Consider, now, the money market. Assume that, in each country, the (transactions) demand for money depends only on national product and that the supply is equal to the sum of the consolidated banking system's domestic assets and foreign-exchange reserves. Suppose also the world's stock of foreign-exchange reserves to be fixed (as it would be under the gold standard if we ignore gold production or under a 'neutral version' of the gold-exchange standard).[12] These assumptions are expressed algebraically by the following three equations:

$$M = \bar{D} + R = L(Y) \tag{3}$$

$$M' = \bar{D}' + \bar{W} - R = L'(Y') \tag{4}$$

$$M + M' = \bar{W} + \bar{D} + \bar{D}' = L(Y) + L'(Y'), \tag{5}$$

where M, M' stand for money supplies, $\bar{D}$ and $\bar{D}'$ for the banking systems' exogenously determined domestic assets, $\bar{W}$ for the fixed world stock of foreign-exchange reserves, R for the reserves of country 1, and L, L' are the demands for money in countries 1 and 2, respectively. In the context of the present money-goods case, $\bar{D}$ can be interpreted as unserviced government debt held by the central bank. Equation (5) is derived directly from (3) and (4).

[10] The proof that D must lie between TT and BB is as follows. Denoting the transfer by τ, $Y'Y'$ shifts to the left by $(1/(m'+s')) \cdot ((s'+m')/m)\tau = (1/m)\tau$. YY shifts upward by $(1/(s+m)) \cdot ((s+m)/m') = (1/m')\tau$. BB is obtained by shifting TT leftward by $(1/m)\tau$ and upward by $(1/m')\tau$. Therefore, BB cuts $Y_* Y_*$ at point E, vertically above A, and $Y'_* Y'_*$ at F, horizontally to the left of A. It follows that D must lie above TT but below BB.

[11] See H. G. Johnson, 'The Transfer Problem and Exchange Stability', Chapter 7 in his *International Trade and Economic Growth*, op. cit.

[12] On the meaning and implications of a neutral gold-exchange standard, see A. K. Swoboda, 'Reserve Policies, Currency Preferences, and International Adjustment', *Yale Economic Essays*, Vol. 10 (Fall, 1970), pp. 83–126.

Equations (1)–(5) are sufficient to describe the nature of equilibrium graphically. Figure 12.2 differs from Figure 12.1 by the adjunction of line *KK*, the locus of combinations of the two countries' incomes for which the world money supply is equal to the sum of the two countries' demands for money. Thus, *KK* depicts equation (5), the constraint that the requirement of monetary equilibrium imposes on admissible values of national incomes. To obtain one point on *KK*, choose a given division of the world stock of money among the

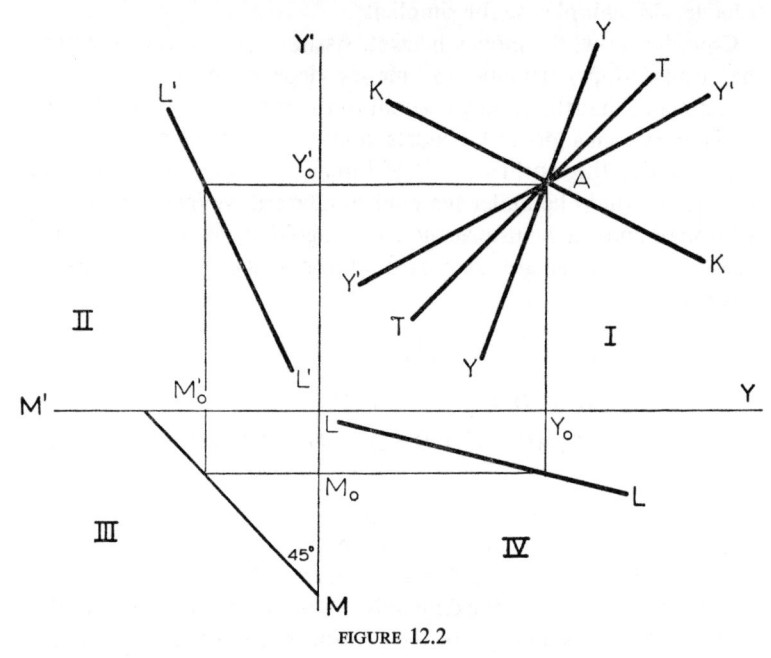

FIGURE 12.2

two countries (e.g. M_0 and M'_0 in Quadrant III) and find the income levels that equate the demand for money in each country (represented by *LL* and *L'L'*) with the pre-assigned national money stocks. The slope of *KK* is negative (and equal to $-L_y/L_{y'}$, where subscripted variables denote partial derivatives with respect to the subscripts) since an increase in one country's income, and hence in its demand for money, can only be accommodated by a decrease in the other country's income, and hence in that country's demand for money. It follows from the construction of *KK* that an upward displacement along that line corresponds to a redistribution of the world money supply from the first to the second country.

Full equilibrium must occur on KK as above (below) that line world excess demand (supply) for money prevails. In addition, equilibrium requires that output be equal to aggregate demand in both countries and that the balance of trade be equal to zero. All three conditions are met at point A.

To discuss the comparative statics (and the stability) of the model, the link between the balance of payments and national money supplies must be taken into account. Under fixed exchange rates, a balance-of-payments deficit (surplus) must lead to a reduction (increase) in foreign-exchange reserves; and, in the absence of policy measures by the central bank, such a change in reserves must be matched by an equivalent change in the money supply.[13] For simplicity, assume that the reserve changes are equal to the balance of payments (here, the balance of trade). Monetary equilibrium is achieved only if and when there is no tendency for the money supply to change. This requirement can be expressed algebraically as:

$$\frac{dR}{dt} = \frac{dM}{dt} = T = \frac{-dR'}{dt} = \frac{-dM'}{dt} = 0 \qquad (6)$$

In addition, note that in our money-goods model an excess demand for money must be reflected in an excess supply of goods and services – a point that equations (1) and (2) do not acknowledge. To take this into account, rewrite equations (1) and (2) as:

$$Y = E(Y,\hat{M}) + T(Y,Y',\hat{M},\hat{M}') \qquad (1')$$

$$Y' = E'(Y',\hat{M}') - T(Y,Y',\hat{M},\hat{M}'), \qquad (2')$$

where $\hat{M} = M - L(Y)$, and $\hat{M} = M' - L'(Y')$. In equilibrium, of course, $\hat{M}$ and $\hat{M}'$ are equal to zero and (1'), (2') reduce to (1) and (2). In disequilibrium, we could postulate a stock-adjustment process that implies equality of the flow excess demand for money with the flow excess supply of goods and services. We are now in a position to establish some comparative statics results.[14] Consider, first, the effect

---

[13] If the banking system keeps a fixed ratio of reserves to monetary liabilities, the money supply changes will be larger than the reserve changes. Such reserve ratios could easily be introduced formally into our analysis, but at the cost of needless complications since none of our results would be modified in an important way.

[14] The appendix and our 'Preliminary Draft', *op. cit.*, pp. 9–11, investigate the stability of the simple monetary model under the dynamic postulates that each income level rises in proportion to the discrepancy between spending on home goods and domestic output and that rates of change in money supplies are equal

of an increase in the stock of money of country 1 brought about by a transitory government budget deficit. This is illustrated in Figure 12.3 by a movement from initial equilibrium at *A* to final equilibrium at *C*. The initial impact of the money supply increase is to shift the *YY* curve to the right creating a balance-of-payments deficit in country 1; the reserve flow to country 2 and the attendant increase in that country's money supply then shifts $Y'Y'$ up (and the outflow of reserves from 1 begins to check the shift in *YY*). Final equilibrium is reached when there is no world liquidity glut or shortage and when payments balance prevails; both conditions are satisfied at *C* the

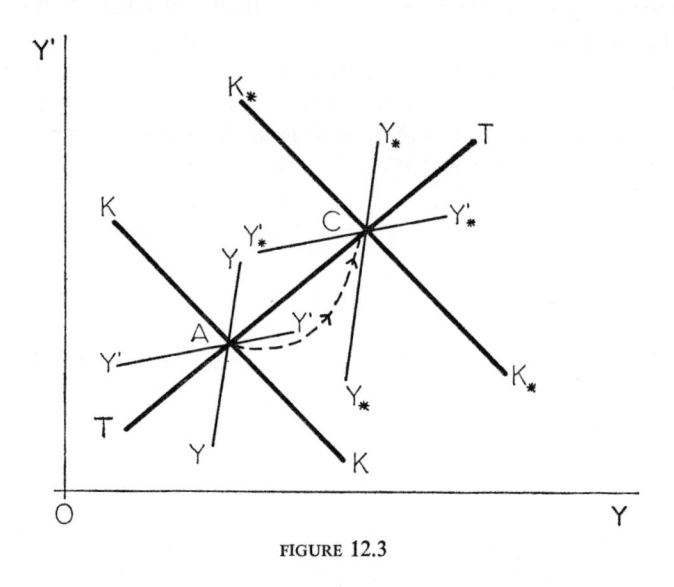

FIGURE 12.3

point of intersection of $K_1 K_1$ (the new *KK* curve corresponding to the higher world money stock) and *TT*. Note that the long-run distribution of income gains among the two countries depends only on, and is proportional to, the slope of the *TT* line, m/m'. Moreover, the location of the final equilibrium point depends only on the magnitude of the money-supply change and not on its geographical

to the balance of trade. Necessary and sufficient conditions are derived and shown to be satisfied if an excess supply of money in one country has a stronger impact on the demand for that country's goods and services than on that for the other country's output. This is similar to the familiar stability requirement for a price system that the excess demand for some good *i* be more sensitive to a change in its own price than to a change in some other good's price.

Adjustment, Policy, and Monetary Equilibrium

origin: had country 2 instead of 1 engaged in monetary expansion, the total increase in the world money stock and the final equilibrium position would have been the same – except for the distribution of world reserves. The country that initiates the money supply increase loses that amount of reserves needed to raise the other country's money supply by enough to maintain money-market equilibrium.

Consider, next, a redistribution of the world money supply, the total stock remaining unchanged, from country 2 to country 1. Such a redistribution leads to only a temporary income gain for country 1 (corresponding to a temporary downward movement along a given KK curve) for it leaves the KK and TT curves undisturbed. A reverse

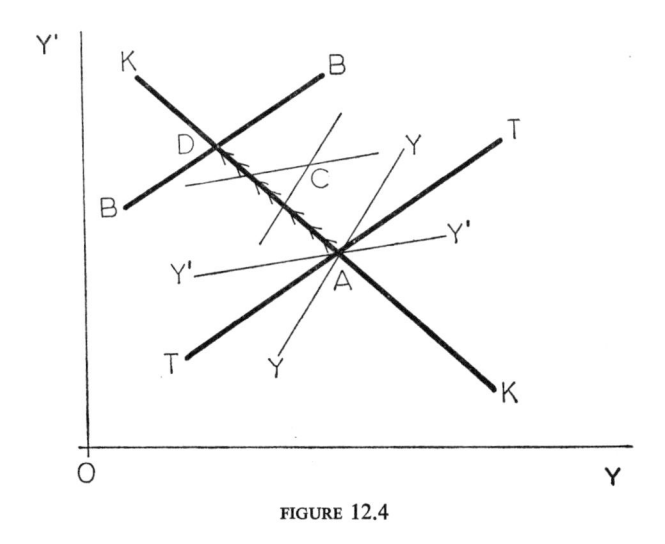

FIGURE 12.4

redistribution of the world money stock – brought about by the reserve flow from country 1 to country 2 that is engendered by the latter's temporary trade surplus – re-establishes the original equilibrium position.

The analysis of an income transfer from country 1 to country 2 is straightforward. For, with a constant world money stock, the final equilibrium point must lie on the original KK line. The effect of such a transfer is illustrated in Figure 12.4 for the simple 'Metzler–Machlup' case. Point C represents, as before, the shift in YY and $Y'Y'$ that would be brought about by the transfer in the absence of a monetary constraint. It has been drawn in for the sake of illustration only and does not possess any relevance to actual adjustment in the present context. Final equilibrium will be at *D* where the transfer is fully effected through whatever changes in reserves are required to supplement the initial expenditure changes, assuming the system to be stable. Full equilibrium requires that the trade balance surplus (saving) of the transferor equal taxation so that the government's tax collection and transfer payments sum to zero and the private sector's tax payments equal its current account surplus. Together these conditions imply that money stocks remain unchanged. The effect of the transfer, in full equilibrium, is entirely determined by the marginal propensities to import and the *marginal* income velocities of circulation of money in the two countries. Algebraically, the changes in incomes due to the transfer are:

$$dY = -\frac{V}{mV + m'V'\left(\frac{\varepsilon}{\varepsilon'}\right)} \cdot \tau < 0$$

$$dY' = \frac{V'}{mV\left(\frac{\varepsilon'}{\varepsilon}\right) + m'V'} \cdot \tau > 0$$

$$\frac{dY'}{dY} = -\frac{\varepsilon V'}{\varepsilon' V} < 0$$

where V, V' are average income velocities, $\varepsilon, \varepsilon'$ income elasticities of the demand for money (i.e. ratios of marginal to average velocities) and τ is the transfer.

This result can be given an intuitive explanation. With a given world money stock, *KK* represents the world's 'income-distribution-possibility' curve. The slope of this curve depends on marginal income velocities of circulation while the specific equilibrium distribution of world income among the two countries depends on the position of the balance-of-payments (balance-of-trade in the absence of transfers) line, *BB*. Although marginal propensities to import and autonomous expenditure levels combine to determine the position of, and shifts in, the *BB* and *TT* curves, income velocities alone determine the ratio of incomes (or income changes) consistent with monetary equilibrium. Therefore, when an income transfer takes place, the increase in the second country's income relative to the decrease in the income of the first depends on velocities of circulation only. When the marginal income velocity of circulation in the recipient country is large relative to that in the donor country, the reserve and money supply changes associated with the transfer will cause a large rise in the recipient's income level and a relatively small decline in the donor's output.

Two propositions summarise this section's results:

(1) With a constant world money supply, monetary disturbances (assuming behaviour parameters to remain constant) will leave the natural distribution of specie and income levels unchanged in the final equilibrium. Equilibrium incomes can change only if the parameters affecting balance-of-payments equilibrium – and hence the position or slope of the *TT* or *BB* curves – change as, for instance, in the case of a transfer. Even then, only the distribution of incomes among the two countries along a given *KK* line can be affected.

(2) A change in the world money supply will affect the incomes of both countries in the same direction and in a proportion that depends uniquely on the ratio of marginal propensities to import. A corollary of this proposition is that the impact of a money supply change on income levels – but not on reserve levels – is independent of the national origin of that change.

III. A MORE GENERAL MODEL UNDER CAPITAL IMMOBILITY

This section incorporates bond markets and interest rates into the analysis though it retains the assumption of capital immobility. The model must be modified to take the interest elasticity of the demand for money and of domestic expenditures on goods and services into account, imports being assumed to depend only on income levels. The system is described by the following equations:

$$Y = E(Y,r) + T(Y,Y') + I \tag{7}$$

$$Y' = E'(Y',r') - T(Y,Y') + I' \tag{8}$$

$$M = \bar{D} + R = L(Y,r) \tag{9}$$

$$M' = \bar{D}' + \bar{W} - R = L'(Y',r') \tag{10}$$

$$\frac{dM}{dt} = \frac{dR}{dt} = T(Y,Y') = -\frac{dM'}{dt} = -\frac{dR'}{dt} \tag{11}$$

where r, r' are the interest rates in countries 1 and 2, respectively,

INTERNATIONAL TRADE AND MONEY

I, I' are shift parameters, and where full equilibrium requires that (11) be equal to zero.

This system is represented graphically in Figure 12.5. Curves LL, XX, and FF, the familiar equilibrium curves that have been used extensively by Mundell,[15] represent those combinations of the first

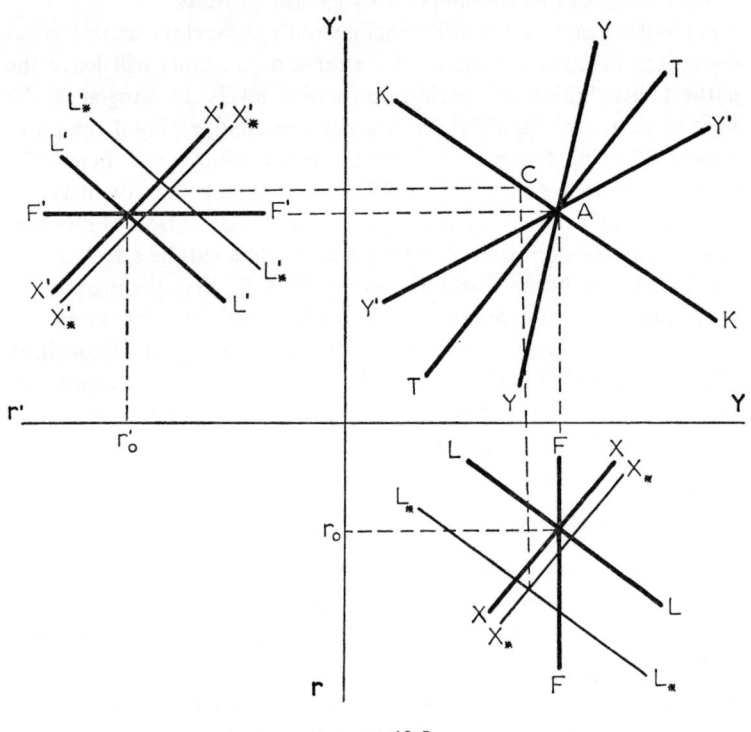

FIGURE 12.5

country's income level and interest rate which – assuming that the second country's income (and hence its import demand) is given and equal to Y'_0 – equate the demand for money with the given supply, the demand for domestic output with the supply of output, and the balance of trade to zero, respectively. Note that FF is vertical (and fixed for the given Y') to reflect the assumption that capital movements and trade are insensitive to the interest rate. Similar definitions hold for $L'L'$, $X'X'$ and $F'F'$. The YY, $Y'Y'$, TT, and KK curves are

[15] See, for instance, R. A. Mundell, 'The International Disequilibrium System', op. cit.

now defined as follows. YY shows those combinations of the two countries' incomes which equate the demand for the goods and services of country 1 with its output when income in the second country varies *and the money supply in country 2 is kept constant* at the level consistent with equilibrium at A (the money stock assumed when drawing LL). Therefore, to each level of the money stock, M, there corresponds a different, but parallel, YY curve. $Y'Y'$ is defined in similar fashion.[16] TT represents those income combinations that maintain balance-of-trade equilibrium. Its slope is m/m', as before; it depends on marginal propensities to import only since we have assumed that the trade balance is not interest-sensitive (which enables us to by-pass some complications that are not essential here). KK represents those combinations of income levels that maintain equality between the demand and supply of money in both countries when a given world money supply is redistributed from one country to the other. It is constructed as follows. Suppose money is redistributed from country 1 to country 2. LL shifts down and $L'L'$ shifts up tending to decrease income in country 1 and to increase income in country 2. The demand for imports increases in country 2 shifting the XX curve of country 1 to the right; by similar reasoning, $X'X'$ shifts to $X'_*X'_*$. The intersections of the shifted money-market equilibrium curves with the shifted XX and $X'X'$ curves (after all income repercussions have been allowed for) determines a new combination of income levels on KK at point C. It follows that all equilibrium conditions, save payments balance, are satisfied along KK since the demand for goods and services is equal to output in each country for points on that locus. General equilibrium prevails at the point of intersection of KK and TT.[17]

It also follows from KK's construction that its slope, given by expression (12) below, may be either positive or negative:

$$\frac{dY'}{dY}\bigg|_{KK} = \frac{E'_r[(s+m)L_r + E_r L_y] - E_r m L'_{r'}}{-E_r[(s'+m')L'_{r'} + E'_{r'} L'_{y'}] + m' E'_{r'} L_r} \gtreqless 0 \qquad (12)$$

[16] The reader can verify that taking monetary equilibrium into account does not modify our previous conclusions as to the slopes of $YY, Y'Y'$, and TT, and as to the relationship of these slopes to each other.

[17] It can be demonstrated that usual assumptions as to the signs of partial derivatives suffice to insure that necessary conditions for stability are met on the dynamic assumptions that incomes change in proportion to the excess demand for output in each country, that each interest rate rises in proportion to the relevant excess demand for money, and that the rate of change of each country's money supply is equal to the balance of trade.

This ambiguity stems from the fact that a redistribution of the world money stock exerts two opposing influences on income levels. Thus, the decrease in the money stock of country 1 tends to lower its equilibrium income; on the other hand, the increase in the second country's income (attendant on the rise in its money supply) tends to raise the exports, and hence equilibrium output, of the first country. Nevertheless, *KK* will usually slope down for at least three reasons. First, it is sufficient that each country's income be more responsive to a change in its own money stock than to an equivalent change in the other country's money supply for *KK* to slope downward.[18] Second, a positive slope of *KK* due to the predominance of indirect money supply effects in one country (or a negative slope due to such predominance in both countries) is likely to be associated with instability of the system.[19] Third, if the two countries are identical with respect to behaviour parameters the slope of *KK* is simply -1; thus, a positive slope of *KK* is associated – at least in the stable case – with strong dissimilarities in economic behaviour. In what follows, we will assume the slope of *KK* to be negative, leaving it to the reader to modify the results for the case of a positively-sloped *KK* curve.

[18] Algebraically, predominance of own money-supply effects implies that the numerator of expression (12) is positive and the denominator negative (the first term outweighing the second in both numerator and denominator).

[19] Assuming that adjustment takes place along *KK* and is governed by the money flows engendered by balance-of-trade disequilibria, it can be shown that equilibrium will tend to be stable when own money-supply effects dominate. In that case, after a temporary disturbance, income tends to rise in the surplus country and to fall in the deficit country restoring payments equilibrium. If indirect money-supply effects predominate in both countries (and, hence, *KK* slopes downward) income movements tend to worsen, rather than correct, payments disequilibria. When *KK* slopes upward because of the predominance of indirect money-supply effects in country 1 (country 2), equilibrium is stable if *KK* cuts *TT* from below (above) and unstable if *KK* cuts *TT* from above (below). More intuitively, suppose indirect effects to predominate in country 1: redistribution of money from 1 to 2 increases income in country 1 since that country's income is more sensitive to the positive effect of the money supply increase in 2 than to the decline in its own stock of money. Hence, when country 1 experiences a deficit both income levels rise and the system slides upward along *KK*. Equilibrium will be re-established if this movement along *KK* restores payments equilibrium, i.e. if *KK* cuts *TT* from below.

Note also that *KK* slopes upward and reduces to the *YY*(*Y'Y'*) curve when liquidity-trap conditions prevail in country 1 (country 2). This case of a positively sloping *KK* curve is consistent with stability. Suppose that the demand for money is infinitely elastic in country 1; the *KK* curve reduces to the *YY* curve and cuts *TT* from below. For an alternative discussion and diagrammatic illustration, see our 'Preliminary Draft', *op. cit.*, pp. 18–19.

Adjustment, Policy, and Monetary Equilibrium

A further complication is introduced by the interest sensitivity of the demand for money: *KK* may shift even though the world money supply remains constant. For instance, an autonomous increase in expenditure tends to raise interest rates; the ensuing reduction in the asset demand for money makes a given world money supply compatible with higher income levels. Graphically, *KK* shifts upward, though its slope remains unchanged, when autonomous expenditures increase. A simple analytical device will prove useful to handle shifts in *KK* when discussing comparative statics results. Decompose the movement from initial to final equilibrium into two steps. First, determine the initial impact of any autonomous disturbance on income levels without allowing any reserve flows to take place through the balance-of-payments adjustment mechanism, i.e. for given national money supplies. Second, determine the reserve flows and income changes required to eliminate the payments disequilibrium created by the first step; this second step yields the final-equilibrium levels of income. Graphically, this procedure corresponds to determining the impact of the autonomous disturbances on the *YY* and *Y'Y'* curves; once the location of their intersection – after the disturbance has occurred – has been determined, move along the *KK* curve that passes through that intersection until the *TT* curve is reached to determine the final equilibrium point. *The new KK curve must pass through the intersection of the shifted YY and Y'Y' curve* since the only equilibrium condition that is not fulfilled at that point is a zero balance-of-payments; this payments disequilibrium results in (and is eliminated by) a redistribution of the world money supply, i.e., in a movement along the *KK* curve.

We can now analyse the comparative statics of reserve redistributions among countries, of monetary policy, of fiscal policy, and of income transfers.

As before a redistribution of money from country 1 to country 2 results only in transitory changes. The redistribution shifts both *YY* and *Y'Y'* up along *KK*. However, both the decreases in the income of the first country and the increase in that of the second lead to a trade deficit for country 2. Reserves flow back from the second to the first country until the initial income levels and distribution of the world money stock are re-established. Note also that, as money is redistributed from 1 to 2 (as the system moves up along *KK*), the interest rate rises in country 1 and falls in country 2.

Figure 12.6 illustrates the impact of monetary policy. Suppose that the authorities of the first country increase the money supply by purchasing bonds in the open market. The initial impact is to increase the first country's output and, indirectly that of the second country through an increase in the latter's exports. YY shifts to Y_*Y_* intersecting the stationary $Y'Y'$ curve at C.[20] At C, however, country 1 experiences a deficit; as it loses reserves both $Y'Y'$ and Y_*Y_* shift up along K_*K_* (the KK curve through C) until their intersection

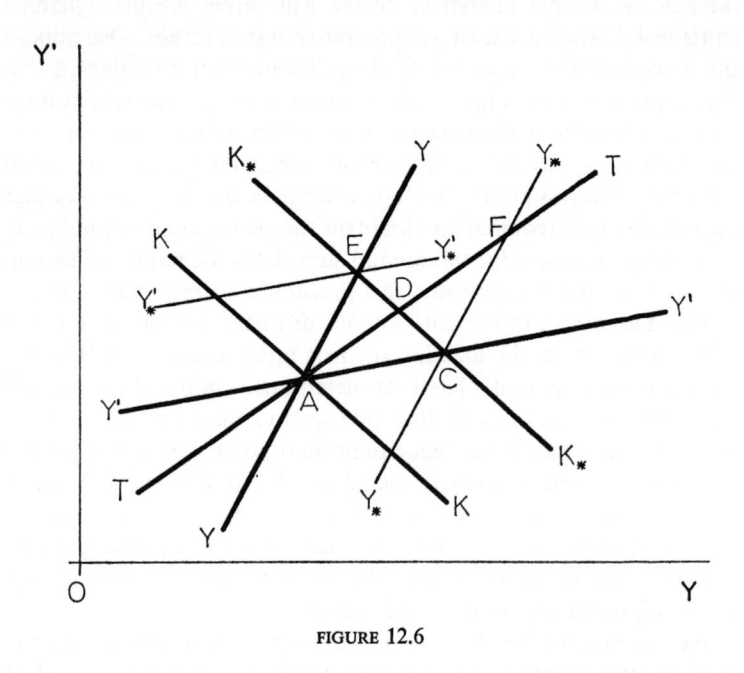

FIGURE 12.6

comes to rest at the final equilibrium point D where balance-of-trade equilibrium is re-established. Had the open-market purchase of bonds taken place in country 2, the same increase in the world money supply would have occurred, the same locus of monetary equilibrium (K_*K_*) would have been relevant, and the same final equilibrium been established. The path to equilibrium (and the change in foreign-exchange reserves), however, would have been different: from A to E and from E to D, as it were.

[20] Algebraically, the magnitude of the movement from A to C is found by differentiating (7) to (10) with respect to an increase in $\bar{D}$ and solving for $dY/d\bar{D}$ and $dY'/d\bar{D}$.

242

This conclusion is similar to that reached in the preceding section for the case of the 'simple' money-goods model. (As a matter of fact, the two models yield exactly the same result if the interest elasticity of the demand for money is zero in both countries.) There are differences, however. For, the initial shift in the YY curve and the slope of KK now both depend on the interest elasticity of spending and of the demand for money as well as on the marginal income velocity of circulation of money. Suppose, for instance, an infinite interest elasticity of the demand for money in country 1; in that case, YY does not shift at all and equilibrium remains at A. Alternatively, imagine an infinite interest elasticity of the demand for money in the second country: an increase in the money supply of the first would have only a transitory effect on income levels. For, the KK curve would now be identical with the $Y'Y'$ curve and the system would have to return from C to A along $KK(Y'Y')$ to re-establish equilibrium. That is, the second country's reserve gains do not affect its income, and imports must return to their initial level to re-establish trade balance.

Our analysis of monetary policy has assumed the absence of sterilisation operations. These can easily be taken into account. Neutralisation operations prevent reserve flows from affecting the money supply of the neutralising country; they prevent the relevant YY curve from moving in response to reserve flows. Thus if both countries sterilise reserve flows, a quasi-equilibrium at C can be maintained until the first country's reserves are exhausted. If, on the other hand, only country 1 neutralises reserve flows full equilibrium is re-established when the second country's money supply has increased sufficiently for balance-of-trade equilibrium to be restored at point F. Monetary policy accompanied by sterilisation operations yields greater income changes for the sterilising country than monetary policy alone. Finally, if country 2 sterilises reserve flows, final and initial equilibrium positions coincide at A. Balance-of-payments equilibrium requires that the money supply of country 1 return to its initial level if country 2 maintains its money supply at its initial level. Accordingly, this conclusion is not limited to the case of perfect capital mobility as previously proved by one of the authors.[21] Its importance appears immediately if we relabel country 1 Europe, country 2 the United States, and we assume that American monetary

[21] See A. K. Swoboda, 'Reserve Policies, Currency Preferences, and International Adjustment', *op. cit.*

policy is entirely governed by internal balance considerations: neutralisation of reserve flows robs European monetary policy of any lasting influence on income and interest rate levels, whatever the size of Europe.

Figure 12.6 can also be used to illustrate the effects of debt-financed fiscal expansion.[22] Starting from equilibrium at A, let autonomous expenditure increase in country 1 shifting the YY

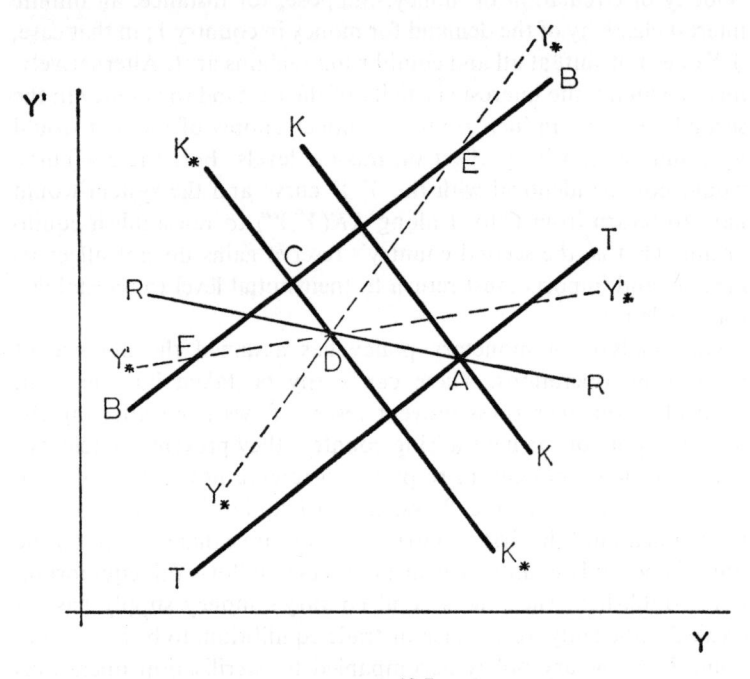

FIGURE 12.7

curve to Y_*Y_* until it intersects the $Y'Y'$ curve at C. The analysis is exactly the same as in the case of monetary policy; final equilibrium is again at D. However, here, the initial shift in YY will be the larger

[22] An analysis of tax-financed fiscal policy would have to be carried out along slightly different lines. Suppose, for instance, that the government increases its spending by dG and finances this increase by raising poll taxes by the same amount. Initially, at least, disposable income does not change and output increases by dG. This is all that need happen if (a) imports and (b) the demand for money are a function of disposable income. If imports and the demand for money are a function of output, however, an excess demand for foreign goods and for money emerges, the consequences of which can be traced through the model.

Adjustment, Policy, and Monetary Equilibrium

the greater the interest elasticity of the demand for money in country 1 and the lower the interest elasticity of domestic expenditure. Moreover, the source of the shift in KK resides now in higher interest rates permitting an economy of 'speculative money balances' rather than in an increase in the stock of money. Note also that neutralisation by both countries would lead to a quasi-equilibrium at C, the result predicted by the 'pure-income' models (except that here the initial shift in YY and the location of point C depend on monetary parameters as well as on marginal propensities to save and import). In other words, the monetary constraint expressed by K_*K_* reduces the income gain of the country where the increase in autonomous expenditure originates and increases that of the rest of the world.

The case of an income transfer from country 1 to country 2 (again for the 'Metzler–Machlup' case) is illustrated in Figure 12.7. The effect of the transfer on the assumption that the distribution of the world money supply is kept constant is to lead the system to point D. At D, however, the transfer is undereffected. The transferor's deficit leads to a redistribution of the world money supply towards country 2 and thus to an upward movement along K_*K_*, the locus of monetary equilibrium through D, until full equilibrium is reached at point C. Again, we find that it is not necessary for price and terms of trade changes to occur for the transfer to be fully effected; reserve flows will intervene to supplement initial income changes. The extent to which the result predicted by the 'pure-income model' is modified by monetary factors depends, of course, on the slope of KK but also on the position of point D. It is possible to define a *transfer line*, RR, on which all points such as D must lie, the exact position of D on RR depending on the direction and magnitude of the transfer. The slope of this line is:

$$\left.\frac{dY'}{dY}\right|_{RR} = -\frac{s+(E_r L_y)/L_r}{s'+(E'_{r'} L'_{y'})/L'_{r'}} < 0 \tag{13}$$

The greater the effect of fiscal expansion (at a constant money supply) in the second country (the lower s', $E'_{r'}$, and $L'_{y'}$, and the larger $L'_{r'}$) relative to the impact of fiscal contraction in the first, the steeper RR and the smaller the relative decrease in the first country's income required by the transfer. Note that if the two countries are identical with respect to behaviour parameters, the slope of RR is equal to that of KK and to -1.

Neutralisation operations afford countries with an interesting possibility of offsetting the effect of income transfers. If both countries neutralise reserve flows a quasi-equilibrium is established at point D; however, if the donor (recipient) country alone neutralises reserve flows a full equilibrium is eventually reached at point E (point F). Point E lies vertically above A, point F horizontally to the left of A.[23] This means that, if only one country neutralises reserve flows, the neutralising country can shift the entire burden of income adjustment necessary to effect the transfer fully to the other country. Consider, for instance, point E. At E, income in the first country remains at its pre-transfer level: expenditure that had been cut by the financing of the transfer is restored to its original level by an increase in exports equal to the transfer; domestic expenditure, the rate of interest, and the money supply stand unaltered. The donor country loses enough reserves to increase the recipient's money supply and expenditure by the amount necessary to generate additional imports equal in value to the transfer.

Analytically, income transfers and expenditure-switching policies present many similarities. A switch in expenditure from foreign to home goods, like an inward transfer but for different reasons, enables a country to maintain balance-of-payments equilibrium while enjoying a higher level of income. The reason for the expenditure switch cannot be analysed within an essentially one-good model if its source is a change in relative prices; its consequences, however, can be traced on the assumptions that no further relative price changes occur and that the impact of the original price change on the demand for real balance can be neglected (a rather untidy assumption). Suppose, for instance, that an autonomous shift of expenditure away from foreign and towards home goods occurs in country 2. Let the magnitude of the shift be denoted by Ω. Its initial impact is to increase the demand for domestic output and improve the balance-of-trade by Ω in country 2. At the same time, this shift creates a decrease of Ω in the demand for the first country's output and an equal worsening of its balance of trade. In other words, an expenditure switch of Ω away from the goods of country 1 onto those of country 2 is exactly equivalent, in its effects on aggregate demands, to an income transfer of Ω from 1 to 2. Moreover, the changes of income necessary

---

[23] The algebraic proof of this statement is similar to that given in footnote 9 above. The reader can verify that the leftward shift in $Y'Y'$ is again $(1/m)\tau$ and the upward shift of YY is again $(1/m')\tau$ (parameters other than marginal propensities to import cancel out in the calculation of the shifts).

to restore balance-of-payments equilibrium after a transfer or an expenditure switch of the same magnitude are identical. In the case of a transfer a trade surplus equal to the transfer must be generated by the donor country; in that of an expenditure switch the balance of trade of the country whose exports have declined must improve by the amount of the switch to re-establish balance in international payments. The difference is that, in the case of a transfer, balance-of-payments equilibrium requires a balance-of-trade surplus for the donor country while, in the case of an expenditure switch, it requires a zero balance of trade. It follows that Figure 12.7 can be used to represent an expenditure switch away from the goods of the first country as well as a transfer from 1 to 2. All that is needed is to relabel BB as $T'T'$, the locus of income combinations that will yield balance-of-trade equilibrium after the switch has occurred. The remainder of the analysis follows on the lines of that of a transfer – as before, of course, under the 'Metzler–Machlup' transfer assumptions.

To summarise, the discussion of this section leads to much the same conclusions as that of the preceding one. A redistribution of the world's money supply will, in the final analysis, leave equilibrium unchanged. An increase in the money supply of one or the other country results in income increases whose distribution (but not magnitude) is governed by marginal propensities to import. It is true that, because of interest rate effects, the position of the KK constraint on potential income levels will now depend on autonomous expenditure levels. However, as long as capital is immobile internationally, the equilibrium distribution of world income among the two countries is governed by the TT curve. That curve's position is not affected by monetary or conventional fiscal policy. Income transfers or switching policies are required to escape from the income distributions it dictates.

IV. CAPITAL MOBILITY

Relevance to policy problems requires that our discussion take into account the interest elasticity of capital flows. We suppose capital flows to be a function of interest-rate differentials. This assumption is adopted for the sake of manageability and conformity with the bulk of the 'policy-mix' literature. Alternatively, we could have assumed that changes in the interest-rate differential lead to a change in the aggregate amount and/or location of the desired stocks of various types of assets and that capital flows are a function of the speed at which actual and desired stocks of assets are brought into equality. Our treatment of capital flows assumes, as it were, that a given interest-rate differential produces an adjustment of stocks that gives rise to capital movements occurring continuously at a constant rate. It is thus a device for the analysis of short-run changes, on the assumption that complete stock adjustment is achieved only in the long run.[24]

One need only replace equation (11) by (11′) below in system (7)–(11) to take induced capital movements into account:

$$\frac{dR}{dt} = \frac{dM}{dt} = T(Y,Y') + K(r-r') = \frac{-dR'}{dt} = \frac{-dM'}{dt}, \quad (11')$$

where K is the net capital inflow into country 1, and full equilibrium requires (11′) to be equal to zero. An increase in the interest differential, $r-r'$, is assumed to lead to an increased net capital inflow (reduced net outflow) into country 1. Graphically, define a family of lines, labelled BB, which represent those combinations of the two countries' income levels that satisfy the condition (11′) = 0; one such line exists for each value of the interest-rate differential. The slope of each BB line is equal to that of the TT line since the level of capital flow is given along any one of them. The larger $(r-r')$, the larger the net capital inflow into country 1, the higher the level of income and imports into that country that is compatible with balance-of-payments equilibrium, and the further down and to the right will BB lie. Comparative statics analysis now requires that the impact of any autonomous disturbance on $(r-r')$ be determined, at first under the assumptions that national money stocks are kept constant. The magnitude and direction of the change in $(r-r')$ will then determine, together with the sensitivity of capital flows (denoted by K_r) to a change in the interest differential, the magnitude and direction of the shift in BB caused by the autonomous disturbance. For an analysis of full-equilibrium comparative statics it is sufficient to determine the impact of an autonomous disturbance on the interest differential in full equilibrium; that differential determines the trade surplus or deficit (and hence relative income levels) necessary to

[24] For a discussion of these assumptions, see, for instance, R. I. McKinnon, 'Portfolio Balance and International Payments Adjustment', in R. A. Mundell and A. K. Swoboda (Eds.), *Monetary Problems of the International Economy* (The University of Chicago Press, Chicago, 1969), pp. 199–234.

Adjustment, Policy, and Monetary Equilibrium

maintain balance-of-payments equilibrium. It follows that the comparative statics of disturbances that do not affect that differential are invariant to the degree of capital mobility; the latter plays a role only in determining the magnitude of balance-of-payments disequilibria when the system is not at rest and the speed of adjustment to a given autonomous disturbance.[25]

Consider, first, the consequences of redistributing the world money supply from country 2 to country 1 (Figure 12.8). The initial impact

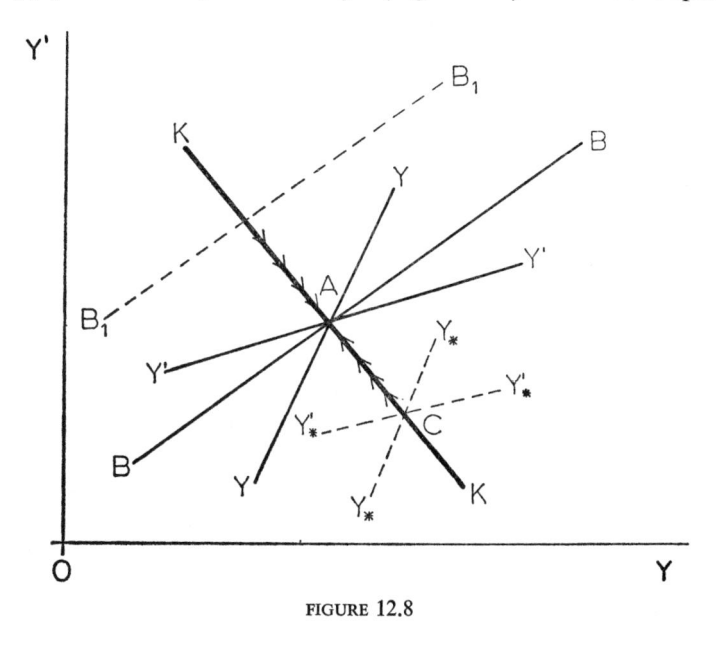

FIGURE 12.8

is to move incomes from A to C; the attendant lowering of the interest-rate differential shifts the balance-of-payments schedule up to B_1B_1. The reserve flows associated with country 1's deficit will return the system to A, as when capital is immobile internationally. The dynamics of adjustment, however, are affected by the degree of capital mobility. For, the deficit per unit of time at a disequilibrium

[25] For a more detailed discussion of the role of capital mobility along these lines but in the context of the single 'small' open economy, see A. K. Swoboda, 'Equilibrium, Quasi-Equilibrium, and Macroeconomic Policy under Fixed Exchange Rates', *op. cit.* Note also that in the case of perfect capital mobility, a further simplification of the model used for comparative statics can be made since, in that case, $r = r'$ in equilibrium. See R. A. Mundell, 'A Reply: Capital Mobility and Size', *op. cit.*

R 249

point such as C is larger the higher the interest sensitivity of capital flows. The larger the initial deficit, the more rapid adjustment is likely to be (assuming the system to be stable) and the more difficult it is to reach and maintain by neutralisation operations a quasi-equilibrium point such as C.[26]

Suppose, next, that the monetary authorities of country 1 purchase bonds in the open market. As before, the system would shift to point C (Figure 12.6) in the absence of reserve flows. At the same time, the balance-of-payments schedule shifts up to some position $B_1 B_1$ (not drawn) since at C the interest differential is lower than at A.[27] That is, the deficit per unit of time experienced by country 1 at C is larger than it would be were capital immobile internationally. Final equilibrium, however, must again be at D. For, as reserves flow from 1 to 2, point C moves up $K_* K_*$ and $B_1 B_1$ shifts down as $(r - r')$ increases. At D, the trade balance has the same value as at A and, hence, the net capital flow must be the same as at A. It follows that the movement from C to D restores the interest differential to its initial equilibrium value although both interest rates will have declined as a consequence of the expansion in the world money supply. To summarise, the comparative statics of adjustment to money-supply disturbances are not affected by the degree of capital mobility, though the dynamics of adjustment and the effectiveness of neutralisation operations are. The equilibrium interest-rate differential is invariant with respect to autonomous money-supply changes.

The equilibrium interest-rate differential, however, does depend on the level of autonomous expenditure. Therefore, the impact of fiscal policy and of income transfers will depend on the responsiveness of capital movements to interest-rate changes. Consider an autonomous increase in expenditure in country 1 (Figure 12.9). The impact effect is to shift YY so that it intersects $Y'Y'$ at C. Final equilibrium must again take place on $K_* K_*$; however, BB shifts since the interest-rate differential changes. Assume, first, that it changes in favour of

[26] As a matter of fact, when $K_r \longrightarrow \infty$, the deficit in the first country's balance of payments tends to infinity as soon as the interest differential deviates from its equilibrium level and it may be impossible even to reach a point such as C.

[27] Differentiating (7) and (10) and solving for the change in the interest differential brought about by a change in money supply (before reserve flows take place) yields:

$$d(r-r')/d\bar{D} = (1/\Delta)[(ss' + sm' + ms')L'_{r'} + (s+m)E'_{r'}L'_{y'} + mE_r L'_{y'}] < 0,$$

where

$$\Delta = (ss' + sm' + ms')L_r L'_{r'} + (s+m)E'_{r'}L_r L'_y + (s' + m')E_r L'_{r'}L_y + E_r I'_{r'}L_y L'_{y'} > 0.$$

Adjustment, Policy, and Monetary Equilibrium

country 1, as it usually, though not necessarily, does.[28] *BB*, therefore, shifts down. Two cases can be distinguished. (1) *BB* shifts to the same position, B_1B_1, between *D* and *C*; in that case, country 1 experiences a *deficit* at *C*, the *YY* and *Y'Y'* curves shift up and B_1B_1 shifts down along K_*K_* until final equilibrium is reached at some point such as *E*. (2) *BB* shifts by a more substantial amount to, say,

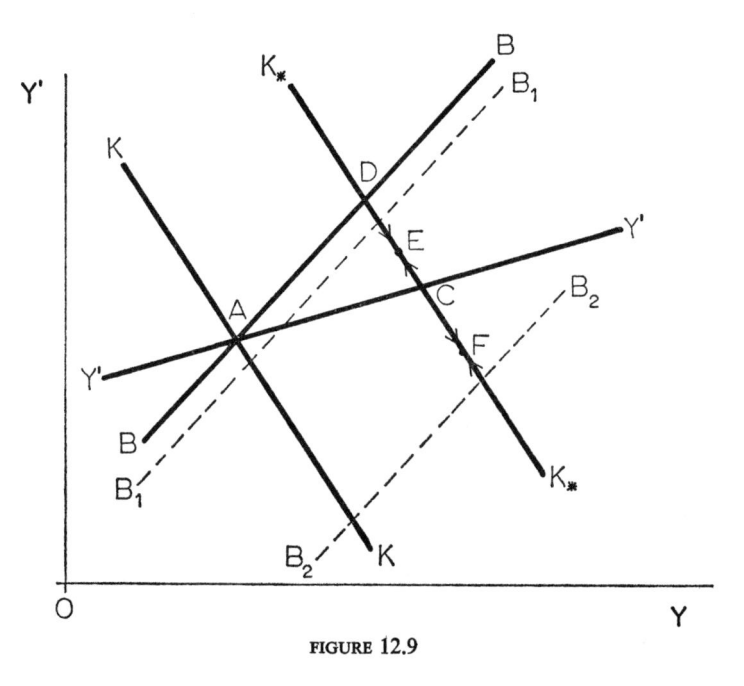

FIGURE 12.9

B_2B_2 (as it would for a large K_r); country 1 now experiences a *surplus* as a result of fiscal expansion, gains reserves, and the *YY* and *Y'Y'* curves shift down and B_2B_2 shifts up along K_*K_* until final equilibrium is reached at some point such as F.[29]

[28] Differentiating (7) to (10) and solving yields:
$$d(r-r')/dI = (1/\Delta)[(s'+m')L_yL'_{r'} + E'_{r'}L_yL'_{y'}] + (1/\Delta)(mL_rL'_{y'}) \gtreqless 0.$$
The first term on the right-hand side of this expression represents the impact of dI on r, the second its impact on r'. The first term will dominate and the expression will be positive, for instance, if $m = m'$, $L_r = L'_{r'}$ and $L_y = L'_{y'}$.

[29] This result in a two-country framework has as counterpart in the one-country case the fact that whether fiscal expansion results in a balance-of-payments deficit or surplus depends on whether the *FF* curve is more or less steep than the *LL* curve.

Note that F may (but need not) imply a level of the second country's income that is lower than that prevailing at the initial equilibrium position, A. This is the diagrammatic counterpart to Mundell's disturbing finding that, under perfect capital mobility and fixed exchange rates, fiscal expansion by one country may turn out to be a 'beggar-my-neighbour' policy.[30] Our analysis makes the reason for this clear: fiscal expansion tends to widen the interest differential in favour of the expanding country and may cause a capital outflow from the rest of the world that is large enough to 'suck out' money in an amount sufficient to counteract the expansionary impact of the increase in the second country's exports. Perfect capital mobility, however, is neither a necessary (though some interest sensitivity of capital flows is) nor sufficient condition for this special case to arise.

In any event, the role of capital mobility, in addition to speeding up the process of adjustment, is to reduce (or even reverse) the income changes necessary to re-establish balance-of-payments equilibrium after fiscal expansion has taken place. The one exception to this statement concerns the case where fiscal expansion in country 1 decreases $(r-r')$; this would result in an upward shift in BB and in final equilibrium at point D (as in the case of capital immobility).

The analysis of an income transfer from the first to the second country is simpler as, under the 'Metzler–Machlup' assumptions, the interest differential at constant money supplies unambiguously changes in favour of the recipient country.[31] This means that the deficit experienced by the transferring country in the absence of money supply changes is larger than it would be were capital immobile internationally. However, the secondary income adjustments needed to effect the transfer fully may be larger or smaller than those required under capital immobility. For, as reserves flow from the donor to the recipient the interest differential now changes in favour of the donor. Whether this improvement for the donor offsets the initial worsening of the differential before or after the final equilibrium that would have been established under capital immobility is reached cannot be ascertained *a priori* by graphical methods. Figure 12.10 illustrates the case where the transfer line is assumed for

[30] See R. A. Mundell, 'A Reply: Capital Mobility and Size', *op. cit.*
[31] At constant money supplies, the effect of a transfer on the interest differential is given by

$$d(r-r')/d\tau = (1/\Delta)[s'L'_{r'}L_y + sL_rL'_{y'} + L_yL'_{y'}(E'_{r'} + E_r)] < 0.$$

Adjustment, Policy, and Monetary Equilibrium

simplicity to coincide with the *KK* line. At constant interest rates – or under capital immobility – payments balance inclusive of the transfer would be reached along B_1B_1. However, at constant national money stocks, the system moves to point *C*, the interest differential is lowered and, hence, the balance-of-payments schedule inclusive of the transfer that corresponds to this lowered value of $(r-r')$ will lie

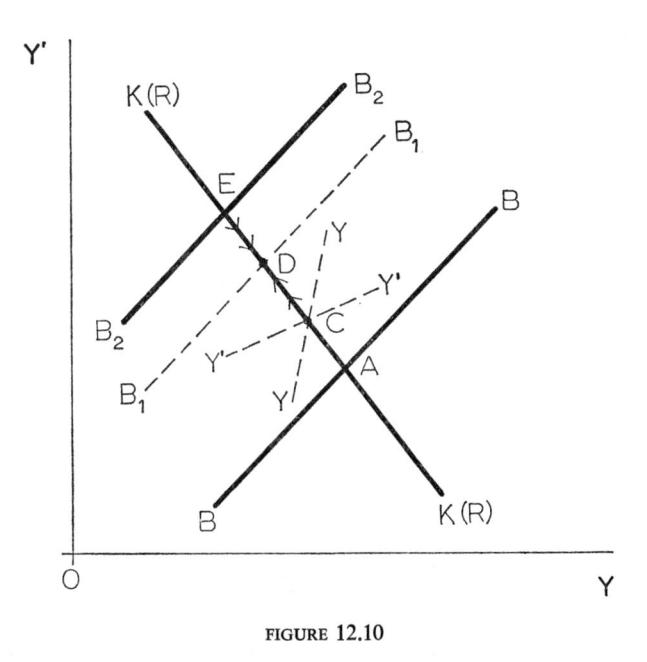

FIGURE 12.10

somewhere above B_1B_1, say, at B_2B_2. As reserves flow from the donor to the recipient, *YY* and *Y'Y'* shift up and B_2B_2 shifts down. Final equilibrium is reached along *KK* (*RR*), either below or above *D* (the capital immobility equilibrium point) but, in any event, above *C*, as before. The analysis of switching policies follows on similar lines.

To summarise, the responsiveness of capital movements to interest-rate movements does not affect the comparative statics analysis of monetary disturbances. However, the equilibrium interest-rate differential does depend on autonomous expenditure levels and, therefore, the comparative statics analysis of income transfers and of fiscal and expenditure-switching policies is not invariant with respect to the degree of capital mobility. Although, in full equilibrium, the position of the *BB* curve is not affected by changes in money supplies, it does depend on fiscal policies.

V. GLOBAL POLICIES

Problems of global policy – in particular, that of reconciling national income targets in an interdependent world economy – can now be briefly illustrated with the help of our diagrammatic apparatus.

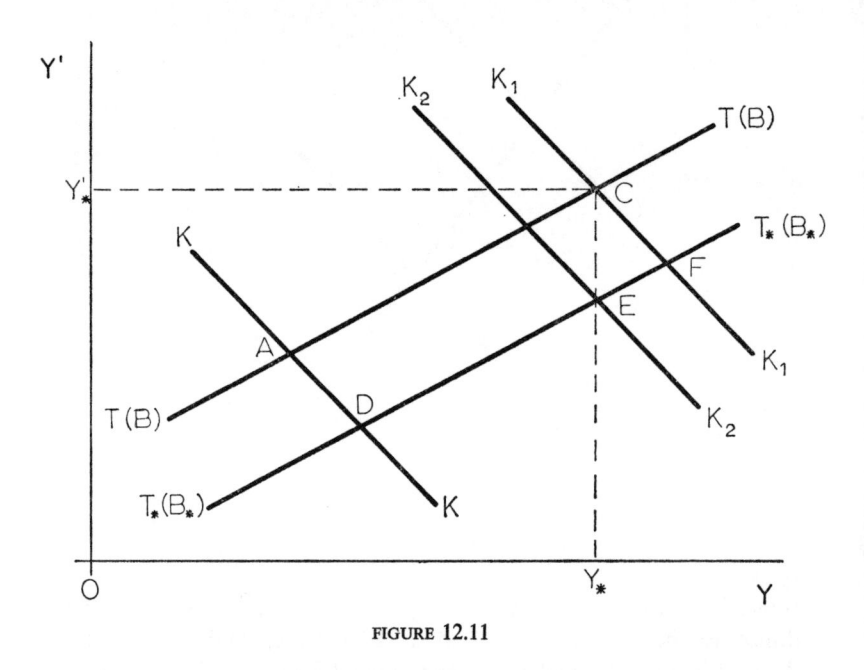

FIGURE 12.11

Consider the situation illustrated in Figure 12.11. Suppose that capital is immobile internationally, and that full-employment income in countries 1 and 2 is at Y_* and Y'_*, respectively, and that the trade-balance equilibrium line is TT. Internal and external balance is achieved simultaneously by both countries at C. A liquidity problem is associated with points lying off the K_1K_1 curve, an adjustment problem with those lying off the balance-of-payments schedule, and a mixture of both problems with points that are on neither schedule. At A, for instance, there is a liquidity shortage that can be eliminated

Adjustment, Policy, and Monetary Equilibrium

by increasing – in any available fashion – the world money stock, *or* by increasing autonomous expenditure and thereby increasing interest rates and reducing the asset demand for money. Note that the liquidity problem at hand is one of shortage (or glut) of money and not of foreign-exchange reserves, the so-called 'international liquidity' problem. The latter problem arises if, at *C*, the level or distribution of world reserves is considered inadequate (or excessive).[32] At *F*, on the other hand, the policy problem is one of adjustment; income in the deficit country must decrease, income in the surplus country increase, to restore payments equilibrium. Adjustment, in this particular case, is automatic and does not conflict with internal policy objectives.

The more difficult policy problem arises when internal and external balance objectives conflict. Suppose, for instance, that the relevant trade-balance line is T_*T_*. Internal balance in both countries implies a balance-of-trade deficit for the second country, payments equilibrium the frustration of internal balance objectives in at least one country. In the balance of induced capital movements, the only means of achieving internal and external balance simultaneously in both countries is to effect an income transfer from 1 to 2 or an expenditure switch onto the good of the second country and away from those of the first sufficient to shift the payments-equilibrium line from T_*T_* to TT. This, of course, is Meade's celebrated policy-conflict model and his proposed solution.[33] As in the one-country case, an appropriate division of labour between monetary and fiscal policy makes it possible to achieve internal and external balance simultaneously without having recourse to expenditure switching or income transfers when capital is mobile internationally. This can be shown with the help of Figure 12.11. Relabel T_*T_* as B_*B_* and TT as BB. Suppose we start at point *E* where balance-of-payments

---

[32] An international liquidity problem could arise in one or several of the following guises: (*a*) Countries attempt to maintain a given ratio of foreign-exchange reserves to money supply and, in the absence of fiscal expansion, this limits equilibrium to under-employment income levels at, say, *A*. (*b*) No country is willing to expand its money supply or budget deficit unilaterally as this would lead to a reserve loss (this type of problem can be overcome by joint expansion of income levels in a ratio m/m' to maintain the initial distribution of reserves). (*c*) The existing stock of reserves is considered to be inadequate to finance the higher volume of trade (or potential trade imbalances) that would prevail at point *C*.

[33] See J. E. Meade, *The Balance of Payments*, *op. cit.*, especially Chapters 10 and 11.

and monetary equilibrium prevail but where Y' is below its target level Y'. Our problem is to apply fiscal and monetary policies in such a way as to shift K_2K_2 to K_1K_1 and B_*B_* to BB. Fiscal policy should be used to deal with the discrepancy of income in the second country from its target value since an increase in spending by that country's government will cause the interest differential to change in its favour and the B_*B_* curve to shift up; monetary expansion by country 2, on the other hand, would lead to a (temporary) downward shift of the B_*B_* curve, that is, a movement away and not towards the desired equilibrium position of BB. The movement towards point C would of course, in a decentralised system of policy responses, most likely involve an intricate series of steps, especially if it is desired to keep the same distribution of the world's foreign-exchange reserves at C as at E. One point, however, is clear: gearing monetary policies to desired reserve distributions and fiscal policies to income targets constitutes a stable assignment of instruments to targets while the reverse pairing does not.[34]

Expenditure-switching policies, however, retain their importance even when capital is mobile internationally and fiscal and monetary instruments are available. In the first place, the extent to which capital movements can be relied on to finance trade imbalances may be limited both in scope and in time – a point that has been emphasised by some of the 'policy-mix' literature. Second, it may be desirable to speed up the adjustment process through recourse to switching policies. Finally, and perhaps most important, the structure of the balance-of-payments itself constitutes a policy target in addition to over-all balance. To achieve a certain level of the trade balance while preserving balance-of-payments equilibrium and full employment requires the use of switching policies (or income transfers) in addition to that of fiscal and monetary instruments.

VI. CONCLUSION

The conclusions reached in this paper have been established under the assumptions underlying models of the IS-LM variety, namely, unemployment and fixed prices. However, many of our results

[34] Actually, one of the instruments is redundant since one country's surplus is the other's deficit and there is only one independent balance-of-payments target. See R. A. Mundell, 'The Redundancy Problem and the World Price Level', in R. A. Mundell and A. K. Swoboda (Eds.), *Monetary Problems of the International Economy, op. cit.*, pp. 379–82.

would hold, qualitatively, in a world of full employment and flexible prices. Two features of our model are worth an additional comment before we conclude. First, implicit in our conclusion that equilibrium is invariant with respect to a (*ceteris paribus*) redistribution of the world money supply is the assumption that the impact of such redistributions on wealth is transitory only, or alternatively, that current behaviour depends only on current income. This assumption would be inappropriate were our model extended to analyse the impact of changes in exchange-rate parities, especially when the public holds foreign assets. A more precise analysis would take into account the redistribution of wealth (or change in expected permanent income) associated with a reserve redistribution. With known marginal propensities to spend out of wealth, the analysis could then proceed along the lines suggested by that of a transfer or expenditure switch, once the capital levy-subsidy effect of the redistribution of reserves has been ascertained. Second, as was pointed out in section IV, the concept of capital mobility used in this paper constitutes a useful first approximation mainly for short-run analysis. For longer-run purposes, the capital immobility model, together with its emphasis on expenditure-switching policies and on the role of transfers, becomes quite relevant.

In spite of its abstract character, the model used in this paper does yield interesting conclusions – conclusions that are, incidentally, also relevant to the analysis of domestic income re-distribution and to the impact of regional fiscal policy. In particular, the degree of capital mobility is seen not to affect the impact of money-supply disturbances after full adjustment has taken place; the importance of capital mobility resides in its role in speeding up the process of adjustment. One important corollary of this proposition is that the monetary-policy results derived under the assumption of perfect capital mobility do not, as was previously thought, constitute an exception but the general rule. The lesson for stabilisation policy under fixed exchange rates is an important one: the effectiveness of monetary policy varies inversely with the size of countries, changes in national money supplies become generalised into changes in the world money stock, and neutralisation operations by one country rob the other country's monetary policy of its influence on income levels – irrespective of the degree of capital mobility. Furthermore, if one country, say, the United States, is very large relative to any single foreign country, and if foreign countries do not act in concert, its economic policy will largely determine income and interest-rate trends in the rest of the world (this is of course one feature of the so-called dollar standard). Again, this conclusion holds irrespective of the degree of capital mobility although the latter plays a role in determining the speed with which developments in the dominant country are transmitted to the rest of the world. Second, the model emphasises the importance of monetary factors in determining the impact of transfers and expenditure-switching policies on the level of world income and its distribution among countries. Finally, the concept of a 'natural distribution of specie' retains its importance even in a world of underemployment. This distribution does depend in general, it is true, on autonomous expenditure levels; however, the smaller the interest sensitivity of the demand for money the less the influence of exogenous changes in spending.

The main point is simply that 'Hume's Law' with its monetary mechanism of payments adjustment holds in the face of unemployment and wage rigidities.[35]

Appendix

This appendix provides an algebraic statement of the stability conditions of (1) the non-monetary model of section II, and (2) the simple money-goods model of section II.

I

The derivation of stability conditions for the non-monetary model of section II is straightforward.[36] Let income movements be governed by the following two equations:

$$dY/dt = k_1(E+T-Y) \tag{A1}$$
$$dY'/dt = k_2(E'-T-Y'). \tag{A2}$$

After expansion into a Taylor series and omitting non-linear terms we obtain an equation system with characteristic equation:

$$\begin{vmatrix} \lambda+k_1(s+m) & -k_1m' \\ -k_2m & \lambda+k_2(s'+m') \end{vmatrix} =$$
$$\lambda^2 + \lambda[k_1(s+m)+k_2(s'+m')] + k_1k_2[(s+m)(s'+m')-mm'] = 0.$$

[35] This is, of course, also the conclusion reached by Mundell with the help of the one-country model. See his 'The International Disequilibrium System', *op. cit*.

[36] This derivation is similar to that used by L. A. Metzler in 'Underemployment Equilibrium in International Trade' *op. cit*.

The value of the roots λ_1, λ_2 of this equation is given by

$$\lambda_1, \lambda_2 = \frac{-k_1(s+m)-k_2(s'+m')}{2}$$

$$\pm \frac{\sqrt{[k_1(s+m)+k_2(s'+m')]^2 - 4k_1k_2[(s+m)(s'+m')-mm']}}{2}$$

It is clear that if $s, s', m, m' > 0$, the roots will be real and negative, i.e. the system will approach equilibrium without oscillations. A necessary condition for the roots to have negative real parts is that $s+m>0$, $s'+m'>0$. A sufficient condition for λ_1, λ_2 to be negative when real is that $(s+m)(s'+m')-mm' > 0$ which is equivalent to the condition that $(s+m)/m' > m/(s'+m')$, that is, to the requirement that YY be steeper than $Y'Y'$. If this last condition is fulfilled the approach to equilibrium will be a direct (non-oscillatory) one.

II

Consider, first, the one-country version of the simple money–goods model. Assuming that income rises in proportion to the excess demand for goods and services and that changes in the money supply are equal to the balance of trade, expanding into a Taylor series and linearising, we obtain

$$\begin{bmatrix} dY/dt \\ dM/dt \end{bmatrix} = \begin{bmatrix} -k_1(s+m+hL_y) & k_1h \\ -(m-tL_y) & -t \end{bmatrix} \begin{bmatrix} Y-Y_0 \\ M-M_0 \end{bmatrix}, \quad \text{(A3)}$$

$$\text{where } h = \frac{\partial E}{\partial M}$$

$$t = \frac{\partial T}{\partial M}.$$

The characteristic equation of this system is

$$\lambda^2 + \lambda[t + k_1(s+m+hL_y)] + k_1[ts + m(t+h)] = 0.$$

(A3) is stable since the coefficients of this quadratic equation are all positive.

Turn, now, to the two-country case. After expansion into a Taylor series and omission of non-linear terms, equations (1'), (2') and (6) of the text become

$$\begin{bmatrix} dY/dt \\ dY'/dt \\ dM/dt \end{bmatrix} = \begin{bmatrix} -k_1(s+m+hL_y) & k_1(m'-t'L_{y'}') & k_1(h-t') \\ k_2(m-tL_y) & -k_2(s'+m'+h'L_{y'}') & -k_2(h'-t) \\ -(m-tL_y) & (m'-t'L_{y'}') & -(t+t') \end{bmatrix}$$

$$\begin{bmatrix} Y-Y_0 \\ Y'-Y_0' \\ M-M_0 \end{bmatrix} \quad \text{(A4)}$$

The characteristic equation of (A4) is

$$\begin{vmatrix} \lambda+k_1(s+m+hL_y) & -k_1(m'-t'L_{y'}') & -k_1(h-t') \\ -k_2(m-tL_y) & \lambda+k_2(s'+m'+h'L_{y'}') & k_2(h'-t) \\ (m-tL_y) & -(m'-t'L_{y'}') & \lambda+(t+t') \end{vmatrix} = \quad \text{(A5)}$$

$$= \lambda^3 - D_1\lambda^2 + D_2\lambda - D_3 = 0,$$

where D_i is the sum of the i-th order principal minors of the coefficient matrix of (A4). Necessary conditions for stability are that these minors alternate in sign, with $D_1 < 0$.

Let $(s+m+hL_y) = A$, $(s'+m'+h'L_{y'}') = A'$, $(m-tL_y) = B$, and $(m'-t'L_{y'}') = B'$. It can be verified that

$$D_1 = -[k_1A + k_2A' + (t+t')] < 0$$

$$D_2 = k_1k_2[(AA'-BB')] + k_2[(t+t')A' + B'(h'-t)] + \\ + k_1[(t+t')A + B(h-t')] \gtrless 0$$

$$D_3 = -k_1k_2[h'B'(A-B) + tA(A'-B') + t'A'(A-B) + hB(A'-B')]$$

$$= -k_1k_2[(m'g' + t's')(s+gL_y) + (mg+ts)(s'+g'L_{y'}')] < 0,$$

where $g = h+t$, and $g' = h'+t'$. The only principal minor whose sign is ambiguous is D_2. By expanding D_2 and cancelling terms, it can be shown that the $k_1[\ldots]$ and $k_2[\ldots]$ terms are both positive. Thus necessary conditions for stability will obtain if $[AA'-BB'] > 0$. By expanding, we find that this requirement can be rewritten as

$$[AA'-BB'] = 1 + B/(s+gL_y) + B'/(s'+g'L_{y'}') > 0. \quad \text{(A6)}$$

Thus, necessary conditions for stability are met when $B, B' > 0$. (By expanding and manipulating (A6) it can be shown that either $B > 0$

or $B'>0$ suffices for necessary conditions.) By the Routh–Hurwitz criterion, necessary *and* sufficient conditions for stability obtain when $D_3 - D_1 D_2 > 0$.

The reader can verify that this condition is met if $B, B' > 0$. An intuitive explanation of these results can be given as follows. When $B, B' < 0$, an increase in a country's income causes an excess demand for money so large that it reduces its demand for the other country's goods. Other things equal, this implies a balance-of-payments surplus for the expanding country and an inflow of reserves, reinforcing the initial rise in income rather than stabilising it. Furthemore, it can be shown that $(AA' - BB')$ will be positive if $hh' > tt'$ (or $h'/t' > t/h$). That is, the system will tend to be stable if an excess supply of a country's money has a stronger impact on the demand for that country's goods than on that for the other country's output. This is similar to the familiar stability requirement for a price system that the excess demand for some good i be more sensitive to a change in its own price than to a change in some other good's price.

Index

Absorption approach, 175ff., 183, 209
Adjustment
　balance-of-payments, 206-13
　burden of, 197ff.
Alexander, S. S., 209
Amano, A., 108n, 117n
Arbitrage, 113ff.
'Arm's length' rule, 79, 84
Assignment, 256

Balance of payments, 107ff., 128ff., 142, 145, 197
　adjustment policy and, 225ff.
　devaluation and, 170, 185ff.
　in Hecksher–Ohlin model, 16, 19, 20ff.
　Keynesian and monetarist models, 210ff.
　monetary approach to, 206ff.
Balance of trade
　adjustment of, 225
　currency devaluation and, 174, 185
　new technology and, 60, 63, 69
Baldwin, R. E., 9, *29*, 36n, 46
Bartolomei, J. A., 107n
Base money, 129ff., 141, 142, 146
Basevi, G., 10, *107*
Batra, B., 45ff.
Beggar-my-neighbour policy, 227, 252
Bentzel, R., 86, 95
Bertrand, T., 51n
Bhagwati, J. N., 9, *45*, 51n, 177n
Bickerdike, C. F., 16n
Black, S. W., 107n, 110, 112n, 114n, 120n
Bloomfield, A. I., 108n
Borrowing short and lending long, 22
Branson, W. H., 107n
Brehmen, E., 108n
Brunner, K., 10, *127*, 128n

Capital, 22ff.
　long-term, 113, 171
　short-term, 11, 115, 116
Capital accumulation, 51
Capital immobility, 229-47

Capital mobility
　adjustment and, 225, 227ff., 247-54
　fiscal-monetary mix and, 210
　fiscal policy and, 226
　monetary policy and, 109, 127
Capital movements, 23ff.
　balance of payments and, 226, 248
　(*see also* Capital mobility)
　foreign-exchange market and, 107ff., 114
　tariff-induced, 45, 50ff.
Cassel, G., 207
Colonial type of investment, 24
Confidence, 21, 22
Connolly, M. B., 10, 45n, *55*, 225n
Cooper, C. A., 35n
Cooper, R. N., 10, *167*, 177n, 186n
Covering *see* Hedging
Crawling peg, 109
Customs unions, 29ff.

D'Adda, C., 109n
Dandekar, V. M., 86
Devaluation
　deflationary impact of, 157, 175-83
　evidence on, 183ff.
　forward exchange and, 113
　in developing countries
　　types of, 170-1
　　elasticities and, 172-5, 177
　　absorption approach and, 175ff.
　　monetary approach to, 206, 222ff.
Diaz-Alejandro, C. F., 180
Distortion
　in consumption, 52
　in wages, 45ff.
Distribution (of income), 85ff., 236, 237, 257
　customs union and, 40ff., 69
　devaluation and, 179
Dobb, M., 18n
Dollar, 22, 258
Dornbusch, R., 10, 166n, *225*

Effective demand, 16
Elasticity approach, 172ff., 185, 208

262

INDEX

Euro-dollar, 144
Exchange rate, 107, 142, 153, 167ff., 257
Expenditure-switching policy, 209, 246, 253, 255

Factor endowments, 20
Factor-price equalisation theorem, 20
Fair-share rule, 73, 83, 84
Family planning, 97, 100
Financial policy, 151
Fiscal-monetary mix, 210, 226, 247, 255ff.
Fiscal policy, 108, 171, 181n, 210, 225ff.
Flatters, F., 51n
Floating exchange rate, 207, 223
Fixed exchange rates, 20, 124, 157, 197, 208, 226, 233, 257
Foreign exchange, 107ff., 208
 rationing of, 174
Forward exchange rate, 107ff., 110ff., 128ff., 142, 154
Free trade, 16, 31ff., 46, 51
Frevert, P. A., 107n, 110n
Full employment, 16, 17

Galbraith, J. K., 191
German mark, 21
Goldsmith, S. F., 97
Gold standard, 21, 22, 23, 232

Haberler, G., 45, 225n
Hagen, E., 46
Harrod, R. F., 20
Hecksher–Ohlin Theory, 19, 68, 69n
Hedging, 110ff., 119–21, 142, 144
Helliwell, J., 108n
Hicks, J. R., 30
Horst, T., 10, 55n, *72*
Hume, D., 67n, 206

International Monetary Fund (IMF), 123, 167, 204, 206
Immiserizing growth, 45ff.
Imported inflation, 127, 153
Interest rate
 and foreign-exchange market, 107ff.
 monetary policy in open economy and, 127ff., 141ff., 210, 226, 237, 248
International investment, 22
International liquidity, 197, 202, 255, 255n

International reserves, 207
 foreign exchange market and, 112, 122, 127ff.
 money supply and, 215, 218, 229ff.

Johnson, H. G., 10, 50ff., 51n, 55n, 81n, 83, *206*, 225, 226n, 231

Keat, P. G., 92
Kemp, M. C., 29, 30, 31, 79n, 182n
Kenen, P. B., 107n
Keynes, J. M., 108, 109
Keynesian revolution, 208
Kindleberger, C. P., 81n
Kolm, S. C., 124n
Koopmans, T. C., 206
Kravis, I., 55n

Laissez-faire, 46
Lampman, R. J., 97
Leamer, E. E., 117n
Learning by doing, 56
Lee, C. H., 117n
Levin, J. H., 107n
L'Huillier, J., 10, *197*
Liberalisation
 of imports, 171, 172, 176, 185
Lydall, H. F., 91

Machlup, F., 170, 225n
Market size, 79
Marshall, A., 18, 19, 21, 55
Marshall–Lerner Condition, 178, 208
Masera, F., 108n
Massel, B. F., 35n
Maxwell, T., 108n
McKinnon, R. I., 248n
Meade, J. E., 29n, 108n, 209, 210, 225, 226, 255
Meltzer, A. H., 127n, 128n
Metzler, L. A., 225, 258n
Miller, N. C., 23n, 117n
Mobility of factors, 15
Modigliani, F., 108n
Monetary base *see* Base money
Monetary-fiscal mix *see* Fiscal-monetary mix
Monetary policy, 107, 127ff., 141, 148, 171, 181n
 balance of payments and, 215, 226ff.
 capital movements and, 109, 141ff., 210
Money illusion, 212

INDEX

Monopoly, 59ff.
  discriminating, 74
Multi-national firm, 72ff.
Mundell, R. A., 55n, 108n, 109, 206, 210, 225, 226, 227, 238, 248n, 249n, 252, 256n

Neo-neoclassical system, 20, 22
Neutralisation, 226, 243, 245ff., 250
Nicholson, J. L., 87, 95, 97

Offer curve, 18, 48, 49
Open-market operations, 129, 147, 152, 250
Operation twist, 108
Optimum tariff, 29, 48, 188

Pattanaik, P., 45, 46
Pigou, A. C., 21
Preferential systems, 29, 38ff.
Price-specie-flow mechanism, 206, 207
Production function, 17, 19, 56
Protection, 16
Public good
  technology as, 59n, 81
Purchasing-power-parity, 207

Quantity theory of money, 20, 200, 213, 228

Ranis, G., 184n, 186n
Rate of profit, 17ff., 19
Rath, N., 86
Real balance effect, 209
Real money balances, 176, 182
Research and Development
  in multi-national firm, 80ff.
  terms of trade and, 58ff., 66, 68, 69
Reserve currency, 220, 224
Reserve ratio, 133
Ricardo, D., 17ff., 18n
Robinson, J., 9, *15*, 16n, 208
Robinson, R., 230n
Roosa bond, 204
Ross, S., 55n
Rybczynski
  line, 51
  theorem, 68
Rybczynski, T. M., 51, 68, 69

Samuelson, P. A., 16, **17,** 17n, 19, 20, 30, 59n

Scitovsky, T., 30
Scully, G., 45ff.
Second best, 29
Sliding parity, 109
Social welfare function, 31
Sohmen, E., 107n, 115n, 182n
Solow, R. M., 20n
Soltow, L., 92, 93
Special Drawing Rights (SDRs), 170, 204, 229
Speculation, 110ff., 118–19, 142, 179
Spot exchange rate, 107ff., 112–13
Sraffa, Piero, 18n
Stein, J. L., 107n
Sterilisation, 109, 243
Sterling, 21ff.
Stern, R. M., 117n
Stevens, G., 72n
Stoll, H., 107n
Sutch, R., 108n
Swap, 109
Swoboda, A. K., 10, *225*, 226, 232n, 243n, 248n, 249n, 256n

Tan, A. H., 51
Tariff
  customs union and, 30ff.
  devaluation and, 171, 173
  immiserizing growth and, 48, 50
  multi-national firm and, 74, 77, 79
Technical change, 55ff.
Technology, 73, 80, 83
  spillover of, 65ff.
  transmission of, 73, 80ff.
Terms of trade
  balance of payments and, 199, 201
  devaluation and, 169, 175, 185, 187ff.
  gains from trade and, 17
  immiserizing growth and, 45ff.
  technical change and, 56, 59ff., 62n, 68, 69
Tinbergen, J., 10, *85*, 108n
Transfers, 55ff., 111, 112, 231ff.
Tsiang, S. C., 107n
Two-by-two model, 15ff., 20, 57, 66n

Vanek, J., 29, 31, 41, 43

Wage-price spiral, 172, 185, 187, 189ff.
Whitman, M. von N., 117n
Willett, T. D., 117n

264